New York Legal Research

Carolina Academic Press
Legal Research Series

Suzanne E. Rowe, Series Editor

❧

Arizona — Tamara S. Herrera

Arkansas — Coleen M. Barger

California — Hether C. Macfarlane & Suzanne E. Rowe

Colorado — Robert Michael Linz

Connecticut — Jessica G. Hynes

Federal — Mary Garvey Algero, Spencer L. Simons, Suzanne E. Rowe, Scott Childs & Sarah E. Ricks

Florida, Third Edition — Barbara J. Busharis & Suzanne E. Rowe

Georgia — Nancy P. Johnson, Elizabeth G. Adelman & Nancy J. Adams

Idaho — Tenielle Fordyce-Ruff & Suzanne E. Rowe

Illinois, Second Edition — Mark E. Wojcik

Iowa — John D. Edwards, M. Sara Lowe, Karen L. Wallace & Melissa H. Weresh

Kansas — Joseph A. Custer & Christopher L. Steadham

Louisiana — Mary Garvey Algero

Massachusetts — E. Joan Blum

Michigan, Second Edition — Pamela Lysaght & Cristina D. Lockwood

Minnesota — Suzanne Thorpe

Missouri, Second Edition — Wanda M. Temm & Julie M. Cheslik

New York, Second Edition — Elizabeth G. Adelman, Theodora Belniak & Suzanne E. Rowe

North Carolina — Scott Childs

Ohio — Katherine L. Hall & Sara Sampson

Oregon, Second Edition — Suzanne E. Rowe

Pennsylvania — Barbara J. Busharis & Bonny L. Tavares

Tennessee — Sibyl Marshall & Carol McCrehan Parker

Texas — Spencer L. Simons

Washington, Second Edition — Julie Heintz-Cho, Tom Cobb & Mary A. Hotchkiss

Wisconsin — Patricia Cervenka & Leslie Behroozi

❧

New York Legal Research

Second Edition

Elizabeth G. Adelman

Theodora Belniak

Suzanne E. Rowe

Suzanne E. Rowe, Series Editor

Carolina Academic Press

Durham, North Carolina

Library of Congress Cataloging-in-Publication Data

Adelman, Elizabeth.
New York legal research / Elizabeth G. Adelman, Theodora Belniak, and Suzanne E. Rowe. -- 2nd ed.
p. cm.
Includes bibliographical references and index.
ISBN 978-1-59460-980-0 (alk. paper)
1. Legal research--New York (State) I. Belniak, Theodora. II. Rowe, Suzanne E., 1961- III. Title.

KFN5074.A34 2012
340.072'0747--dc23

2011046084

Carolina Academic Press
700 Kent Street
Durham, North Carolina 27701
Telephone (919) 489-7486
Fax (919) 493-5668
www.cap-press.com

Printed in the United States of America.

For my supportive law library colleagues near and far. Thank you.
EGA

To J.R.F., who brewed endless cups of tea and gave endless encouragement during this project. Thank you.
TB

To Donna, for many years of outstanding work and warm support. Thank you.
SER

Summary of Contents

Contents

List of Tables and Figures

Tables

Figures

Appendices

Series Note

The Legal Research Series published by Carolina Academic Press includes titles from many states around the country. The goal of each book is to provide law students, practitioners, paralegals, college students, laypeople, and librarians with the essential elements of legal research in each state. Unlike more bibliographic texts, the Legal Research Series books seek to explain concisely both the sources of state law research and the process for conducting legal research effectively.

Preface and Acknowledgments

The goal of *New York Legal Research 2d* is to explore concisely both the sources of New York state law research and the process of conducting research using those sources. New to the second edition is a chapter on New York City law.

Writing a book like this is a collaborative effort, and this is as true in this edition as it was in the first. In the first edition, each author took a leading role in various chapters. Elizabeth Adelman was responsible for drafting chapters on statutes, constitutions, local law, and court rules; legislative history; administrative law; updating; and ethics. She also provided current expertise on New York resources. Suzanne Rowe was responsible for drafting chapters on research techniques, judicial opinions, and research strategies, as well as the introductory chapter and the citation appendix. Both authors contributed portions to the chapter on secondary sources.

In the second edition, Elizabeth Adelman took a leading role in updating the chapters on judicial opinions; legislative history; administrative law; ethics; and research strategies. Theodora Belniak, our new co-author, was responsible for drafting a new chapter on New York City law and for a complete re-write of the secondary sources chapter. In addition, she took a leading role in updating the chapters on the research process; legal research techniques; statutes, constitutions, local law, and court rules; updating; and the citation appendix. Suzanne Rowe contributed to each chapter in an editorial capacity. Two of the authors have written other titles in the Legal Research Series, and portions of their earlier work are reflected here.

We gratefully acknowledge the substantive contributions of Alison F. Alifano and Marshall R. Voizard. For superb research and editing assistance, we appreciate the work of Mason Whitcomb. Due to the small size of this book, some screens have been cropped and some page excerpts slightly modified. Please note that further reproduction is prohibited.

Elizabeth G. Adelman
Theodora Belniak
Suzanne E. Rowe
October 2011

New York Legal Research

Chapter 1

The Research Process and Legal Analysis

I. New York Legal Research

The fundamentals of legal research are the same in every American jurisdiction, though the details vary. While some variations are minor, others require specialized knowledge of the resources available and the analytical framework in which those resources are used. This book focuses on the resources and analysis required to be thorough and effective in researching New York law. It supplements this focus with brief explanations of federal research and research into the law of other states, both to introduce other resources and to highlight some of the variations.

II. Legal Research and Legal Analysis

The basic process of legal research is simple. For most print resources, you will begin with an index, find entries that appear relevant, read those sections of the text, and then find out whether more recent information is available. For most online research, you will search particular websites or databases using words likely to appear in relevant documents.

Legal analysis is interwoven throughout this process, raising challenging questions. In print research, which words will you look up in the index? How will you decide whether an index entry looks promising? With online research, how will you choose relevant words and construct a search most likely to produce the documents you need? When you read the text of a document, how will you determine whether it is relevant to your client's situation? How will you learn whether more recent material changed the law or merely applied it in a new situation? The answer to each of these questions requires legal analysis. This intersection of research and analysis can make legal research very difficult, especially for the novice. While this book's focus is legal research, it also includes the fundamental aspects of legal analysis required to conduct research competently.

This book is not designed to be a blueprint of every resource in the law library or search engine on the Internet; many resources contain their own detailed explanations in a preface or a "Help" section. This book is more like a manual or field guide, introducing the resources needed at each step of the research process and explaining how to use them. You will benefit most from this book by reading it in the library near the sources being discussed or with your computer open to relevant websites.

III. Types of Legal Authority

Before researching the law, you must be clear about the goal of your search. In every research situation, you want to find constitutional provisions, statutes, administrative rules, and judicial opinions that control your client's situation. In other words, you are searching for primary, mandatory authority.

Law is often divided along two lines. The first line distinguishes primary authority from secondary authority. *Primary authority* is law produced by government bodies with law-making power. Legislatures write statutes, courts write judicial opinions, and administrative agencies write rules (also called regulations). *Secondary authorities*, in contrast, are materials that are written about the law, generally by practicing attorneys, law professors, or legal editors. Secondary authorities include law practice guides, treatises, law review articles, and legal encyclopedias. These secondary sources are designed to aid researchers in understanding the law and locating primary authority.

Table 1-1. Examples of Authority in New York Research

	Mandatory Authority	Persuasive Authority
Primary Authority	New York constitution New York statutes New York Supreme Court cases	New Jersey constitution Massachusetts statutes Pennsylvania Supreme Court cases
Secondary Authority	—	Treatises Law review articles Legal encyclopedias

The second line is drawn between mandatory and persuasive authority. *Mandatory authority* is binding on the court that would decide a conflict if the situation were litigated. In a question of New York law, mandatory or binding authority includes New York's constitution, statutes enacted by the New York legislature, opinions of the New York Court of Appeals,[1] and New York administrative rules. *Persuasive authority* is not binding, but may be followed if relevant and well reasoned. Authority may be merely persuasive if it is from a different jurisdiction or if it is not produced by a law-making body. In a question of New York law, examples of persuasive authority include a similar California statute, an opinion of a Florida state court, and a law review article. Notice in Table 1-1 that persuasive authority may be either primary or secondary authority, while mandatory authority is always primary.

1. An opinion from the Appellate Division is binding on the trial courts if the New York Court of Appeals has not addressed the particular topic. Trial courts are bound by the precedent of the department of the Appellate Division where the trial court sits. If there is no precedent in that department, the trial court must follow the precedent of other departments. If there is a split in the Appellate Divisions outside the trial court's department, the trial court has the discretion to follow the precedent of either court. *See Mountain View Coach Lines, Inc. v. Storms*, 102 A.D.2d 663, 476 N.Y.S.2d 918 (1984).

Within primary, mandatory authority, there is an interlocking hierarchy of law involving constitutions, statutes, administrative rules, and judicial opinions. The constitution of each state is the supreme law of that state. If a statute is on point, that statute comes next in the hierarchy, followed by administrative rules. A judicial opinion may interpret the statute or rule, but the opinion cannot disregard either. A judicial opinion may, however, decide that a statute violates the constitution or that a rule oversteps its bounds. If there is no constitutional provision, statute, or administrative rule on point, the issue will be controlled by *common law*, also called judge-made law or case law.[2]

IV. Overview of the Research Process

Conducting effective legal research means following a process. This process leads to the authority that controls a legal issue as well as to commentary that may help you analyze new and complex legal matters. The outline in Table 1-2 presents the basic research process.

If you are unfamiliar with an area of law, you should follow each step of the process in the order indicated. Beginning with secondary sources will provide both context for the issues you must research and citations to relevant primary authority. As you gain experience in researching legal questions, you may choose to modify the process. For example, if you know that a statute controls a situation, you may choose to begin with that step.

A. Getting Started

1. Gathering Facts and Determining Jurisdiction

The first step in any research process is to gather the facts of the client's situation. In law practice, gathering facts may include inter-

---

2. Common law is derived from judicial decisions, rather than statutes or constitutions. *Black's Law Dictionary* 313 (Bryan A. Garner ed., 9th ed. 2009).

Table 1-2. Overview of the Research Process

1. Gather facts, decide which jurisdiction controls, and generate a list of *research terms.*
2. Consult *secondary authorities* such as treatises, legal encyclopedias, and law review articles. Secondary authorities explain the law and refer to primary authorities.
3. Search *enacted law,* including *constitutional provisions, statutes,* and *rules* by reviewing their indexes or searching online for your research terms. Read these primary authorities carefully, update them if necessary, and then study their annotations for cross-references to additional authorities and explanatory materials.
4. Research *case law.* Find citations to *cases* by searching *digests* (topical indexes) or *online databases.* Read the cases either in *reporters* (books that publish cases) or online.
5. *Update* legal authorities by using a citator such as Shepard's or KeyCite to (a) ensure that an authority is still respected and (b) find additional sources that may be relevant to the research project.
6. *End your research* when you have no holes in your analysis and when you begin seeing the same authorities repeatedly.

viewing the client, reviewing documents, and talking to colleagues who are also working for the client.

An early question that arises for any research project is which jurisdiction's law controls. This book assumes that the client's situation is controlled by New York law, but you must determine whether federal law, the law of another state, tribal law, or local law is binding.

2. *Generating Research Terms*

After gathering facts and determining the jurisdiction, generate a list of research terms. Many legal resources in print use lengthy indexes as the starting point for finding legal authority. Electronic sources often require the researcher to enter words that are likely to appear in a synopsis or in the full text of relevant documents. To ensure you are thorough in beginning a research project, you will need a compre-

Table 1-3. Generating Research Terms

Journalistic Approach	
Who:	Person with strong religious beliefs, prisoner
What:	Personal hygiene, beards
How:	Forced shaving
Why:	Religious freedom, cultural freedom, personal autonomy
When:	Post-arrest, during incarceration
Where:	Prison

hensive list of words, terms, and phrases that may lead to law on point. These may be legal terms or common words that describe the client's situation. The items on this list are *research terms* or *keywords.*

Organized brainstorming is the best way to compile a comprehensive list of research terms. Some researchers ask the journalistic questions: Who? What? How? Why? When? Where? Others use a mnemonic device like TARPP, which stands for Things, Actions, Remedies, People, and Places. Whether you use one of these suggestions or develop your own method, generate a broad range of research terms regarding the facts, issues, and desired solutions of your client's situation. Include in the list both specific and general words. Try to think of synonyms and antonyms for each term since at this point you are uncertain which terms an index may include. Using a legal dictionary or thesaurus may help you generate additional terms.

Consider the following example: A friend's uncle was recently arrested. In keeping with his cultural and religious beliefs, the uncle has long hair and a beard. The local prison required that the uncle cut his long hair and shave his beard, citing safety and the need to be able to identify the man while in holding. Your friend would like you to represent the uncle, and you need to know about any laws, statutes, or regulations governing the alteration of a prisoner's personal appearance and whether such alterations are a violation of the uncle's rights. Table 1-3 provides examples of research terms you might use to begin work on this project.

In initial brainstorming, the goal is to produce as many terms as possible. But when you begin researching, use the terms that appear on the list most often or that seem most important. As your research progresses, you will learn new research terms to include in the list and decide to take others off. For example, a secondary source may refer to a *term of art*, a word or phrase that has special meaning in a particular area of law. Later in your research, you may read cases that give you insights into the key words judges tend to use in discussing this topic. These terms and words need to be added to the list.

Review the list periodically to help you refine your research. If an online search produces far too many results, review the list for more specific search terms. On the other hand, if the terms you use initially produce no hits, review the list for alternative, more general terms.

B. Conducting Research—Organization of This Book

The remainder of this book explains how to use your research terms to conduct legal research. Chapter 2 both reviews print research techniques and introduces fundamental online research techniques. Then the book turns to specific resources. It begins with secondary sources in Chapter 3 because those sources are often the first that a researcher turns to in a new research project. Then the book covers primary authority, which is the goal of legal research. Chapter 4 addresses case law, including an introduction to judicial opinions and techniques for researching to find relevant cases. Chapter 5 begins the book's coverage of enacted law, explaining research of the New York Constitution, New York statutes, local law, and New York court rules. Chapter 6 is devoted to legislative history research. Chapter 7 addresses administrative law.

Following this discussion of secondary and primary authority, Chapter 8 explains how to update legal authority using KeyCite and Shepard's citators. Chapter 9 outlines New York City research. Chapter 10 addresses ethical rules that govern New York law practice. Finally, Chapter 11 discusses research strategies as well as how to organize your research. You may prefer to skim that chapter now and refer to it frequently, even though a number of references in it will not become clear until you have read the intervening chapters.

Appendix A provides an overview of the conventions lawyers follow in citing legal authority in their documents. Appendix B contains a selected bibliography of texts on legal research and analysis. The general research texts tend to concentrate on federal resources, supplementing this book's brief introduction to those resources.

Chapter 2

Legal Research Techniques

Legal research uses print sources, government websites, and online providers like Lexis and Westlaw. While each resource is slightly different, they share some basic research techniques in common. This chapter covers the basic techniques for using print and online legal resources. Researchers experienced in both print and online resources will find here a helpful review. Those with less experience in one type of resource will need to consider these techniques carefully, as later chapters assume familiarity with them. The chapter closes with important questions to ask in deciding whether to use print or online sources—a decision you should make at each step of the research process.

I. Print Research Strategies

Today, fewer researchers approach legal problems with a firm foundation in print research techniques. In large part, this is because so much information is available online, which has decreased the demand for print sources among college students and professionals. In legal research, however, not all material is available online. Even when sources are available both in print and online, print sources are sometimes more efficient to use. The efficiency may be simply because the sources are free in a library. More often, the efficiency results from the way the resources are organized.

A. Finding a Legal Source by Citation

Retrieving a document in a print source is easy when you have its citation. Simply find the relevant book, and turn to the portion indicated by the citation. The citation may be to a particular volume and page (e.g., for a judicial opinion), a code name and section (e.g., for a statute), or a volume and section number (e.g., for a treatise). Example citations are listed below.

Example judicial opinion:	*People v. Carmona*, 606 N.Y.S.2d 879
Example statute:	New York Civ. Prac. L. & R. § 4505
Example treatise:	5 N.Y. Practice, Evidence in New York State and Federal Courts § 5:36

B. Table-of-Contents Searching

Most print sources begin with a table of contents. One way to begin searching these sources is to skim the table of contents for your research terms. The table of contents will refer to relevant pages, section numbers, or paragraph numbers, depending on how the source is organized.

Because a table of contents lists the headings used in that volume, it provides an analytical overview of the topics covered. Skimming the table of contents of an encyclopedia can show how lawyers typically organize concepts in a particular area of law. Reviewing a table of contents for a statutory provision can provide context for the analysis of a single statute. Thus, you can use the table of contents as an overview of the law and to find specific portions of the volume that may contain helpful information.

C. Topic Searching with a Print Index

The index is another frequent starting point in print resources. Using research terms you generated based on the client's problem, search the index for references to particular pages or sections of the volume. Often, it is wise to spend several minutes in the index looking for a number of research terms. This technique ensures that you begin your research in the most helpful part of the volume, not just the part you encountered first.

It is common for an index to contain cross-references to other entries. Sometimes cross-references can be confusing as to whether they refer to different subheadings or to different main headings. Take a few moments to learn the cross-reference signals of a new book, as they vary among resources.

In multi-volume series, the index is likely to be located in the last volume. Separate indexes may be provided for each volume or for each legal topic. In a case digest, for example, the "Analysis" outline at the beginning of a topic can provide context for the concepts covered and suggest particular portions of the topic that may lead to relevant cases.

D. Pocket Parts and Supplements

Many print sources are updated using pocket parts. These are extra pages sent by the publisher to be inserted in the back cover of a particular volume. Pocket parts often contain the most recent material available in print, so it is important to check any volume used in research to see whether it has a pocket part. If a pocket part becomes too large to fit in the back of a volume, it will be published as a softcover supplement and placed next to the volume.

In addition to updates to single volumes, a softcover supplement may exist for an entire series of books. This supplement will likely be shelved at the end of the series. It will contain the most up-to-date information available in print.

II. Online Legal Research

Online research is often necessary for conducting effective and cost-efficient legal research. Unlike other online research, however, legal research requires a high level of precision, both in deciding where to search and in constructing searches. The following examples show why. If you are searching for a hotel where you can stay while taking depositions in Albany, a quick Internet search could return dozens of possible hotels that fit your price range. Selecting the first one on a results list carries no special advantage or disadvantage. In online legal research, however, you cannot simply follow whichever case you find first. Overlooking a recent case by the New York Court of Appeals could result in malpractice.

Online legal research can be conducted on a variety of sites; some of the key sites are listed in Table 2-1. New York primary authority is widely available from the websites of the State Senate, the Department of State, and the New York State Unified Court System.

Some of the more common commercial providers of online legal sources are HeinOnline, FindLaw, Lexis, Loislaw, VersusLaw and Westlaw. The most widely used providers with the largest databases are Lexis and Westlaw. The rest of this chapter focuses on their services, though the explanations will be generally applicable to other online providers as well.

In addition to these sources, many legal researchers use "gateway" sites that link to a variety of online resources. Two university-provided gateway sites are Cornell University Law School's Legal Information Institute at www.law.cornell.edu and Washburn University School of Law's WashLaw at www.washlaw.edu.

If the information you need is available for free on one of the government or university sites, think carefully before using a costly commercial provider. Sometimes a commercial provider's extensive database or sophisticated search engine will make the cost worthwhile, but you need to consider the costs and efficiencies involved in every search.

A. Finding a Legal Source by Citation

When working online, retrieving a document is as simple as typing the citation into a designated box on the proper screen. On Lexis,

Table 2-1. Selected Websites for Online Research

Provider	Web Address
State Sites	
New York Senate	www.nysenate.gov
New York Department of State	www.dos.state.ny.us
New York State Unified Court System	www.nycourts.gov
Commercial Sites	
FindLaw	www.findlaw.com
Lexis	www.lexisnexis.com
Loislaw	www.loislaw.com*
VersusLaw	www.versuslaw.com
Westlaw	www.westlaw.com
HeinOnline	http://home.heinonline.org
Gateway Sites	
Cornell University Law School's Legal Information Institute	www.law.cornell.edu
Washburn University School of Law's WashLaw	www.washlaw.edu

* Loislaw is free to members of the New York State Bar. Enter through the bar's website at www.nysba.org. Click on "Membership" and then "Member Benefits and Savings Programs."

this function is called "Get a Document"; on Westlaw, it is called "Find by citation." Figure 2-1 provides a sample Lexis search screen, while Figure 2-2 shows a New York case retrieved through that search.

Note that online services typically use the print citation to identify particular documents. In other words, to retrieve a case from Lexis, you will enter the volume and page of the print reporter. Most online providers list accepted citation formats, which vary from one online site to another.

Figure 2-1. "Get a Document" on Lexis

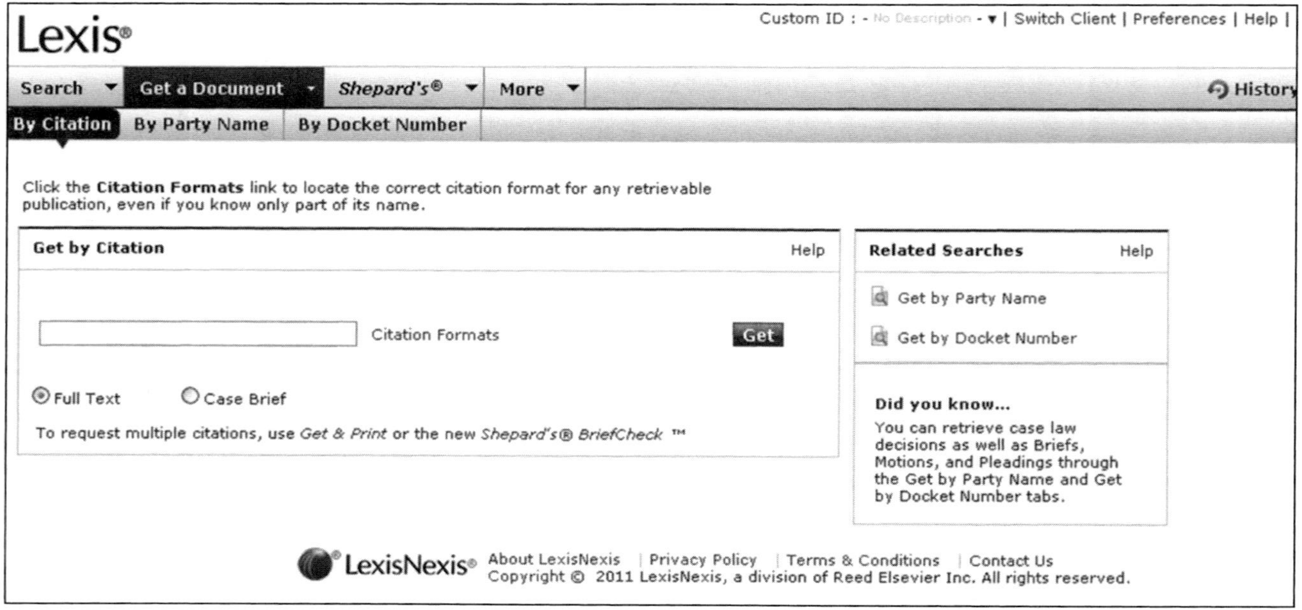

Source: Copyright 2011 LexisNexis, a division of Reed Elsevier Inc. All Rights Reserved. LexisNexis and the Knowledge Burst logo are registered trademarks of Reed Elsevier Properties Inc. and are used with the permission of LexisNexis.

Figure 2-2. Sample New York Case on Lexis

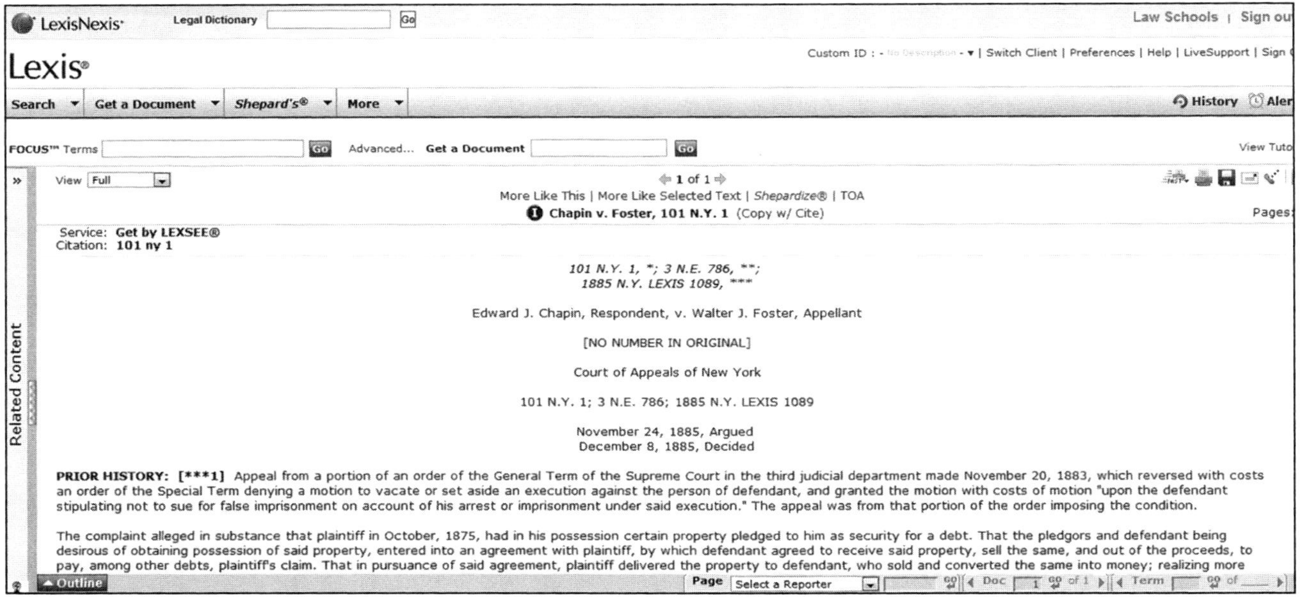

LexisNexis® Legal Dictionary Go Law Schools | Sign ou

Lexis® Custom ID : - No Description - ▾ | Switch Client | Preferences | Help | LiveSupport | Sign

Search ▾ | Get a Document ▾ | *Shepard's®* ▾ | More ▾ History Aler

FOCUS™ Terms Go Advanced... Get a Document Go View Tuto

View Full

1 of 1

More Like This | More Like Selected Text | *Shepardize®* | TOA

Chapin v. Foster, 101 N.Y. 1 (Copy w/ Cite)

Pages:

Service: **Get by LEXSEE®**
Citation: **101 ny 1**

*101 N.Y. 1, *; 3 N.E. 786, **;*
*1885 N.Y. LEXIS 1089, ****

Edward J. Chapin, Respondent, v. Walter J. Foster, Appellant

[NO NUMBER IN ORIGINAL]

Court of Appeals of New York

101 N.Y. 1; 3 N.E. 786; 1885 N.Y. LEXIS 1089

November 24, 1885, Argued
December 8, 1885, Decided

PRIOR HISTORY: [*1]** Appeal from a portion of an order of the General Term of the Supreme Court in the third judicial department made November 20, 1883, which reversed with costs an order of the Special Term denying a motion to vacate or set aside an execution against the person of defendant, and granted the motion with costs of motion "upon the defendant stipulating not to sue for false imprisonment on account of his arrest or imprisonment under said execution." The appeal was from that portion of the order imposing the condition.

The complaint alleged in substance that plaintiff in October, 1875, had in his possession certain property pledged to him as security for a debt. That the pledgors and defendant being desirous of obtaining possession of said property, entered into an agreement with plaintiff, by which defendant agreed to receive said property, sell the same, and out of the proceeds, to pay, among other debts, plaintiff's claim. That in pursuance of said agreement, plaintiff delivered the property to defendant, who sold and converted the same into money; realizing more

Related Content | Outline | Page Select a Reporter | Doc 1 of 1 | Term of

B. Table-of-Contents Searching

An increasing number of online sources provide tables of contents. As in print research, the advantages to skimming an online table of contents are (1) seeing how various issues and topics are related in that area of law and (2) finding relevant portions of the document or database.

An online table of contents works just like a table of contents in print, except that the initial page will list only major headings. Subheadings may be accessed by clicking a "plus" symbol next to one of the headings. For example, to find the New York statute on arson in Westlaw, begin by clicking on "Directory" at the top of the Westlaw home page. Locate a New York statutes database, for example, "McKinney's Consolidated Laws of New York Annotated." Next, click on the "Table of Contents" link. Then, click on the "plus" before "McKinney's Consolidated Laws of New York Annotated," and scroll through until you see "Penal Law." Part Three covers specific offenses, and within that part, Title I addresses crimes against property. Article 150 is on arson; individual statutes are listed underneath. See Figure 2-3.

C. Topic Searching Online

Sophisticated online search engines and services have tools for topic searching. The most user-friendly of these tools allows the researcher to begin with a list of broad areas of law and narrow the topic by clicking through successive lists. Topic searching on Lexis uses the tool "Search by Topic," available from the "Search" pull-down menu. On Westlaw, this topic searching tool is called "KeySearch," which is accessed through the "Key Numbers" link at the top of any screen.

In either service, you have the option of entering terms into a search box or clicking through lists of topics. To continue the arson example above, on Westlaw's KeySearch, you could enter the term "arson" in the search box. The search results would be the topics in KeySearch that contain that term. Alternatively, in either service, you could click through successive layers of topics, moving from the general to the specific. Following this approach, you may select the broad

Figure 2-3. Table-of-Contents Search on Westlaw

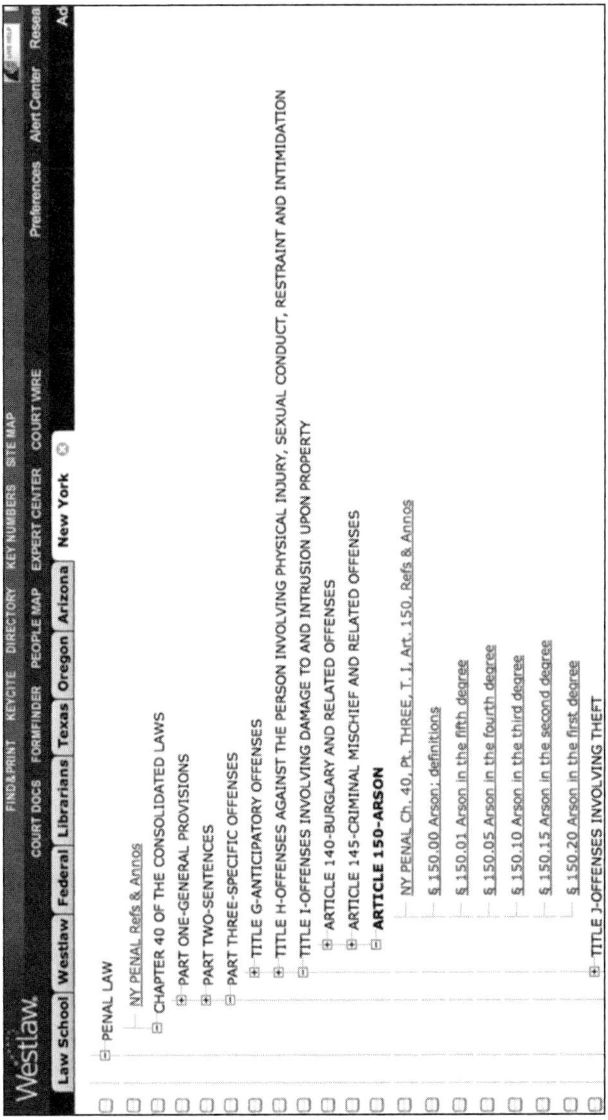

Westlaw
FIND&PRINT KEYCITE DIRECTORY KEY NUMBERS SITE MAP
COURT DOCS FORMFINDER PEOPLE MAP EXPERT CENTER COURT WIRE
Preferences Alert Center Resea
Law School | Westlaw | Federal | Librarians | Texas | Oregon | Arizona | New York
Ad

PENAL LAW
NY PENAL Refs & Annos
CHAPTER 40 OF THE CONSOLIDATED LAWS
PART ONE-GENERAL PROVISIONS
PART TWO-SENTENCES
PART THREE-SPECIFIC OFFENSES
TITLE G-ANTICIPATORY OFFENSES
TITLE H-OFFENSES AGAINST THE PERSON INVOLVING PHYSICAL INJURY, SEXUAL CONDUCT, RESTRAINT AND INTIMIDATION
TITLE I-OFFENSES INVOLVING DAMAGE TO AND INTRUSION UPON PROPERTY
ARTICLE 140-BURGLARY AND RELATED OFFENSES
ARTICLE 145-CRIMINAL MISCHIEF AND RELATED OFFENSES
ARTICLE 150-ARSON
NY PENAL Ch. 40, Pt. THREE, T. I, Art. 150, Refs & Annos
§ 150.00 Arson; definitions
§ 150.01 Arson in the fifth degree
§ 150.05 Arson in the fourth degree
§ 150.10 Arson in the third degree
§ 150.15 Arson in the second degree
§ 150.20 Arson in the first degree
TITLE J-OFFENSES INVOLVING THEFT

Source: Reprinted with permission of West, a Thomson Reuters business.

topic "Criminal Justice," narrow the topic to "Particular Crimes," and finally choose "Arson." See Figure 2-4. Under either approach, the final screen requires you to select a jurisdiction, such as New York state cases, before running the search.

D. Terms-and-Connectors Searching

One of the most common techniques for searching online is with "terms and connectors." These searches use connecting symbols to dictate where search terms should be in relation to each other in the documents retrieved. An outline of the steps to constructing an effective search is provided in Table 2-2.

Table 2-2. Outline for Constructing Terms-and-Connectors Searches

1. Generate search terms, then modify them with expanders and placeholders.
2. Add connectors.
3. Select a database.
4. Use relevant segments or fields to restrict the search by date, court, judge, or other option.
5. Refine the search based on the results.

1. Generate Search Terms

Generate a comprehensive list of search terms, following the suggestions in Chapter 1. This step is critically important in online research, given the literal nature of search engines. If the author of a particular document does not use the exact term you are searching for, that document will not appear in your results.

Next, modify the search terms with expanders and placeholders so that a search will find variations of your words. The exclamation point expands words beyond a common root. For example, "employ!" will find employee, employer, employed, employs, employing,

Figure 2-4. Topic Searching on Westlaw

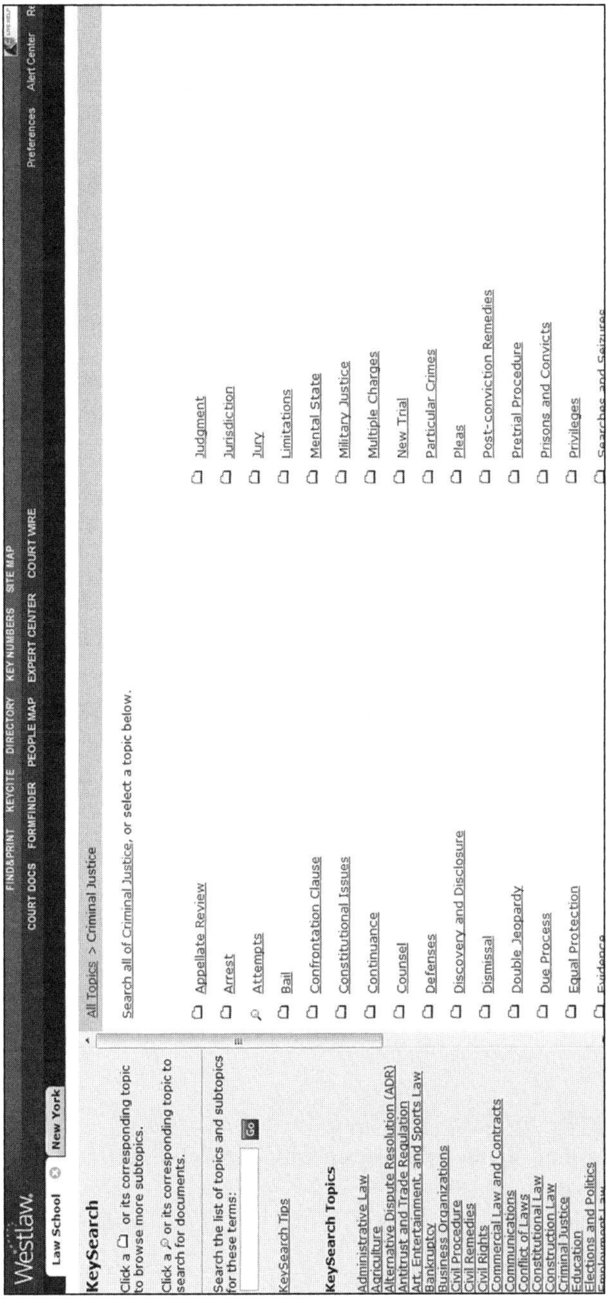

Source: Reprinted with permission of West, a Thomson Reuters business.

etc. The asterisk serves as a placeholder for an individual letter. Up to three asterisks can be used in a single term. This symbol is helpful when you are not sure which form of the word is used, or when you are not sure of the spelling of a word. For example, the search term "dr*nk" will find drink, drank, and drunk. Place holders are preferable to the expander in some instances. Using an expander on "trad!" with hopes of finding trade, trading, trades, etc. will also produce results that include traditional. A better search term may be "trad***."

2. Add Connectors

Connectors determine where search terms will be placed in relation to one another in targeted documents. Effective use of connectors is critical in finding relevant authority. Even minimally sophisticated combinations of parentheses and the various connectors can make your searches much more effective. Table 2-3 summarizes the most common connectors used on Lexis and Westlaw.

Most connectors are the same for the two services. However, two differences can cause some confusion. On Lexis, searching alternative terms requires the use of the connector "or." On Westlaw, a blank space is interpreted as "or," although typing in that connector will produce the same result. The second difference concerns phrases or terms of art. Lexis reads a blank as joining words in a phrase. By contrast, to search a phrase on Westlaw, the terms must be enclosed in quotation marks. Examples are shown in Table 2-4.

In both Lexis and Westlaw, parentheses are used to refine terms-and-connectors searches. Note the following example:

> (covenant or contract) /p (noncompetition or "restraint of trade") /p employ!

This search will look for documents within one paragraph that contain:

- either of the terms (covenant or contract) and
- either of the terms (noncompetition or "restraint of trade") and
- variations of the terms employ, employee, employer, employment, etc.

Table 2-3. Connectors and Commands

Goal	Lexis	Westlaw
Find alternative terms anywhere in the document	or	or blank space
Find both terms anywhere in the document	and &	and &
Find both terms within a particular distance from each other	/p = in 1 paragraph /s = in 1 sentence /n = within *n* words	/p = in 1 paragraph /s = in 1 sentence /n = within *n* words
Find terms used as a phrase	leave a blank space between each word of the phrase	put the phrase in quotation marks
Control the hierarchy of searching	parentheses	parentheses
Exclude terms	and not	but not %
Extend the end of a term	!	!
Hold the place of letters in a term	*	*

Table 2-4. Example Queries

Goal	Lexis Query	Westlaw Query
Search for alternative terms	prisoner or inmate or convict	prisoner inmate convict
Search for a phrase	personal hygiene	"personal hygiene"

Without the parentheses, the search will look for documents containing any one of the following three alternatives:

- the word covenant or
- the word contract within the same paragraph as the word noncompetition or
- the term restraint of trade within the same paragraph as any variation of the terms employ, employee, employer, employment, etc.

3. Select a Database

Terms-and-connectors searches are typically conducted in the full text of documents to look for exact matches. Thus, to begin searching in a service with multiple databases, you must choose which subset of that provider's resources to search. Your research will be more efficient if you restrict each search to the smallest subset of databases that will contain the documents needed. In addition, searches in the smaller subsets are typically cheaper than searches in vast databases.

Lexis and Westlaw divide their resources into subsets by type of document, topic, and jurisdiction. In Lexis, these groups are simply called "sources." In Westlaw, information is grouped into "databases." Both Lexis and Westlaw have directories to allow you to browse among the sources and databases that are available for research. Clicking on the "i" next to the name of a source or database will provide information about its scope.

Both services have compiled New York databases under a tab that you can add to the default set of search tabs. On Lexis, use the "Research System" and then the "Search" tabs, and finally click on "Add/Edit Tabs." Westlaw allows you to do the same from any page by clicking "Add/Remove Tabs." Note that the list of sources or databases shown on a particular page may not include all that are available. On Lexis, you may need to click on "View more." On Westlaw, you may need to add more databases to those shown on a particular tab.

4. Restrict the Search with "Segments" and "Fields"

With terms-and-connectors searching, both Lexis and Westlaw allow you to search specific parts of documents, such as the date, author, or court. On Lexis, these specific parts are called document segments; on Westlaw, they are called fields. The options are available on drop-down menus. A segment or field term is added to the basic search with an appropriate connector.

Three examples demonstrate the usefulness of segment and field searching. First, in conducting a full-text search, you can ensure that the results directly address your topic by searching the syllabi or synopses of the documents. Because this segment or field summarizes the contents of the document, your terms will appear there only if they are the focus of the document. Thus, the search will weed out documents in which your terms are mentioned only in passing or in a footnote. Second, if you know the author of a relevant opinion or article, you can search for her name in the appropriate segment or field, eliminating documents in which the person is referred to only tangentially. Third, to research cases on a statute that was modified five years ago, you could restrict the date of your search to cover that period.

5. *Refine the Search with "Focus" and "Locate"*

With a query of terms and connectors, a search may result in a reasonable number of highly relevant documents, or no documents, or more than one thousand documents. In the latter two instances, refining the search is necessary. When a search produces no results, use broader connectors (e.g., search for terms in the same paragraph rather than in the same sentence), use more general terms, or use a larger set of sources or a larger database. When a search produces a long list of results, skim them to see whether they are on point. If the results seem irrelevant, modify or edit the search query by using more specific terms, more restrictive connectors, or a smaller set of sources or databases.

The "FOCUS™ Terms" feature on Lexis and the "Locate" feature on Westlaw can be used to narrow results further. These features allow a researcher to construct a new search within a prior search, and produce a refined subset of the initial search results. These features can be very cost efficient because they do not result in the additional charges of a new search. Indeed, a good strategy may be to create a broader initial search than you otherwise might and plan to conduct a series of restricting searches on the results.

6. *Example Terms-and-Connectors Search*

Continuing the example from Chapter 1, the following Westlaw search uses the tools described above:

(prisoner inmate convict) /p (hygien! beard!)

The search will look for documents containing any of the terms prisoner or inmate or convict, so long as one of those terms appears in the same paragraph as variations of the terms hygiene or beard. After reviewing some of the documents returned in the search, you may decide to refine the search by omitting the term convict because it is an antiquated identifier. If the results are still not sufficiently focused on your topic, consider adding more narrow terms.

E. Natural-Language Searching

Natural-language search engines allow searches that use a simple question or phrase, as opposed to an arcane series of terms and connectors. These search engines lack the precision of terms-and-connectors searching but allow you to construct a search more quickly and intuitively. A natural-language search for the project in Chapter 1 is "Can an inmate be forced to shave his beard or cut his hair in spite of religious beliefs?"

Natural-language search engines are designed to produce a list of results and to rank the value of the results. Natural-language searching can seem straightforward after the frustration of terms-and-connectors searches that returned no results, but several caveats are important. First, documents are selected based on relevance, but in the computer's selection process relevance could simply mean that the key terms appear frequently in the document, that they appear close to each other in the document, or that they appear in important parts of the document (e.g., the synopsis or the thesis paragraph). Second, on search engines like Google and Yahoo!, some documents appear first in result lists simply because sponsors pay for this privilege. Sometimes the best hit from your perspective will be the search engine's fifteenth result, so skimming through the results is always very important.

On Lexis and Westlaw, the natural-language programs are set to retrieve a particular number of results. Often that number is twenty or one hundred, though you can change the default. The fact that the computer returned one hundred documents does not mean that those one hundred documents are all relevant. Natural-language searching can produce lists of documents that are not very relevant to your research. This may mean that no better matches exist or that the search was not crafted well enough. When conducting the search on the Internet, poor results may mean that this particular search engine did not scan the portion of the Internet that contains the needed documents.

While natural-language searching can be very helpful to the novice online researcher, skilled terms-and-connectors searching will almost always be more powerful and accurate.

F. The Next Generation of Searching: Lexis Advance and WestlawNext

Recently, Lexis and Westlaw introduced researchers to new search interfaces named, respectively, Lexis Advance and WestlawNext. The universe through which a researcher can search remains the same, but the method by which results are gathered and displayed are different from the traditional interfaces. Unlike in Lexis or Westlaw, in which the researcher must select a particular database to search, the new interfaces search the entire universe of material available through a subscription. The results are then organized by type; a single search will return cases, codes, statutes, practice materials, and regulations.

Mimicking popular Internet search engines, Lexis Advance and WestlawNext have single search boxes and default to natural language searches. Unlike in the classic versions of Lexis or Westlaw that require a focused search within a type of document, the researcher need not have an understanding of the structure of government or the origins of legal documents in order to pull results from a search in Lexis Advance or WestlawNext. Much like with Internet search engines, it is a rare search that returns no results. The ease of use for Lexis Advance and WestlawNext is apparent, but the practical application of these new interfaces for complex legal research remains unclear. For the novice researcher, the familiarity of its interface may be a comfort, but, for the seasoned researcher, its broad sweep of resources may be a hindrance.[1]

---

1. Although each new interface has much of the functionality of its older version, much of it is "hidden" in an advanced search feature or a drop-down

G. Moving through Online Documents

In most online services, you can move through the document by scrolling through pages or by clicking through search terms. If the search term feature is not available, try using the "Find" feature on your browser. Some online services attempt to replicate the page turning experience by including a browsing feature so that you can see the previous or next page of a set of documents. In Lexis this feature is "Book Browse" and in Westlaw this feature is "Previous Section" or "Next Section." Reviewing nearby documents through book browsing can help provide context to the original document you were viewing.

H. Printing, Downloading, or E-mailing Results

Both Lexis and Westlaw allow you to download or e-mail documents as opposed to printing them. These options are effective early in a research project because electronic documents allow you to skim quickly to the point where your terms appear using your computer's "Find" function. Moreover, now that most word processors allow highlighting and in-line annotating, you may choose to read and organize your research documents entirely on your computer. However, many researchers still find it easier to read documents carefully on paper as opposed to the computer screen.

I. Keeping Track

Those researchers new to online legal searching may benefit from completing the chart in Table 2-5 before beginning a search. Even experienced researchers should keep notes containing the dates searched, the searches performed, and the search results. These notes will help you stay on track and avoid duplicating research on a later

---

menu. Terms and connectors remain functional, but the importance of their use is not made apparent to those unaware of them.

Table 2-5. Example Notes for Online Searching

Date of Search: *October 31, 2011*

Issue: *Whether a member of a religion that dictates the wearing of a beard may be forced to shave his beard while in the custody of a correctional facility?*

Online Site or Service: *Westlaw*

Source: *New York state cases (short name: NY-CS)*

Search Terms: *[See list in Table 1-3]*

Date Restriction: *None*

Search: *(prisoner inmate convict) /p (hygien! beard!)*

Focus: *hygiene*

Results: *[Either list your results here or print a cite list to attach to your notes.]*

date. Notes will also indicate the time period that needs to be updated as you near your project deadline.

Online services provide lists of past searches and results, and you should form the habit of printing or saving them. On Lexis, click "History." On Westlaw, click "Research Trail." Lexis saves results for thirty days, while Westlaw saves them for fourteen days.

III. Choosing to Research in Print or Online

Even when a document is available both in print and online, the savvy researcher needs to consider the following questions in deciding which media to use.

A. Where Is the Document Available?

Recent primary authority is increasingly available both in print and online. Some important secondary sources may be available only in print, while some resources used to find and update the law are available only online. Do not assume that there is universal overlap between print and online sources.

B. How Fast and How Efficient Will Research Be?

Many researchers find that beginning legal research in print is more productive than beginning online because books tend to provide more context, which keeps the project focused. In addition, most attorneys find it easier to read more carefully and thoroughly in print than on a computer screen. Online research has a number of advantages, though, including the ease of searching and the convenience of downloading or printing important documents.

C. What Is the Document?

Novice legal researchers sometimes find it difficult to distinguish between different types of documents online. In print sources, different types of authorities often appear in separate books, making it easy to tell them apart. In contrast, many documents look the same on a computer screen. Moreover, hyperlinks in online sources allow you to jump from a case to a statute to an article in a few clicks. In an actual library, those moves may take you to different shelves or even different floors. If you favor the tactility of print research, you may prefer researching in a law library instead of online sources.

D. Who Wrote the Document?

Be sure that you know who wrote a document before you base your analysis on it. Remember that only some documents are binding and authoritative. Documents written by courts, legislatures, and administrative agencies are "the law." Articles and treatises written by recognized experts in a field are not binding, but these sources can be very persuasive and are often authoritative. These types of documents are often available both in print and online. However, there are many other documents online with little or no authoritative value and whose authors have only an ill-informed opinion to share. Know who the author is and whether he has the reputation to give weight to his assertions.

E. How Accurate Is the Document?

Print material tends to be more accurate than online versions of the same documents. The very process of publishing, with its numerous stages of editing and revising, ensures a high level of reliability. In contrast, online material is often valued for the speed with which it becomes available. With this speed comes an inevitable sacrifice of accuracy; even reputable services post documents with less editing than a book would warrant. If you need to quote an authority, or are otherwise relying on very precise language from it, print sources are always preferable.

F. Does the Document Provide Pinpoint Citation?

Citations in legal briefs and memoranda require reference to the exact portion of the cited document that provides support. Often this citation will be to a particular page number, section number, or paragraph in a document. While many online services provide these specific references (called *pinpoint citations*), some do not. If the online service you use for research does not provide specific references to page breaks, section numbers, or paragraphs, you will need to consult the resource in print.

G. When Was the Document Published?

Print sources take longer to reach the researcher than online sources. To find the most current material, online sources often provide a clear advantage. But even websites may contain outdated material; you still need to determine whether an online document has a date indicating when it was posted or last updated.

When using an online database, you must also ensure that it covers a period of time relevant to your research. Online sources tend to cover more recent periods; thus, finding older material may require using print sources. A notable exception is HeinOnline at www.heinonline.org, which makes available older law review articles that often are not included in other online sources.

H. How Much Context Is Provided?

Most print sources include tables of contents or outlines that provide an overview of the legal area. These tools can provide context so that a novice researcher can understand the big picture before concentrating on a narrow legal issue. An increasing number of online sources also provide these tools, and when searching online you should use them whenever they are available. Clicking on a table of contents link can show where a document is placed within related material. This tactic is especially helpful when an online search lands you in the middle of a single document and you lack the visual clues or the context to understand how that document relates to the bigger picture.

Many lawyers—from novices to experts—have stories about the great case or article that they stumbled across while looking for something else. These stories result not just from serendipity but from using resources that put related information together. In the library, scan the books shelved nearby helpful sources, and skim through relevant books to see whether other sections are on point. Sometimes online searching also produces serendipitous results; if you feel you may be close to the exact material you need but cannot find it, try using an online table of contents link to reorient yourself.

I. How Much Does It Cost, and Who Is Paying?

Some sources are free to use. Print sources are "free" in the sense that the library has already paid for them. Online sources provided by governments and universities are also free. When cost is an issue, consider using these sources first.

Online research using commercial services, on the other hand, can be very expensive. A single research project, poorly conceived and sloppily done, can cost hundreds or even thousands of dollars. But never assume online research is *too* expensive—its efficiency is often worth its price. Moreover, many law offices negotiate reasonable flat rates that allow them access to the narrow set of online sources they use routinely in their practice.

Check the billing practices in your office before using commercial online sources: What type of contract does your office have with the online provider? How will your office pass along charges to clients? How much are the clients willing to pay? Will the office cover the costs of online pro bono work? Also be sure you know your office's policy regarding the printing of online documents, which often brings extra charges.

Chapter 3

Secondary Sources

I. Introduction

The law is varied and complicated, and no one is an expert in all areas. Fluency in one area of the law is the product of years of practice, but secondary sources can help make you conversant. Penned by experts, secondary sources will provide you with contextual background, terms of art, and major sources of primary law. Secondary sources provide a detailed introduction to an area of law and increase research efficiency.

In the legal world, primary sources are the published materials of a court, legislature, or administrative agency. Secondary sources are editorial offshoots of primary source material; they offer commentaries, proposed definitions, case summaries, legislative histories, and analyses of laws, codes, and judicial opinions. They are updated at various intervals and typically are offered for a fee.

This chapter discusses the common types of secondary sources that you may run across in your research, providing a brief description of format and content. It also offers some tips about how to vet a secondary source and how to optimize your research strategy with secondary sources.

II. Encyclopedias

Similar to general encyclopedias, legal encyclopedias are organized alphabetically by topic and provide summaries of legal topics. Unlike

Figure 3-1. ***New York Jurisprudence*** **Table of Contents Excerpt**

I. IN GENERAL (§§1 TO 11)
II. STATE CORRECTIONAL INSTITUTIONS (§§12 TO 24)
  A. IN GENERAL (§§12 TO 17)
  B. CORRECTIONAL FACILITIES (§§18 TO 24)
III. FACILITIES FOR TREATMENT OF MENTALLY ILL AND RETARDED INMATES (§§25 TO 37)
  A. MENTALLY ILL INMATES (§§25 TO 37)
  B. MENTALLY RETARDED INMATES (§§31 TO 37)
IV. FACILITIES, PROGRAMS, AND SERVICES FOR YOUTH (§§38 TO 61)
  A. FACILITIES (§§38 TO 52)

Source: *New York Jurisprudence, 2d.* Reprinted with permission of West, a Thomson Reuters business.

many discipline-specific encyclopedias, legal encyclopedias are written by staff editors and do not explain the law or attempt to reconcile conflicting definitions.

A. State Encyclopedias

New York Jurisprudence, now in its second series, is published by West. Also known as "New York Jur," it provides brief summaries and definitions of New York state legal topics. In addition to these summaries, each section often provides references to primary sources of law, including cases, statutes, and regulations.

New York Jur is organized by topic and by section within a topic. Figure 3-1 is an excerpt from table of contents to the volume on Penal Law.

Carmody-Wait, 2d, Cyclopedia of New York Practice with Forms, "Carmody-Wait, 2d," is also published by West. Carmody-Wait, 2d focuses on civil practice and criminal procedure, with an in-depth treatment of New York's rules of civil procedure. Like New York Jur, Carmody-Wait, 2d is organized by topic and further divided into sections.

B. Multi-jurisdictional Encyclopedias

American Jurisprudence, or "Am Jur," is published by West and is in its second series. Much like its New York counterpart, Am Jur provides brief summaries and definitions of legal topics. Its content covers all areas of state and federal law and includes references to important primary sources in various jurisdictions. It is organized by topic and then by section number within the topic. Similarly, *Corpus Juris Secundum* (called "CJS") is a national legal encyclopedia, published by West, and organized by topic and section.

C. Using Legal Encyclopedias

Encyclopedias are printed in series, and you need to use the most current series when researching. To figure out if the series is current, check the publication date on the inside cover of the volume and check the stamped pocket part in the back of the volume. Also, encyclopedias sometimes have semi-annual softcover updates, shelved at the end of the hardcover set. If the series has been updated within the last six months, then it is most likely as current as possible. With the exception of the semi-annual updates, volumes will be in hardcover and the finding aids will be in softcover.

Legal encyclopedias often come with an impressive number of finding aids: keyword indexes (also known as general indexes), tables of common words and phrases, tables of cases, and tables of courts and rules. However, the most-used finding aids are the keyword index and the table of cases. The table of cases is an alphabetical list of all cases mentioned in the encyclopedia accompanied by page references to its citing section. The keyword index is an alphabetical organization of topics and subtopics with accompanying references to the title of the volume and the section number. The abbreviations used in the keyword index are explained in the front of the volume. The keyword index also includes suggested topic keywords that serve to redirect. For example, in New York Jur, if you are looking for information about prisoners in New York state and flip to the corresponding section in the index, you will find the directional advice shown in Figure 3-2.

Figure 3-2. *New York Jurisprudence* Excerpt

PRISONS AND PRISONERS
General discussion, **Penal § 1 et seq.**
For detailed treatment see index topic
PENAL AND CORRECTIONAL INSTITUTIONS

Source: *New York Jurisprudence, 2d.* Reprinted with permission of West, a Thomson Reuters business.

For research in an unfamiliar area of law, this advice will help lead you to the proper search term to navigate through the index and volumes.

Unless you have a seminal case in hand, bypass the table of cases and use the keyword index. Begin by looking up any terms of art, topic, or the general area of law, making a note of directional advice (i.e., "See also ...") and citations to topics and sections (i.e., Penal § 184). Next, scan the spines of the hardcover volumes for the topics and section numbers you wrote down, and pull them out. Refer to each section to ascertain its applicability and usefulness, and check for any updates to the particular section within the pocket part at the back of the bound volume. After checking the pocket part, refer to the soft-bound update supplement at the end of the hardbound volumes.

If you want to use the encyclopedias on an online paid service, *New York Jurisprudence, 2d* (NYJUR) and *American Jurisprudence, 2d* (AMJUR) are available on Lexis and Westlaw. *Corpus Juris Secundum* (CJS) is available only on Westlaw. In either service, you can search using natural language, search using terms and connectors, or browse the table of contents. However, take note that neither service provides access to an index or table of cases, and that any general search will search the entire encyclopedia. If you are interested in browsing those tools, begin with the print encyclopedias to narrow your search.

III. Practice Materials

Defined generally, practice materials are the materials produced by:

- attorneys within a field of law,

- bar associations (e.g., continuing legal education materials),
- a private entity to assist directly in the practice of law (e.g., forms and pattern jury instructions).

Practice materials run the gamut from newsletters to sample forms and are usually aimed at a specific audience that is familiar with the basics of an area of law. However, these resources are useful for the novice as well, providing real world insights into and interpretations of an area of law.

A. Bar Association Materials

1. National

Although not New York-specific, the American Bar Association (ABA) publishes helpful online resources, accessible through its website at www.americanbar.org by clicking on "Publications & CLE." The *ABA Journal* is available online and provides information about recent cases, changes in legislation, and current events. In addition, various sections within the ABA publish newsletters, such as *Air & Space Lawyer* and *Construct!*, and access to newsletters is granted with membership to the section. The ABA also publishes its own books and periodicals which are focused in various areas of the law and available for purchase through its website.

2. New York State

The New York State Bar Association (NYSBA) publishes its own journal, focused on New York law. Published nine times a year, much of the material is written by practicing attorneys and is meant for practitioners. In addition, the NYSBA sections publish newsletters, accessible only with section membership. Many of the back issues of the section newsletters are available online for members at www.nysba.org by first clicking on "Publications/Forms" and then "Section Publications."

NYSBA also publishes the *State Bar News*, a compilation of recent Association activities, and the *New York State Law Digest*, a collection of recent New York court decisions of importance.

Much like the national association, NYSBA publishes books, and some are available in e-book format. To review the catalog of offered publications, click first on "Publications/Forms" and then "Attorney Reference Books." The publications are organized by practice area, and clicking on a particular title will provide information such as the author(s), the date of publication, and a table of contents.

3. Finding Bar Association Materials

The majority of NYSBA journals and newsletters are for members only. However, many of the books and guides are available for purchase on the NYSBA's website. In addition, you may want to consult a public law library catalog. If there is a "Search by Publisher" option in the catalog, search using the entire name of the Association and then review the titles.

B. Continuing Legal Education (CLE) Materials

After admittance to the bar, attorneys must maintain membership to a state bar by participating in the bar's mandatory continuing legal education courses, known as CLE.

In New York, CLE can be satisfied by participation in seminars, teleconferences, webinars,[1] and webcasts. The CLE may be hosted by a judge, practitioner, or professor of law, and often is focused on new developments in an area of law. Each CLE produces various resources, such as presentations, audio recordings, and handouts. As the courses should be "'transitional legal education,' i.e., practical skills or basic, entry-level,"[2] they are a source of potential riches for a researcher unfamiliar with an area of law.

Current CLE programs are listed on the NYSBA's website,[3] along with information about purchasing CLE materials. Also, check the

---

1. A webinar is an online seminar, often comprising an online slide presentation, audio, and an instant messenger question service.

2. *See* www.nysba.org/Content/NavigationMenu/CLE/MandatoryCLERules/Mandatory_CLE.htm.

3. *See* www.nysba.org/cle.

catalog of your public law library, as many libraries receive CLE donations from local attorneys.

On the national level, there are various publishers that create CLE programs and materials. The Practising Law Institute (PLI), "a non-profit continuing legal education organization chartered by the Regents of the University of the State of New York,"[4] offers live seminars, webcasts, and on-demand learning. You can browse the various topics on PLI's website at www.pli.edu. The CLE programs are organized by topic and, using the left toolbar while reviewing live seminar offerings, you can reorder your results by location. In addition, PLI publishes treatises and handbooks addressing various areas of law.

C. Forms

A form is a useful starting point for drafting a legal document. Forms provide sample language with blanks that need to be filled in with party names and specifics of an action or claim. However, be aware that the "one-size-fits-all" utility of a form requires that multiple forms be consulted in drafting your specific document.

There are various form books for New York State. *Form books* are compilations of examples and explanations of forms for various topics under New York State law. *Bender's Forms for the Consolidated Laws of New York*, known as "Bender's Forms," is organized in parallel with the state code. *West's McKinney's Forms*, often referred to as "McKinney's Forms," are organized by area of law, including civil practice, matrimonial law, tax, and others. Bender's Forms has many subject-specific forms series, including a series for discovery, pleading, and civil practice, each organized to mirror the relevant sections of the state statutes. McKinney's Forms provide brief explanations of the law and of the relevant form.

In addition to the traditional form books, there are more untraditional routes to finding forms for New York State. In the realm of print materials, *New York Consolidated Laws Service* (CLS) is a com-

4. From PLI's website, www.pli.edu, under "About Us."

pilation of the state code that includes references to forms or sample forms in its entries. Carmody-Wait, 2d is an encyclopedia of criminal and civil practice in New York and contains forms for some of its entries.

McKinney's Forms and Carmody-Wait, 2d are available on Westlaw; Bender's and CLS are available on Lexis.

For online materials, the New York State court website has various forms for different courts within the state available for free.[5] Also, a parallel New York State court website, "CourtHelp," outlines the various forms needed in different court settings.[6] The NYSBA has electronic forms for purchase on its website.[7] The forms are organized topically and are available for purchase to members and nonmembers.

D. Pattern Jury Instructions

Pattern jury instructions (PJI) are meant to be plain language explanations of the law, as applied in a particular jurisdiction. The instructions may serve as a jury's charge during legal proceedings, and therefore are composed with as little legalese as possible to provide clarity and guidelines about the current law within the jurisdiction. Referring to these instructions may inform your research path and help you focus your preparations.

In civil proceedings, the *New York Pattern Jury Instructions* includes the instructions given to a jury and provides cases and statutes that explain the current interpretation of the PJI. Compiled by the Committee on Pattern Jury Instructions of the Association of Supreme Court Justices, the collection is considered the standard. In print, this four-volume set is available for sale from West; it may also be available in your local law library. Online, this set is available on Westlaw.

---

5. *See* www.courts.state.ny.us/forms/index.html.

6. *See* www.nycourts.gov/courthelp/index.html.

7. *See* www.nysba.org, click on "Publications/Forms," then click on "Downloadable Forms."

In criminal proceedings, the Office of Court Administration's Committee on Criminal Jury Instructions oversees the PJI's compilation. As "the only current and official publication,"[8] the Committee has made the entire *Criminal Jury Instructions, Second Edition* (CJI2d) available online.[9] The website includes an overview of the history of changes, how to cite to the CJI2d, and an alphabetical listing of the charges. Please note, however, that CJI2d supersedes all of books II and III, but supersedes only charges of "general applicability" in book I of the first edition.

Available as an unofficial version, *Charges to the Jury and Requests to Charge in a Criminal Case in New York* is on Westlaw and in print.

E. Finding and Using Practice Materials

Because of their disparate natures, practice materials may be found in various locations. To perform a general search in a law library's catalog for bar association material, search the publisher's name. For example, search for publications using the phrase "New York State Bar Association," and then search within those results for topic-specific materials. Alternatively, many of the local bar association publications may be available via the Association website.

For the practice materials and information that are born of CLE classes managed by the state bar association or by the Practising Law Institute, review the organization's website to locate a title and search by title within your local law library catalog. Alternatively, search by publisher in the catalog to locate all associated results.

Be sure to consult multiple resources to assure that you are seeing as much of the "big picture" as possible. The better able you are to discern the local legal landscape around a particular issue, the better able you will be to serve your client. Use the information gleaned from a CLE to pull forms or pattern jury instructions, or use pattern

8. *See* http://www.nycourts.gov/cji/0-TitlePage/1-Preface.html.
9. *See* www.nycourts.gov/cji.

jury instructions to guide you in your choice of bar association newsletters.

IV. Legal Periodicals

A. Academic Legal Periodicals

Articles found in academic legal periodicals are written by law faculty, law students, judges, experts in the field, or practitioners. With few exceptions, the articles are chosen and edited by law students. Law reviews and law journals are rich sources for in-depth discussions of a particular law, statute, or legal issue, replete with extensive annotations.

In general, the articles written by faculty, judges, experts in the field, or practitioners tend toward more detailed analyses of a particular legal issue or trend. These articles may attempt to establish timelines for a law or statute, to balance the various considerations that went into the drafting of a statute, or to provide an analysis of the applicability of a court decision to future cases. Also, many articles are interdisciplinary in nature, reflecting the increasingly interdisciplinary focus of many law faculty members. For example, an article may discuss the sociocultural impact of prisoner hygiene laws on the Amish community or it may compare the biostatistical impact of federal agricultural statutes. The utility of these articles is not merely in the subject matter at hand, but also in the footnotes provided by the writer. These footnotes support almost every statement made by the author with outside authority, such as cases, statutes, or other law review articles, and help provide a research trail for those interested in the topic.

Law student contributions to law reviews and journals often come in the form of *case notes*. These notes are composed to reflect recent changes in a law or a recent court decision. Usually, the case notes summarize the changes briefly and provide a quick overview for the reader. These notes lack the extensive coverage of the longer law reviews and articles but may provide a shortcut for keeping current on changes in case law. Students sometimes write *comments*, which are full-length articles.

B. Finding Law Review and Journal Articles

Some law reviews and journals are focused on particular topics, such as the *Columbia Human Rights Law Review* or the *Tax Law Review*. However, there are many publications that have no prescribed focus, and an article on water rights might be next to an article on commercial transactions in the same issue. With each accredited law school publishing at least one issue a year, there are hundreds of journals and thousands of articles to search for a particular topic. Thankfully, there are many topical finding aids that will assist in your search for useful articles.

1. Indexes

Indexes offer the quickest route to a comprehensive overview of the journals' publications organized by topic. Each article is categorized according to the index's controlled vocabulary or subject headings; in short, editors have tagged the article with key terms and concepts to make it easy to locate. Print indexes will provide you with author, title, and subject searching; electronic indexes will provide you with full-text searching and, in some cases, a full abstract of an article.

In print, consult the *Current Law Index* (CLI) and *Index to Legal Periodicals and Books* (ILPB) (previously titled as the *Index to Legal Periodicals* (1909–1994) and the *Index to Periodical Literature* (1888–1939)). CLI is published monthly and covers over nine hundred journals and law reviews. It is divided into four parts: a subject index, an author/title index, a table of cases, and a table of statutes. ILPB is also comprehensive, indexing written materials from the U.S., Canada, Great Britain, Ireland, Australia, and New Zealand. However, ILPB stretches back only to 1981; for pre-1981 research, check the *Index to Legal Periodicals*. ILPB offers the same features as CLI; in addition, it also lists book reviews.

Both CLI and ILPB/ILP are available on Lexis and Westlaw. CLI is available on Lexis through the "LGLIND" database and on Westlaw through the "LRI" database. Each refers to it as the "Legal Resource

Index," and coverage begins in 1980. ILPB is also available on Lexis and Westlaw in the "ILP" database; however, both services provide access only to the periodicals. They both refer to it as the *Index to Legal Periodicals.* Lexis begins its coverage in 1978, while Westlaw's coverage begins in 1980. Each service uses its Boolean operators to perform searches and offers the possibility of natural-language searching. Although convenient if you have access to either service, searching through journal articles may be difficult without the use of limiters in your search queries.

CLI, ILPB, and ILP have stand-alone databases as well. CLI's database equivalent is LegalTrac, and ILPB and ILP are separate databases that retain their original titles. Each database offers the possibility for sophisticated, multi-faceted searching through use of author name, title, subject, keyword, abstract, case name, statute, publisher, series, and many more. CLI and ILPB's coverage is from 1981 on, and ILP covers 1909 through 1994.

2. Online Journal and Law Review Databases

Lexis and Westlaw offer searchable databases of law reviews and journal articles. Lexis has variable coverage of law reviews and journals, from 1982 to the present in the "ALLUS" database. Westlaw also has variable coverage of law reviews in the "JLR" database. For a full listing of publications, consult the scope note, and scroll down to contents.

Although relatively new among providers of legal articles, HeinOnline is a powerful database for searching law reviews and journals. Unlike CLI or ILPB, HeinOnline offers full-text searching of the article and, unlike Lexis and Westlaw, HeinOnline preserves the original formatting and pagination of the article, providing a text-searchable PDF of the original. In the "Law Journal Library," HeinOnline has around 1,500 journals and law reviews, many of which contain all volumes of a publication. The "Field Search" option allows you to search by title, author, description, or date, and use the subject listing to focus your search on a particular topic. You can search the entire text for words or phrases, as well. Narrow your search by legislation, cases, notes, reviews, comments, and more. While viewing the search results, HeinOnline highlights your search terms and allows you to view snippets of the article in which your term appears.

With the exception of subscriptions to Lexis and Westlaw, most firms do not purchase access to the stand-alone databases listed above. However, most academic law libraries have access to ILPB/ILP, LegalTrac, and HeinOnline. In addition, some libraries keep the print version of CLI and ILPB up-to-date in the stacks. Although there may be some restrictions because of licensing agreements, these resources usually are available to law students, faculty, and law library patrons.

V. *American Law Reports*

American Law Reports (ALR) is a cross between a case reporter and a treatise. Recent cases that establish or transform an area of law are selected, and editors create *annotations* that delve deeply into the particular issues of law that arise in the case. To illustrate the depth of coverage, consider that many volumes of ALR are at least eight hundred pages long and each volume often discusses as few as ten distinct legal issues. Figure 3-3 is an example of how an annotation is organized.

These extensive annotations consist of a lengthy index, a full case, tables of authorities, multi-jurisdictional surveys of the topic, and commentary from lawyers. Written for the practitioner, these annotations are extremely helpful if you can find one on topic.

A. ALR in Print

ALR has been published in various series since 1919. Currently, ALR is in its sixth series (ALR 6th) and ALR Federal is in its second series (ALR Fed. 2d). ALR covers state and constitutional issues; ALR Federal covers only federal topics.

Each series has its own quick index, and ALR Index collates the topics found in all of ALR. You may also peruse ALR Digest. ALR is updated through pocket parts, and some annotations may be com-

Figure 3-3. *American Law Reports* Example

ANNOTATION

VALIDITY UNDER FEDERAL LAW OF PRISON REGULATIONS RELATING TO INMATES' HAIR LENGTH AND STYLE

By

Glenn A. Guarino, J.D.

I. PREFATORY MATTERS

§ 1. Introduction:
  [a] Scope
  [b] Related matters

§ 2. Summary and comment:
  [a] Generally
  [b] Practice pointers

II. LEGAL BASES OF INMATES' CHALLENGES TO PRISON HAIR REGULATIONS

§ 3. First Amendment free exercise of religion:
  [a] Infringement of First Amendment rights held established or supportable
  [b] Infringement of First Amendment rights held not established

§ 4. Equal protection
§ 5. Due process
§ 6. Personal preference
§ 7. Medical necessity

III. GOVERNMENTAL JUSTIFICATION FOR PRISON HAIR REGULATIONS

§ 8. Generally—view that restriction must be in furtherance of important state interest and achieved by the least restrictive alternative
§ 9. –Fifth Circuit cases
§ 10. Particular justifications considered—prisoner identification:
  [a] Justification held established
  [b] Justification held not established

§ 11. –Personal hygiene
  [a] Justification held established
  [b] Justification held not established

§ 12. –Maintenance of institutional security and preventing concealment of contraband.

Source: Glenn A. Guarino, Annotation, *Validity Under Federal Law of Prison Regulations Relating to Inmates' Hair Length and Style,* 62 A.L.R. Fed. 479 (1983). Reprinted with permission of West, a Thomson Reuters business.

pletely superseded by future additions. To be sure that you are consulting the most recent annotations, check the Annotation History table in the indexes.

B. ALR's Electronic Databases

ALR is also available on Lexis in the "LEDALR" database and Westlaw in the "ALR" database. Each contains the full collection of ALR and ALR Federal, which are both updated weekly. Both services omit the full cases included in annotations but provide hyperlinks to these cases in other databases.

VI. Treatises, Hornbooks, and Nutshells

As an area of law garners more attention through an increase in case law or statutory provisions, an expert will often "write the book" on the topic. This book may take the form of a treatise, hornbook, or Nutshell. A treatise presents the deepest coverage on a topic, a hornbook is a quicker overview, and the Nutshell series from West is the most condensed overview of the topic. A researcher can choose the approximate depth of coverage by focusing on any or all of the three types.

The Nutshell series by West provides a basic overview and often is used by students when first introduced to a legal topic. The series focuses on outlining the major issues in an area of law and mentions seminal cases and changes in law.

Hornbooks are frequently used as textbooks in law school. Usually, they are written by law professors and other subject experts, and they outline major landmark cases in more detail. They are useful for the researcher in that they provide the pertinent text of many important judicial opinions.

There is no uniformity in length, organization, updating conventions, jurisdictional scope, or contents of treatises, reflecting the variability of topics found in law. However, there are many treatises that practitioners know by name and reputation. Often, depending on the topic, these treatises will be the starting point for research. For example, those interested in property in New York may begin with "Warren's Weed," a treatise titled *Warren's Weed New York Real Property*, or, in corporate law, "White on Corporations," a treatise titled *White, New York Business Entities.*

When using a treatise for the first time, familiarize yourself with its organizational structure. Some treatises are loose-leaf and portions of them are updated as the law changes; look to the front of the volume where update notices are filed to ascertain whether it's current. If the treatise is in a bound volume, check the front matter for the publication date. After determining that the treatise is recent, browse the index for a topic with which you are familiar, and review the entry to learn the author's style. Many treatises include historical background, case law, statutory law, and commentary from experts in the field.

VII. Restatements, Model Codes, and Uniform Laws

A. Restatements

Restatements of the Law are published by the American Law Institute (ALI). ALI is a non-profit corporation that enlists the help of member lawyers, judges, and professors of law to draft proposed and final restatements of common law topics with the purpose of clarifying and reconciling the differences in common law. The Restatements are not binding interpretations of the law, but are considered persuasive.

Each Restatement follows the development of case law and attempts to distill basic, universal principles of a particular area of law. For example, the *Restatement of Property* (First) is broken down into topical chapters, including a chapter devoted to defining common terms of art in property law. Figure 3-4 provides an example of a Restatement.

Figure 3-4. Example of a Restatement

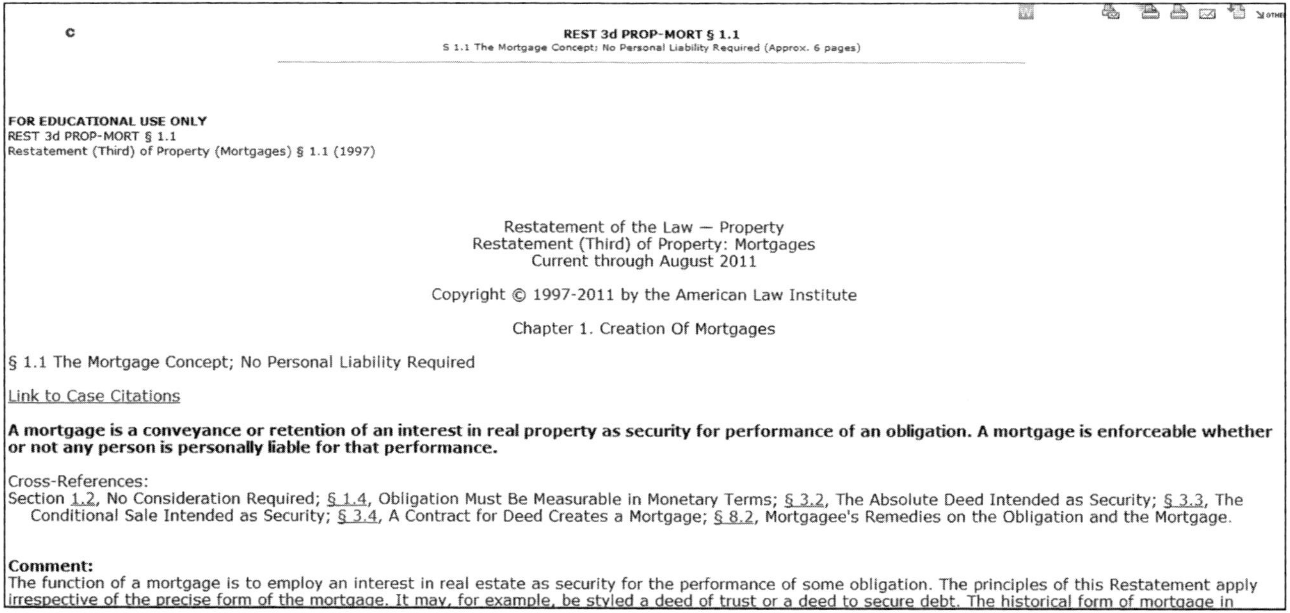

C

REST 3d PROP-MORT § 1.1

§ 1.1 The Mortgage Concept; No Personal Liability Required (Approx. 6 pages)

FOR EDUCATIONAL USE ONLY
REST 3d PROP-MORT § 1.1
Restatement (Third) of Property (Mortgages) § 1.1 (1997)

Restatement of the Law — Property
Restatement (Third) of Property: Mortgages
Current through August 2011

Copyright © 1997-2011 by the American Law Institute

Chapter 1. Creation Of Mortgages

§ 1.1 The Mortgage Concept; No Personal Liability Required

Link to Case Citations

A mortgage is a conveyance or retention of an interest in real property as security for performance of an obligation. A mortgage is enforceable whether or not any person is personally liable for that performance.

Cross-References:
Section 1.2, No Consideration Required; § 1.4, Obligation Must Be Measurable in Monetary Terms; § 3.2, The Absolute Deed Intended as Security; § 3.3, The Conditional Sale Intended as Security; § 3.4, A Contract for Deed Creates a Mortgage; § 8.2, Mortgagee's Remedies on the Obligation and the Mortgage.

Comment:
The function of a mortgage is to employ an interest in real estate as security for the performance of some obligation. The principles of this Restatement apply irrespective of the precise form of the mortgage. It may, for example, be styled a deed of trust or a deed to secure debt. The historical form of mortgage in

Source: Westlaw, 2011. Reprinted with permission of West, a Thomson Reuters business.

Table 3-1. Restatement Topics

Restatements exist for the following areas and topics of law:

- Agency
- Conflict of Laws
- Contracts
- Employment Law
- Foreign Relations
- Judgments
- Law Governing Lawyers
- Property
- Restitution
- Torts
- Trusts
- U.S. Law of International Commercial Arbitration
- Unfair Competition

Note that each section in a Restatement includes a statement of law, a comment on any nuance within the statement, an illustration of the statement and underlying principles, research references to digests and ALR, and extensive case citations organized by court. In addition, commentary may include the historical background of the term of art and its relationship to other terms of art within the area of common law. Although not New York-specific, the Restatements elucidate general principles of law and are helpful in summarizing the law. Consult Table 3-1 for an idea of the topics addressed in various Restatements.

Restatements are available in print, as well as online. When searching a library catalog for a print copy, search for the word "Restatement" in a title search first, and drill down by area of law. Lexis creates a database for each Restatement. Westlaw, however, combines all of the Restatements into one database, "REST," with an extensive table of contents and also allows you to search through individual restatements. HeinOnline also makes the Restatements available in its American Law Institute Library, including council, preliminary, and final drafts.

B. Model Codes and Uniform Laws

Much like the Restatements, model codes and uniform laws are meant to reconcile the differing landscapes of states' statutory laws. Two of the major contributors to this process are the National Conference of Commissioners on Uniform State Laws (NCCUSL), also known as the Uniform Law Commission, and the American Law Institute (ALI). Experts are called upon to propose and draft sample codes and laws for implementation across the states. After a comment period, revisions are made and a final version is written.

ALI and the Uniform Law Commission are responsible for the oft-discussed *Uniform Commercial Code* and *Model Penal Code*. The Uniform Law Commission has tackled many statutory laws, including everything from the Anatomical Gift Act to the Unclaimed Property Act. Each model act and code includes suggested statutory language and an explanation of its construction. However, keep in mind that these acts are not primary law until a state adopts them through the legislative process. Also, a state may adopt only portions of an act or code, so be sure to check the state's statutory text for omissions and revisions.

Consulting a uniform law's accompanying commentary may be useful if your state has adopted any portion of the uniform law. To determine whether your state has adopted a suggested statutory format, you can review two sources:

1. The Uniform Law Commission website at www.nccusl.org; under the "Acts" drop-down menu in the top toolbar. Here, you will find a brief explanation of the drafting process and an alphabetical listing of the proposed acts. Each act listed has, at minimum, a legislative fact sheet. Some acts have the full final act, an act summary, model testimony, fact sheets, amendments, and a list of recent introductions to different state jurisdictions with corresponding bill numbers. In addition to the aforementioned list, each act page has an "Enactment Status Map" of the fifty states (grey color indicates that the act has been enacted in the state). For example, as of May 12, 2011, the Uniform Collaborative Law Act has

been introduced in the legislatures of Alabama (Bill SB 18), Hawaii (Bill HB 626), Massachusetts (Bill HB 31), and others.[10]

2. Cornell's Legal Information Institute (LII) website at www.law.cornell.edu/uniform; under the heading "In this collection." Click on the relevant law, and on that particular law's page, you will see a list of states that have adopted the laws, often with the pertinent state statutory citation. For example, the Uniform Interstate Family Support Act of 1996 has been adopted by Arizona (A.R.S. §§ 25-621 to 25-661).[11] In addition, the text of the original uniform act or code will be linked.

To find other sample codes, consult the Uniform Law Commission and the ALI websites. Many law libraries have print copies of the more popular uniform codes. In addition, Lexis and Westlaw have much of the Uniform Commercial Code (UCC) (search their respective directories for specific articles). HeinOnline offers the 1984 and 1995 versions of the UCC drafts in its American Law Institute Library.

VIII. Loose-leaf and Newsletter Services

Loose-leaf services and newsletters are one way in which practitioners stay current with the trends and changes in an area of law. Loose-leaf services are named as such because they are kept in a three-ring binder and interfiled with frequent updates. Newsletters are published frequently—at least once a month.

Loose-leaf services offer a survey of pertinent and current primary and secondary authority for a particular area of law, and are a great place to start researching a legal issue. For example, imagine you are researching a decision made by an agency like the Internal Revenue Service. A loose-leaf service might bring together statutes, case law,

---

10. *See* www.nccusl.org/Act.aspx?title=Collaborative%20Law%20Act.

11. *See* www.law.cornell.edu/uniform/vol9.html#pater.

agency rulings, agency memoranda, income portfolios, and the Internal Revenue Code. The convenience of "one-stop" shopping cannot be understated, and consulting a loose-leaf service first may save a significant amount of time during your research process.

To discover a topical loose-leaf service in print, you may want to consult *Legal Looseleafs in Print* or *Legal Newsletters in Print*, compiled and edited by Arlene Eis. These titles are available for purchase in print or online at www.infosource.pub. These extensive compilations include current loose-leafs and newsletters, listed both by publication title and by subject for ease of browsing. Contact and pricing information is included in each entry, as well as information about online equivalents. Bureau of National Affairs (BNA) and Commerce Clearing House (CCH) are the most prolific publishers of loose-leaf series.

To use a loose-leaf service in print, first ascertain its currentness by consulting the filing update notices in the front of the volume(s). Then, search the index or the table of contents for your legal issue. Online equivalents now exist for most BNA and CCH publications on subscription-based platforms. Online, BNA publishes various reporters (similar to newsletters) and aggregates many of its print services into online "Centers." For example, the Tax and Accounting Center is home to its state, federal, and weekly tax reports, and its tax portfolios.

CCH presents its various loose-leaf services as browseable, searchable databases with a simple tree structure. Figure 3-5 illustrates its tree structure.

In addition to the standalone options, BNA products purchased as packages can be accessed through Lexis and Westlaw gateways. Westlaw can provide access to your CCH subscriptions. Each online option offers its proprietary search box features.

Regardless of online or print format, a loose-leaf service will provide detailed information about primary and secondary authorities. This information may be focused on a particular jurisdiction, such as *Drafting New York Wills and Related Documents*, or offer a more general overview in different jurisdictions, such as *Collier on Bankruptcy*.

Figure 3-5. CCH Federal Tax Practice Area Menu

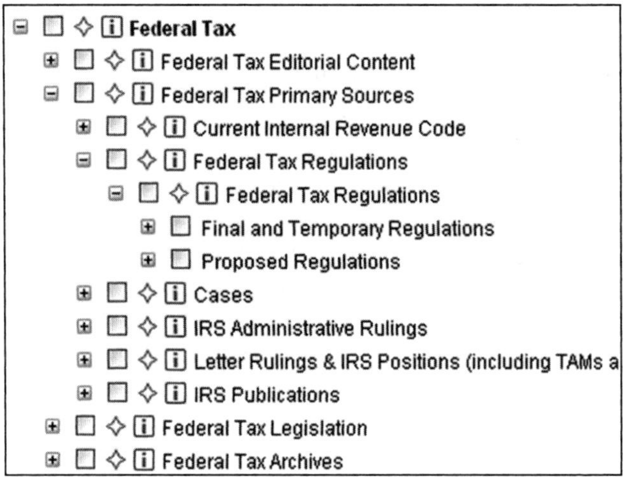

- **Federal Tax**
  - Federal Tax Editorial Content
  - Federal Tax Primary Sources
    - Current Internal Revenue Code
    - Federal Tax Regulations
      - Federal Tax Regulations
        - Final and Temporary Regulations
        - Proposed Regulations
    - Cases
    - IRS Administrative Rulings
    - Letter Rulings & IRS Positions (including TAMs a
    - IRS Publications
  - Federal Tax Legislation
  - Federal Tax Archives

IX. Using Secondary Sources

To begin, a caveat: secondary sources are not primary authority. They may contain primary source material and will lead you to this material with extensive citations, but they are not primary authority. If a primary authority is cited, always be sure to verify its validity in the most up-to-date official version of the authority. A court does not look kindly on shortcuts no matter how popular the secondary source may be.

A. Choosing a Secondary Source

In the context of a research problem, reviewing every source mentioned in this chapter is not recommended. Secondary sources stretch across a spectrum of complexity, and choosing the right point in that spectrum will save you time.

Dictionaries and encyclopedias are on one end of the spectrum, representing the more basic resources. If you are looking for a quick, no-frills explanation of a legal topic without much detail or exposition, begin at this end and work forward by following annotations. Moving toward the other end of the spectrum, if you are more comfortable with the basics and have a good grasp on the terms of art within the area of law, a treatise or loose-leaf service may be the best point of entry. In addition, practice materials may offer a jurisdiction-specific interpretation of a particular legal issue.

In addition to considering where the resource sits on the spectrum, you will need to check for currentness. A treatise, no matter how well written, will do you no favors if it is twenty years old. Loose-leaf services, because they incorporate recent changes in law, should have recent updates; be sure to consult the filing notices in the front of the volume for the date. With any of the resources mentioned in this chapter, try to find the most current reflections on the topic. A persuasive argument needs to be thorough and current.

B. Citing a Secondary Source

Returning to the caveat at the beginning of this section—secondary sources are not primary authority. Cite primary authority whenever possible. Using a secondary source to bolster a legal argument is a clear sign that no primary law exists in favor of your argument. Rarely are sources like journal articles or treatises cited in a memoranda, and some of the secondary sources, like CLE or loose-leaf materials, are never cited. Sometimes, secondary sources are used to back up primary authority, but usually this occurs if the primary authority has origins in a different jurisdiction.

However, there are rare occasions when citing a secondary source may be your only option. If you are arguing against the current interpretation of the law, you might use a heavily cited journal article from a well-known author that was published in a nationally recognized journal or law review. If you want to provide a brief overview of an area of law without searching through case law, you might refer to an established treatise's interpretation, particularly if that treatise's interpretation has been cited and received well in your jurisdiction.

Chapter 4

Cases, Digests, and Online Searching

Courts write judicial opinions—informally called cases—to explain their decisions in litigated disputes. Cases are published in rough chronological order in books called *reporters*. Some reporters include cases decided by only a certain court, for example, the New York Court of Appeals. Other reporters include cases from courts within a specific geographic region, for example, the northeastern United States.[1] Reporters are fundamental tools of legal research, regardless of whether a researcher is using print or online sources. This is because case citations are keyed to print reporters, even by online services.

This chapter begins with an overview of court systems in New York and at the federal level. Then it explains reporters and the features added to opinions when they are published in reporters. Next the chapter discusses how to use digests—topical indexes of cases—and online resources to find cases in conducting legal research. The chapter ends with suggestions for reading cases effectively.

I. Court Systems

The typical American court structure resembles a pyramid.[2] At the base is a broad set of trial courts that hear many cases. In the middle

1. Still other reporters publish only those cases that deal with a certain topic, such as bankruptcy, media law, or rules of civil and criminal procedure.

2. The following discussion omits tribal courts in New York. Information is available online for a number of tribal courts. For example, links are avail-

are the intermediate courts of appeals, which hear only those cases that have been appealed from the trial courts. At the top is the ultimate appellate court, which hears cases on appeal from an intermediate appellate court.[3]

Most states use this structure, as does the federal government. New York's court system, called the Unified Court System, is essentially the same, but a little more complex.[4] See Figure 4-1 for a graphical display of the civil court system in New York.

A. New York State Unified Court System

The highest court in New York is the Court of Appeals. It hears appeals from intermediate appellate courts. There are seven judges on the New York Court of Appeals.

New York has three types of intermediate appellate courts: the Appellate Divisions of the Supreme Court and two inferior appellate courts called the Appellate Terms of the Supreme Court and the County Courts. The state is divided geographically into four judicial departments, each with an Appellate Division of the Supreme Court. The Appellate Divisions hear appeals from the two inferior appellate courts, from some trial courts, and from administrative agencies.

The Appellate Terms of the Supreme Court hear appeals from some trial courts in the first and second judicial departments. The County Courts are primarily trial courts, but they hear appeals from various trial-level courts in the third and fourth departments.

---

able from the Federal-State Tribal Courts Forum, at www.nyfedstatetribalcourtsforum.org, and the National Indian Law Library, at www.narf.org/nill (click on "Tribal Law Gateway").

3. Some decisions are appealed directly to the highest court, such as criminal cases concerning the death penalty.

4. One complicating factor in New York's Unified Court System is that it is different in New York City than it is in the rest of the state, particularly at the trial court level. New York City courts are discussed in Chapter 9, Part VI.

Figure 4-1. Civil Court Structure

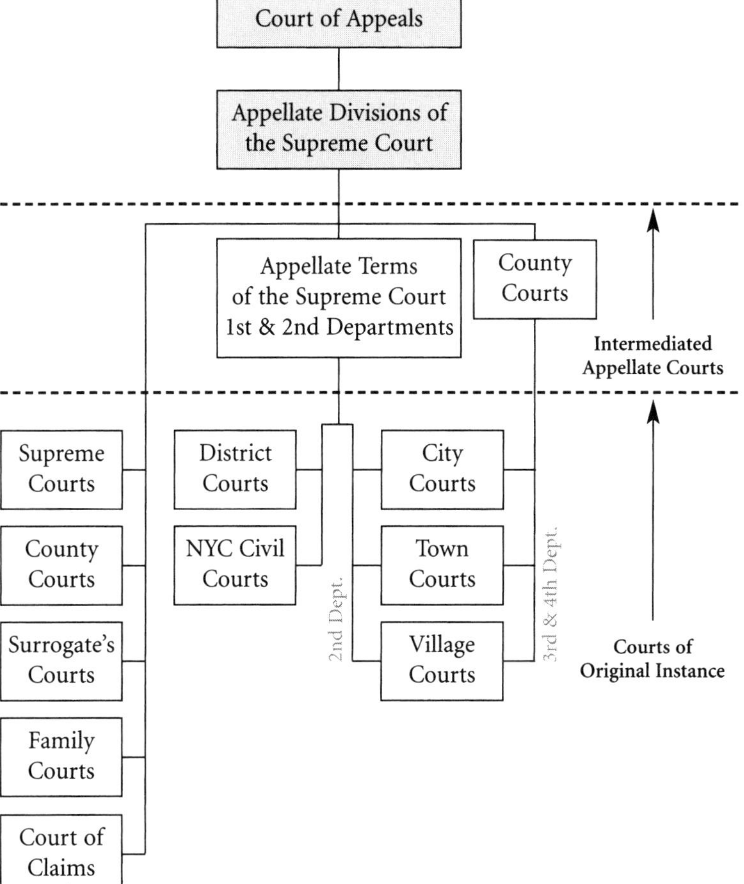

Source: New York Unified Court System website at www.courts.state.ny.us/courts/structure.shtml.

There are many trial courts in New York. Trial courts of superior jurisdiction include the Supreme Court,[5] the County Courts, the Sur-

5. New York's Supreme Court is not to be confused with the United States Supreme Court. In this book, the federal Supreme Court will be preceded by "U.S." to distinguish it from the New York trial court.

rogate's Courts, the Family Courts, and the Court of Claims. Trial courts of limited jurisdiction include City Courts, District Courts, and others. There are some major differences between the New York City courts and the upstate courts.[6]

B. Federal Courts

In the federal judicial system, the trial courts are called United States District Courts. There are ninety-four district courts in the federal system, with each district drawn from a particular state. A state with a relatively small population might not be subdivided into smaller geographic regions, while states with larger populations and higher caseloads are subdivided into multiple districts. The entire state of Vermont, for example, makes up the federal District of Vermont. Meanwhile, New York has four districts: northern, southern, eastern, and western. District courts are located in several cities within each district.

Intermediate appellate courts in the federal system are called United States Courts of Appeals. There are courts of appeals for each of the thirteen federal circuits. Twelve of these circuits are based on geographic jurisdiction. Eleven numbered circuits cover all the states; the twelfth is the District of Columbia Circuit. The thirteenth circuit, called the Federal Circuit, hears appeals from district courts in all other circuits on issues related to patent law and from certain specialized courts and agencies. A map showing the federal circuits is available at www.uscourts.gov/courtlinks. Circuit maps may also be found in the front of the *Federal Supplement* and the *Federal Reporter*, books that publish the cases decided by federal courts.

New York is in the Second Circuit. This means that cases from the United States District Courts in New York's four federal districts are

6. For detailed information, visit the New York State Unified Court System website at www.courts.state.ny.us/courts and click on "Introduction to the Courts" in the left frame.

appealed to the United States Court of Appeals for the Second Circuit. This circuit encompasses New York, Vermont, and Connecticut.

The highest court in the federal system is the United States Supreme Court. It decides cases concerning the United States Constitution and federal statutes. This court does not have the final say on matters of purely state law; that authority rests with the highest court of each state. Parties who wish to have the U.S. Supreme Court hear their case must file a petition for *certiorari*, as the court has discretion over which cases it hears.

The website for the federal judiciary contains maps, court addresses, explanations of jurisdiction, and other helpful information. The address is www.uscourts.gov.

C. Courts of Other States

While New York has a relatively complicated court structure, most states have a simpler three-tier court system that is more like the federal court structure. Most states have just one intermediate appellate court rather than the two levels that exist in New York, and a few states have no intermediate appellate court. Moreover, unlike New York, most states label their ultimate appellate court the "Supreme Court," and label their intermediate appellate court the "Court of Appeals." Two other states, Massachusetts and Maine, call their highest court the "Supreme Judicial Court."

Citation manuals are good references for learning the names and hierarchy of the courts, as well as for learning proper citation to legal authorities. The two most popular are *The Bluebook: A Uniform System of Citation*[7] and the *ALWD Citation Manual: A Professional System of Citation*.[8] The first appendix of both manuals provides information on state and federal courts.

---

7. *The Bluebook: A Uniform System of Citation* (Columbia Law Review Ass'n et al. eds., 19th ed. 2010) ("Bluebook").

8. ALWD & Darby Dickerson, *ALWD Citation Manual* (4th ed. 2010) ("ALWD Manual").

II. Reporters

A. Reporters for New York Cases

The New York State Reporter is responsible for the three official reporters for New York state cases: *New York Reports* publishes cases of the Court of Appeals; *Appellate Division Reports* publishes cases of the Appellate Divisions of the New York Supreme Court; and *Miscellaneous Reports* publishes cases of lower appellate courts and trial courts.

Additionally, West publishes New York Court of Appeals cases in a regional reporter called *North Eastern Reporter*. As with other regional reporters, *North Eastern Reporter* combines several courts' opinions under a single title. *North Eastern Reporter* publishes cases from the appellate courts of Illinois, Indiana, Massachusetts, New York, and Ohio.[9] Other West regional reporters are *Atlantic Reporter*, *South Eastern Reporter*, *Southern Reporter*, *South Western Reporter*, *North Western Reporter*, and *Pacific Reporter*. Because the publisher decided which states to group together in regional reporters, these groupings have no legal impact. Moreover, the coverage of each regional reporter is not the same as the composition of the federal circuits.[10]

West also publishes a separate series called *West's New York Supplement*, with cases from the Court of Appeals as well as other lower courts in New York. The various reporters for New York's cases are summarized in Table 4-1.

Reporters are published in series. *New York Reports* began a third series in 2004. *North Eastern Reporter* is in its second series, though it will begin a third series soon. To find a case in a reporter with multi-

9. While *North Eastern Reporter* includes only Court of Appeals cases from New York, it includes cases from both the intermediate and highest appellate courts of the other states.

10. Remember that the Second Circuit contains New York, Connecticut, and Vermont, while *North Eastern Reporter* publishes cases from New York, Illinois, Indiana, Massachusetts, and Ohio.

Table 4-1. Reporters for New York Cases

Court	Reporter Name	Abbreviation
New York Court of Appeals	*New York Reports* (official) *North Eastern Reporter* *New York Supplement*	N.Y., N.Y.2d N.E., N.E.2d N.Y.S., N.Y.S.2d
New York Supreme Court, Appellate Division	*Appellate Division Reports* (official) *New York Supplement*	A.D., A.D.2d, A.D.3d N.Y.S., N.Y.S.2d
New York's lower intermediate courts and trial courts	*New York Miscellaneous Reports* (official) *New York Supplement*	Misc., Misc. 2d N.Y.S., N.Y.S.2d

ple series, you must know which series the case was reported in. This information is included in the citation to the case, as explained below.

Another mode of publication is electronic publication. The opinions of courts in New York and the rest of the United States can be found on two fee-based services, Lexis and Westlaw.[11] Selected court opinions can also be found on FindLaw, which is owned by West. Other electronic databases, such as Google Scholar, also include New York cases. Finally, the opinions of New York courts are published on the official website of the courts, www.courts.state.ny.us/courts under the "Decisions" tab in the left frame.

1. Citing New York Cases

A citation to a New York case requires the name of the parties, the volume and abbreviation for the reporter, the initial page of the case, and the date.[12] *New York Reports* is abbreviated as "N.Y." The case *Peo-*

11. Both services are available to law students through their school's subscription. While the students are not charged, the schools pay fees that are based on the number of students enrolled.

12. The following citations adhere to the style of the Bluebook's format for practice documents. For format adhering to the *New York Law Reports Style Manual* or the ALWD Manual, see Appendix A at the end of this book.

ple v. Lewis, 68 N.Y.2d 923 (1986), can be found in volume 68 of the second series of *New York Reports*, starting on page 923. The case was decided in 1986.

In New York, all documents submitted to New York courts must cite the official reporters;[13] citing additional reporters is optional. For documents that are not going to be submitted to a New York court, lawyers usually follow the custom of their firm or office. Often that customary reporter will be the West regional reporter listed above. Especially when writing a memo for a firm outside of New York, you would likely cite the New York case mentioned above to *North Eastern Reporter* or *West's New York Supplement*. To indicate which state's courts decided cases cited to a regional reporter, include an abbreviation at the beginning of the date parenthetical.

EXAMPLE: *People v. Lewis*, 502 N.E.2d 988 (N.Y. 1986).

Sometimes you will want to include citations to all reporters that have published an opinion. Multiple citations that refer to the same case in different reporters are called *parallel citations*.

EXAMPLE: *People v. Lewis*, 68 N.Y.2d 923, 510 N.Y.S.2d 73, 502 N.E.2d 988 (1986).

Note that the New York Court of Appeals case in the example has three parallel citations; most state cases appear in just two reporters, so the cases have just two parallel citations.

2. Features of a Reported Case

The following discussion relates to cases published in *North Eastern Reporter* or *New York Supplement*. Both of these reporters are published by West. Because West publishes most American cases, this discussion of the features of a reported case applies to cases in many reporters. Knowing how West organizes its cases will also provide you with the tools to understand what you see in a case published by a different publisher or available online.

---

13. N.Y. C.P.L.R. § 5529(e).

A case printed in a reporter contains the exact language of the court's opinion. Additionally, the publisher adds supplemental information intended to aid researchers in learning about the case, locating the relevant parts of the case, and finding similar cases. Some of these research aids are gleaned from the court record of the case while others are written by the publisher's editorial staff. Most reporters will include most of these items, though perhaps in a different order. To best understand the following discussion, select from the library shelves a volume of *North Eastern Reporter*, preferably a volume containing a case you are familiar with. You might instead retrieve the case on Westlaw and open the PDF version. Alternatively, refer to the case excerpt in Figure 4-2 for examples of most of the concepts explained below. (The *New York Reports* version is printed in an appendix to this chapter.)

Parallel citation. The reporter provides the citation for the case in any official or other unofficial reporter in which the case is also printed.

Parties and procedural designations. Most reported cases are from appellate courts. The appealing party is called the *appellant*; the other party is the *respondent.*[14]

Docket number. The docket number is assigned by a court for keeping track of documents pertaining to a particular case.

Deciding court. The opinion gives the full name of the court that decided the case.

Date of decision. Each case begins with the date of the court's decision. Some reporters include additional dates, such as the date the case was argued or submitted to the court. For citation purposes, only the year the case was decided is important.

Synopsis. The synopsis is a short summary of the key facts, procedure, legal points, and disposition of the case. Reading a synopsis can quickly tell you whether a case is on point. You cannot rely exclusively on a synopsis and you must never cite it, but it is a very useful research tool.

---

14. In the federal system and in some states, the terms *appellant* and *appellee* are used when a party has a right to appeal, while the terms *petitioner* and *respondent* apply to parties when the court has discretion to hear the appeal.

Disposition and opinions. The disposition of the case is the court's decision to affirm, reverse, remand, or vacate the decision below. If the appellate court agrees with only part of the lower court's decision, the appellate court may affirm in part and reverse in part. If some judges filed concurring or dissenting opinions, the opinions will be noted in this section.

Headnotes. A headnote is a sentence or short paragraph that sets out a single point of law in a case. Most cases will have several headnotes. The text of each headnote often comes directly from the text of the opinion. But because only the opinion itself is authoritative, do not rely on headnotes in doing research and do not cite them in legal documents. At the beginning of each headnote is a number identifying it in sequence with other headnotes. Within the text of the opinion, the same sequence number will appear in bold print or in brackets at the point in the text supporting the headnote. Using these headnote numbers to find the point of law in the text is a quick way to locate particular points that interest you.

Just after the sequence number, each headnote begins with a word or phrase, a key symbol, and a number. These are *topics* and *key numbers*, which are used in subject indexes to locate other cases that discuss similar points of law. These subject indexes, called *digests*, are discussed later in this chapter.

Headnotes are generally the product of a given reporter's editorial staff, even when the text of the headnote is identical to language used in the opinion. Thus, the number of headnotes—and the text of the headnotes—will differ depending on which publisher's reporter is being used. Because the official and unofficial reporters are published by different publishers, the headnotes in *New York Reports*, *Appellate Division Reports*, and *New York Miscellaneous Reports* (the official reporters), and the headnotes of *North Eastern Reporter* and *New York Supplement* (West reporters), are quite different.

Procedural information. Most reporters provide a variety of procedural information. For example, the attorneys who argued for each party will be listed. Some reporters indicate the court from which the case was appealed, the judges who heard the case, and the judge who wrote the decision. Note that following a judge's name may be the initials "C.J." for the chief judge (or "P.J." for the presiding justice in the intermediate appellate courts) or "J." for another judge or justice.[15]

Opinion. In *West's North Eastern Reporter*, the actual opinion of the court begins immediately following the name of the judge who wrote the opinion. If the judges who heard the case do not agree on the outcome or the reasons for the outcome, there may be several opinions. The opinion supported by a majority of the judges is called the *majority opinion*. An opinion written to agree with the outcome but not the reasoning of the majority is called a *concurring opinion*. An opinion written by judges who disagree with the outcome supported by the majority of the judges is called a *dissenting opinion*. While only the majority opinion is binding precedent, the other opinions provide valuable insights and may be cited as persuasive authority. If there is no majority on both the outcome and the reasoning, the case will be decided by whichever opinion garners the most support, which is called a *plurality decision*.

Cases decided by the New York Court of Appeals are heard by all seven of its judges. Cases decided by the Appellate Division are heard by four or five justices sitting as a panel of the full court.

3. *Tables in Reporters*

Most reporters contain the following tables: (a) a list of the judges serving during the period in which the reported cases were decided, (b) an alphabetical table of cases reported in that volume, (c) a list of cases in which the highest court of appeals has granted or denied petitions for review,[16] (d) a section called Words and Phrases that lists cases in that volume of the reporter that define particular legal terms,

15. In New York, appellate court judges at the Appellate Division, Appellate Term, and Supreme Court level are called justices. Judges in the Court of Appeals and most trial courts are called judges. The terms vary from state to state and in federal courts also.

16. This feature is more common in state reporters. Note that a court rarely issues opinions when it grants, denies, or dismisses petitions. Instead, a court issues a *memorandum* decision that simply records its action on the petition. You can identify these cases by the abbreviation "(Mem.)" following the case name. While most petitions for review by the New York Court

Figure 4-2. Case from *West's North Eastern Reporter* *People v. Lewis*, 502 N.E.2d 988 (N.Y. 1986)

988 N.Y. **502 NORTH EASTERN REPORTER, 2d SERIES**

68 N.Y.2d 923

923**The PEOPLE of the State of New York, Plaintiff,**

v.

Alfredo LEWIS, Defendant.

Alfredo LEWIS, Respondent,

v.

COMMISSIONER OF DEPARTMENT OF CORRECTIONAL SERVICES OF the STATE OF NEW YORK, Appellant.

Court of Appeals of New York.

Nov. 11, 1986.

Prisoner awaiting sentencing and transfer to correctional facility brought declaratory judgment action challenging validity of directive of Department of Correctional Services requiring that male prisoners receive initial haircut. The Supreme Court, Queens County, Dunkin, J., held that directive was unconstitutional as applied to prisoner, and State appealed. The Supreme Court, Appellate Division, 115 A.D.2d 597, 496 N.Y.S.2d 258, affirmed. On appeal, the Court of Appeals held that prisoner who had not cut his hair for over 20 years due to his sincere religious beliefs was not required to comply with directive mandating that all newly received inmates have haircut for reasons of health and sanitation as well as to permit taking of initial identification photographs.

Order affirmed.

1. Constitutional Law ⚷82(13)

Prison regulation challenged on ground that it impinges on First Amendment rights will be upheld, giving due deference to discretion and expertise of prison authorities, if regulation furthers substantial governmental interest of security, order or rehabilitation, and its encroachment on First Amendment freedom is no greater than necessary to protect interest involved. U.S.C.A. Const.Amend. 1.

2. Prisons ⚷4(14)

Prisoner who had not cut his hair for over 20 years due to his sincere religious beliefs was not required to comply with directive of State Department of Correctional Services mandating that all newly received inmates have haircut for reasons of health and sanitation as well as to permit taking of initial identification photographs, where identification photographs could be successfully taken if prisoner simply pulled his hair back, and there was no regulation governing length of hair following initial haircut. U.S.C.A. Const.Amend. 1.

Robert Abrams, Atty. Gen. (Esther Furman, New York City, O. Peter Sherwood, Albany, and Howard L. Zwickel, New York City, of counsel), for appellant.

Alan E. Kudisch, Kew Gardens, for respondent.

924Arnold S. Cohen and Caesar D. Cirigliano, New York City, for Legal Aid Society and another, amici curiae.

Janet Packard, Michael Raskin, Robert Selcov, Poughkeepsie, Stephen M. Latimer and David C. Leven, New York City, for Prisoners' Legal Services of New York, amicus curiae.

OPINION OF THE COURT

MEMORANDUM.

The order of the Appellate Division, 115 A.D.2d 597, 496 N.Y.S.2d 258, should be affirmed.

Plaintiff, a convicted felon, challenges as a violation of his First Amendment rights the application to him of defendant's directive requiring that male prisoners receive an initial haircut. Plaintiff is an avowed Rastafarian, wears his hair in dreadlocks, and has not cut his hair for 20 or more years. It is undisputed that he is sincere in his beliefs, that they are of religious nature, and that a haircut would impinge on those beliefs. The challenged directive provides that males received as new commitments have an initial haircut and

Source: *North Eastern Reporter, 2d.* Reprinted with permission of West, a Thomson Reuters business.

Figure 4-2. Case from *West's North Eastern Reporter, continued*
People v. Lewis, 502 N.E.2d 988 (N.Y. 1986)

ITOMAN (U.S.A.), INC. v. DAEWOO CORP. N.Y. **989**
Cite as 502 N.E.2d 989 (N.Y. 1986)

shave for reasons of health and sanitation as well as to permit the taking of the initial identification photographs; following the initial haircut, there is no restriction on the length of an inmate's hair. On this appeal, defendant urges only that the initial haircut is essential to prison security in that photographs taken at that time facilitate quick identification of inmates and escapees.*

[1] A prisoner retains First Amendment rights "not inconsistent with his status as a prisoner or with legitimate penological objectives of the corrections system." (*Pell v. Procunier,* 417 U.S. 817, 822, 94 S.Ct. 2800, 2804, 41 L.Ed.2d 495.) A regulation challenged on the ground that it impinges on First Amendment rights will be upheld if—giving due deference to the discretion and expertise of prison authorities—the regulation furthers substantial governmental interests of security, order or rehabilitation, and its encroachment on First Amendment freedoms is no greater than necessary to protect the interest involved (*Wali v. Coughlin,* 2nd Cir., 754 F.2d 1015, 1029; *Phillips v. Coughlin,* 586 F.Supp. 1281, 1283).

[2] Plaintiff urges that the regulation must be stricken because it does not constitute the "least intrusive means" of satisfying ⌊925defendant's administrative concern; defendant contends that the regulation should be upheld because it does not represent an "exaggerated response" to his legitimate penological interests. Both lower courts found that, as to plaintiff, the asserted objective of the regulation in issue could be fully achieved simply by pulling his hair back when the initial identification photographs are taken. This affirmed finding is supported by the testimony of a deputy commissioner in the Department of Correctional Services; and a sufficient showing was not made here of administrative burden. In this instance, therefore, defendant's interest can be readily satisfied without any interference with plaintiff's beliefs. Thus, whichever test is adopted, on this record the regulation as applied to plaintiff needlessly infringes on his beliefs, and cannot stand.

WACHTLER, C.J., and MEYER, SIMONS, KAYE, ALEXANDER, TITONE and HANCOCK, JJ., concur.

Order affirmed, without costs, in a memorandum.

68 N.Y.2d 925

⌊925In the Matter of the Arbitration between ITOMAN (U.S.A.), INC., Respondent,

and

DAEWOO CORPORATION, Appellant.

Court of Appeals of New York.

Nov. 11, 1986.

In connection with dispute over quality of fabric imported from Korea, New York importer demanded arbitration in New York in accordance with salesnote, and Korean exporter insisted that arbitration should proceed in Korea in accordance with confirmation order. The Supreme Court at Special Term, New York County, White, J., granted motion of importer to compel arbitration in New York, and appeal was taken. The Supreme Court, Appellate Division, 115 A.D.2d 1023, 495 N.Y.S.2d 880, affirmed. On appeal, the Court of Appeals held that remand was required, where record contained three confirmation orders, each somewhat different, one confirmation order

* The following issues are not reached on this appeal. First, no State constitutional argument is properly presented. Second, plaintiff has agreed to comply with the shave requirement. Third, we do not consider whether Rastafarianism is a religion entitled to First Amendment protection. (*See, Overton v. Department of Correctional Servs.,* 131 Misc.2d 295, 499 N.Y.S.2d 860.)

Source: *North Eastern Reporter, 2d.* Reprinted with permission of West, a Thomson Reuters business.

and (e) a subject index. In West reporters, this subject index is called the Key Number Digest. The topics and key numbers at the beginning of each headnote are included in the index. Searching the index can point you to additional cases that are on point, as addressed later in this chapter.

4. *Advance Sheets*

The bound volumes of reporters can take months to publish, with official reporters usually taking much longer than commercial reporters. To make cases available in print sooner, some publishers supply subscribers with softbound booklets called *advance sheets*. The advance sheets are typically published weekly.

5. *Other Sources for Finding New York Cases*

To provide access to cases even faster than advance sheets can be published, slip opinions are available either from the court that decided the case or online at www.courts.state.ny.us/decisions. A *slip opinion* is the actual document produced by the court, without the editorial enhancements normally added by the publisher. Slip opinions are added to court websites within two or three business days. In addition, cases are added daily to both Lexis and Westlaw, which are often the fastest way to find a new opinion.

B. Reporters for Federal Cases

Reporters are also published for cases decided by federal courts. Table 4-2 lists the federal court reporters, along with their citation abbreviations.

Decisions of the United States Supreme Court are reported in *United States Reports* (official); *Supreme Court Reporter* (West); and *United States Supreme Court Reports, Lawyers' Edition* (LexisNexis). Although the official *United States Reports* should be cited if possible,

---

of Appeals are denied, denying a petition does not mean that the court agrees with the outcome or analysis in the lower court's opinion.

Table 4-2. Reporters for Federal Court Cases

Court	Reporter Name	Abbreviation
U.S. Supreme Court	*United States Reports* (official) *Supreme Court Reporter* *United States Supreme Court Reports, Lawyers' Edition*	U.S. S. Ct. L. Ed., L. Ed. 2d
U.S. Courts of Appeals	*Federal Reporter*	F., F.2d, F.3d
U.S. District Courts	*Federal Supplement*	F. Supp., F. Supp. 2d

that series frequently publishes cases several years after they are decided. Thus, for recent cases, lawyers often cite the *Supreme Court Reporter*. Another source for finding recent cases from the U.S. Supreme Court is *United States Law Week*. This service publishes the full text of cases from the U.S. Supreme Court and provides summaries of important decisions of state and federal courts.

Cases decided by the federal intermediate appellate courts are published in *Federal Reporter*, now in its third series. Some Court of Appeals cases that were not selected for publication in *Federal Reporter* may be published in a relatively new reporter series, *Federal Appendix*.[17] Selected cases from the United States District Courts, the federal trial courts, are reported in *Federal Supplement* and *Federal Supplement, Second Series*.

U.S. Supreme Court opinions are widely available online. The Court's website[18] includes slip opinions soon after the decisions are rendered. Limited access to court of appeals and district court cases may be available from the individual court's website. An educational site supported by Cornell University also publishes federal cases

17. The precedential value of opinions published in *Federal Appendix* varies by federal circuit. Check the rules of the court with jurisdiction over your case.

18. The address is www.supremecourt.gov/opinions/slipopinions.aspx.

quickly.[19] Lexis and Westlaw publish federal opinions soon after they are released. Remember that Lexis and Westlaw make available selected "unpublished" opinions, including those published in *Federal Appendix* and those not published in any reporter. Check court rules to determine the weight each court gives to unpublished opinions.

III. West Digests

A digest is a multivolume or online index in which cases are organized by subject. Under each subject, the digest provides one or more headnotes from each case that addresses that particular subject and a citation to the case. The digest does not reprint the entire case. Digests are important research tools because reporters organize cases chronologically rather than by subject. The digest serves as a subject index to reporters. This part of the chapter concentrates on digests published by West because West digests are the most widely used throughout the country. Much of the information provided here also applies to any other case digest.

The print digest most often used in New York for researching New York law is *West's New York Digest, 4th.*[20] It includes headnotes of cases from state and federal courts in New York from 1978 to the current date. Earlier series of the digest index earlier cases. This digest also includes references to articles published by New York law reviews and to the legal encyclopedia *Corpus Juris Secundum*. An example of an entry in *West's New York Digest, 4th* is given in Figure 4-3.

Some digests index cases from a number of different jurisdictions. *West's Federal Practice Digest* provides an index to cases decided by federal trial and appellate courts. West's *Decennial Digest* indexes cases from all United States jurisdictions that are reported in West's na-

---

19. The address is www.law.cornell.edu.

20. While West publishes some regional digests to accompany its regional reporters, there is no longer a West digest for the *North Eastern Reporter*.

Figure 4-3. Excerpt from *West's New York Digest, 4th*

Headnote under Prisons 🔑 153

N.Y. 1986. Prisoner who had not cut his hair for over 20 years due to his sincere religious beliefs was not required to comply with directive of State Department of Correctional Services mandating that all newly received inmates have haircut for reasons of health and sanitation as well as to permit taking of initial identification photographs, where identification photographs could be successfully taken if prisoner simply pulled his hair back, and there was no regulation governing the length of hair following initial haircut. U.S.C.A. Const.Amend. 1.

People v. Lewis, 510 N.Y.S.2d 73, 68 N.Y.2d 923, 502 N.E.2d 988.

Source: *West's New York Digest, 4th.* Reprinted with permission of West, a Thomson Reuters business.

tional reporter system.[21] Each of these digests is published by West and uses the West topic and key number system.

A. Digest Features

1. Topics and Key Numbers

West digests index cases according to the West system of *topics* and *key numbers*. West assigns a topic and key number to each headnote in a case based on the legal point that is the focus of the headnote.

---

21. The *Decennial Digest* was originally published every ten years. While it still digests cases in ten-year increments, West published the Tenth series in two parts and the Eleventh series in three parts. The *Decennial Digest* may be helpful when (1) your library does not contain a digest for the jurisdiction whose laws you are researching or (2) there is no law on point in your jurisdiction, requiring you to search the laws of other jurisdictions for persuasive authority.

The West *topic* places the headnote within a broad subject area of the law. Examples of West topics include "Criminal Law," "Health and Environment," and "Witnesses." The *key number* relates to a subtopic within that area of law.[22] When performing research in a digest, it is necessary to have both the topic and key number. An analogy is the necessity to have both a number and street name to have a complete street address. In both cases, having only one part is not enough information to guide you to your destination.

The topic used for the example in this chapter is "Prisons." It contains over four hundred key numbers on subtopics addressing such issues as care of inmates, type of confinement, prisoner grievances, and prisoner hygiene. Key number 153 has been assigned to the subtopic "Hair, grooming, and clothing." Thus, the topic and key number "Prisons 153" is a research tool that will lead to cases West has indexed together because they all address issues surrounding prisoner hygiene and dress.

2. Headnotes

The digest entries under each topic and key number are the actual headnotes found in cases. The bulk of each headnote entry is a sentence that summarizes the point of law that is the specific subject of the topic and key number assigned to that headnote. Each case is indexed in the digest under as many topics and key numbers as it had headnotes in the reporter.

In a digest, headnotes are arranged under each topic and key number according to the court that decided the case. Federal cases are listed first, followed by state court cases. Within the federal and state systems, cases are listed according to judicial hierarchy: cases from the highest appellate court are listed first, followed by decisions of intermediate appellate courts, then trial court cases. Cases from courts with more than one division, e.g., the Appellate Division of the

---

22. In general, parentheses are used in headnote key numbers to denote subheadings, while decimals are used to insert new key numbers. A topic outline may omit a key number that is no longer used.

Supreme Court, are listed by division. Cases from each court are given in reverse chronological order. This order is helpful because recent cases, which are listed first, are more likely to be pertinent to your research.

At the beginning of each headnote is a court abbreviation and date. The abbreviations are explained in tables at the beginning of each digest volume. At the end of the digest headnote are citations to any statutes that are cited in the case. This information is followed by the case citation and any parallel citations.

Although West may have assigned a topic and key number to a particular point of law, a given jurisdiction may not have decided a case on that point. In that instance, no entries will appear under the topic and key number of that jurisdiction's digest. However, the topic and key number system makes it easy to research cases in other jurisdictions using West digests, which may lead to persuasive authorities.

3. Topic and Key Number Conversions

Various topics and key numbers may change over time in response to developments in the law. Researching with the second headnote of the case *People v. Lewis*, shown in Figure 4-2, provides an example. That headnote was initially assigned the topic and key number Prisons 4(14). To locate additional cases on this subject using *West's New York Digest 4th*, select the volume(s) containing the topic "Prisons" and open to key number 4(14). When browsing the digest volume for this topic and key number, you see the following notation indicating that Prisons 4 is no longer a valid key number:

> PRISONS Key Numbers 1 to 18
> are no longer valid and have been
> replaced by new Key Numbers. See
> topic analysis and translation tables.

Translation tables can be found at the beginning of the Prisons topic either in the main volume or in the pocket part. Figure 4-4 is an example of a translation table. It shows that Prisons 4(14) has been con-

Figure 4-4. *West's New York Digest, 4th* Key Number Translation Table Showing Prisons ⚿ 4(14) Converted to Prisons ⚿ 153

Former PRISONS Key Number	Present PRISONS Key Number
1	101
2, 3	214
4(1)	103, 111, 112
4(2.1, 3)	105, 112
4(4)	350–374
4(5)	113, 123
4(6)	129, 130, 142, 143, 149
4(7)	132, 135–139
4(8)	140
4(9)	145–148
4(10.1)	260
4(11)	262, 263, 267, 268
4(12)	264
4(13)	265–268
4(14)	152–155
6	390, 391
7	391–394, 396

Source: *West's New York Digest, 4th.* Reprinted with permission of West, a Thomson Reuters business.

verted to the key number range 152–55. Browsing the digest in this key number range, you locate Prisons 153, *Hair, grooming, and clothing*. In sum, the headnote formerly under Prisons 4(14) is now located under Prisons 153.

B. Digest Research in Print

1. *Beginning with a Relevant Case*

If you begin a research project knowing one case on point, read the case in a West reporter and identify the headnotes that are rele-

Table 4-3. Outline for Digest Research with the Descriptive-Word Index

1. Find your research terms in the Descriptive-Word Index (and its pocket part), which will list topics and key numbers relevant to those terms.
2. Review the headnotes under each topic and key number in the main volumes of the digest.
3. Update each topic and key number by checking the pocket parts or volume supplement, the cumulative supplementary pamphlets, and the digests contained in the reporter's most recent advance sheets.

vant to your issue. Note the topic and key number given for each relevant headnote. Select a digest volume containing one of the relevant topics. Within that topic, find the key number given in the related headnote. Under the key number, all the headnotes of cases with that topic and key number will be listed. Repeat this step for each relevant topic and key number in your original case. Remember to update the search to find the most recent cases on point.

2. *Beginning with the Descriptive-Word Index*

Most digest research begins with the Descriptive-Word Index, which translates research terms into the topics and key numbers used by the digest to index cases. See Table 4-3 for an outline of this process.

To begin, use an organized method of brainstorming to generate a list of research terms that describe the situation you are analyzing. Then look up each term in the Descriptive-Word Index (contained in several volumes at the end of the digest) and write down the topic and key number for each. Record both the topic and the key number. Many topics have the same key numbers, so a number alone is not a helpful research tool. Check each volume's pocket part for the most recent information. Figure 4-5 shows an excerpt from the Descriptive-Word Index in *West's New York Digest, 4th.* Note that some topics may be abbreviated in the Descriptive-Word Index. A list of top-

Figure 4-5. Excerpt from the Descriptive-Word Index in *West's New York Digest, 4th*

48C N Y D 4th–57 PRISONS

References are to Digest Topics and Key Numbers

PRISONS—Cont'd

RELIGIOUS practices,
Generally, **Prisons** 🔑 **152**
Ablution, **Prisons** 🔑 **155**
Ceremonies, **Prisons** 🔑 **155**
Cleansing, **Prisons** 🔑 **155**
Clergy, **Prisons** 🔑 **152, 155**
Clothing, **Prisons** 🔑 **153**
Crowns, wearing of, **Prisons** 🔑 **153**
Diet, **Prisons** 🔑 **154**
Facial Hair, **Prisons** 🔑 **153**
Food, Prisons 🔑 154
Freedom of Religion. *See heading RELIGION, FREEDOM OF, PRISONS and pretrial detention*
Grooming, **Prisons** 🔑 **153**
Hair, **Prisons** 🔑 **153**
Hygiene, **Prisons** 🔑 **153**

Source: *West's New York Digest, 4th.* Reprinted with permission of West, a Thomson Reuters business.

ics and their abbreviations is included at the front of each index volume.

Using the topics and key numbers you recorded from the Descriptive-Word Index, select a digest volume that contains one of the topics. At the beginning of each topic is a list of "Subjects Included" as well as "Subjects Excluded and Covered by Other Topics." These lists will help you decide whether that topic is likely to index cases most relevant to your research. The list of excluded subjects may contain references to other relevant topics found elsewhere in the digest. After these lists is the key number outline of the topic, under the heading "Analysis," as seen in Figure 4-6. Longer topics will contain a

Figure 4-6. Excerpt from *West's New York Digest, 4th* Analysis for Prisons

Analysis

I. IN GENERAL, 🔑 100–109.
II. PRISONERS AND INMATES, 🔑 110–349.
  (A) IN GENERAL, 🔑 110–119.
  (B) CARE, CUSTODY, CONFINEMENT, AND CONTROL, 🔑 120–169.
  (C) LABOR AND EMPLOYMENT, 🔑 170–189.
  (D) HEALTH AND MEDICAL CARE, 🔑 190–209.

  . . .

III. PRETRIAL DETENTION, 🔑 350–379.
IV. NONPRISONERS, 🔑 380–389.

  . . .

Source: *West's New York Digest, 4th*. Reprinted with permission of West, a Thomson Reuters business.

short, summary outline and then a detailed outline. Many topics follow a general litigation organization, so that elements, defenses, pleadings, and evidence are discussed in that order. Take a moment to skim the Analysis outline to ensure that you found in the Descriptive-Word Index all the relevant key numbers within that topic.

Next, turn to each of the relevant key numbers and carefully review each of the case headnotes listed there. Write down the citation for each case that you decide you need to read. At this point, the cites do not have to be complete or conform to any system of citation. Recording the last name of one party, the volume, reporter, and page number will often be sufficient.

To find more recent topics, key numbers, and case headnotes, check the back of the volume for pocket parts. A softbound volume of updated material may be provided instead, if the material is too thick to fit in a pocket part. These supplements are in turn updated by cumulative supplementary pamphlets, which contain updates for all topics.[23] For same day currency, you must go to an online database, such as Lexis or Westlaw, which are explained later in this chapter.[24]

Reviewing headnotes and recording possibly relevant case citations is time consuming but critical work. To analyze a client's situation accurately, you need to read every relevant case, as the cost of skipping a key case is high. However, you may be selective in deciding which cases to read first. Additionally, when a topic and key number contain many pages of case headnotes, or when you are working under tight deadlines, you may need to be selective in choosing the cases you are able to read. First, read those cases that are binding authority in your jurisdiction. Within that subset, read the most recent cases. If a headnote includes facts similar to your client's, read that case, too.

3. *Beginning with the Topic Analysis*

After researching a specific area of law many times, you may be very familiar with the topics under which cases in that area are indexed. If so, you can begin your research using the Analysis outline that appears at the beginning of each relevant topic. Scan the list of key number subtopics, and then review the headnotes under each key number that appears to be on point. As always, remember to check the pocket parts, supplementary pamphlets, and reporter advance sheets for more recent cases under the topics and key numbers you are searching.

4. *Words and Phrases*

To learn whether a court has defined a term, refer to the Words and Phrases volumes at the end of the digest.[25] While a dictionary like

---

23. You may find coverage after the cumulative supplements by going to a particular reporter's most recent volumes and advance sheets and using the digest contained in each. A table at the beginning of each digest volume will indicate which reporter volumes are indexed there. Updating requires you to check the digest sections of subsequent reporters.

24. Note that only Westlaw allows you to continue research using West topics and key numbers.

25. West also produces a multivolume set, *Words and Phrases*, containing court definitions from federal and state jurisdictions combined.

Black's Law Dictionary will provide a general definition of a term, Words and Phrases will direct you to a case that defines the term for a particular jurisdiction. Judicial definitions are especially helpful when an important term in a statute is vague.

5. Table of Cases

The Table of Cases lists all the cases indexed in a particular digest series by both the primary plaintiff's name and the primary defendant's name. The table is helpful when you do not know the citation to a relevant case but do know the name of one or both parties. This situation may occur (1) because a colleague recommended the case, (2) because you used it in previous research, or (3) because the only citation you have is to the official reporter, which does not use West's topics and key numbers. The Table of Cases provides the full name of the case, the citation for the case, and the relevant topics and key numbers. After consulting the Table of Cases, you could either read the case in a reporter or continue working in the digest using the listed topics and key numbers to find more related cases.

IV. Online Subject Searching[26]

A. Westlaw and Lexis

Both Westlaw and Lexis offer ways to search for cases by subject. On Westlaw, options include the "Key Number Digest" feature for searching by digest topic and key number, and the "KeySearch" feature for searching by subject. On Lexis, the feature for subject searching is "Search by Topic or Headnote."

26. This section addresses searching Westlaw's and Lexis's "classic" versions. See Chapter 2 for a brief discussion of WestlawNext and Lexis Advance.

These features on Westlaw and Lexis have a number of aspects in common. First, both systems display breakdowns of topics that resemble the Analysis outline of a print digest. In both systems, you can expand the list of general topics to search more specific subtopics by clicking on a symbol or icon at the left of the general topic listing. This expander feature is most commonly a plus (+) symbol. The approach here, as with print digest searching, is to decide where in the larger scheme of legal topics your more specific topic is likely to be located.

1. Westlaw's Key Number Digest

Currently, you can access the digest feature on Westlaw by clicking on the "Site Map" tab at the top of the Westlaw research system page, and then choosing "West Key Number Digest Outline (Custom Digest)" under "Search Westlaw." Alternatively, click on "Key Numbers" at the top of any Westlaw screen, and then select "West Key Number Digest Outline." A third possibility, also available from the "Key Numbers" link, is to type terms into a search box. The computer will return a list of relevant topics and key numbers.

Like its print counterpart, Westlaw's digest is organized around topics and key numbers. For example, "Prisons" is its own topic in *West's New York Digest, 4th*, and that topic also appears in Westlaw's digest feature. See Figure 4-7. Note that when topics and key numbers are represented online, the topic is sometimes converted to a number. "Prisons" is topic 310, and the topic and key number "Witnesses 153" is represented as 310k153.

The results of a search in the digest function are headnotes from relevant cases. Review these headnotes with the same care that you would review headnotes in a print digest. Skimming the entries is easier in online research because they are hyperlinked to the list of cases.

2. Westlaw's KeySearch

To use the subject searching function on Westlaw, click on "Key Numbers" at the top of any screen, and then click on "KeySearch." From there, you have two options. First, you can simply type terms into the search box in the left frame and Westlaw will return a list of

Figure 4-7. Westlaw's Key Number Digest "Prisons"

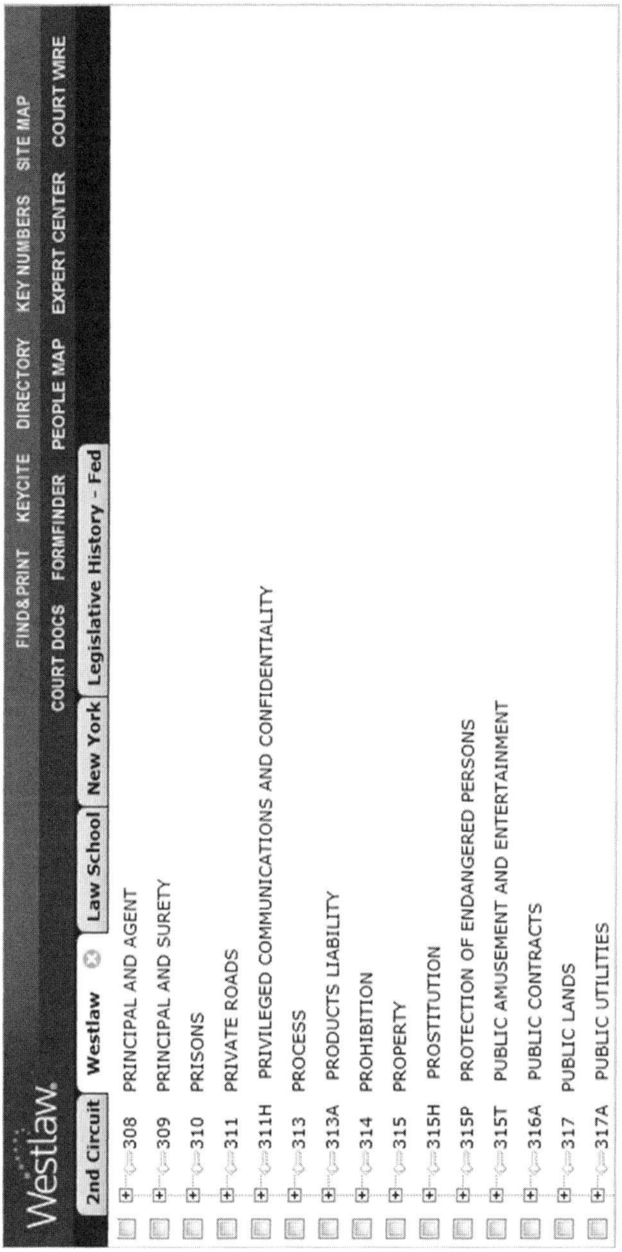

Westlaw.

FIND&PRINT KEYCITE DIRECTORY KEY NUMBERS SITE MAP

COURT DOCS FORMFINDER PEOPLE MAP EXPERT CENTER COURT WIRE

2nd Circuit | Westlaw | Law School | New York | Legislative History - Fed

308 PRINCIPAL AND AGENT
309 PRINCIPAL AND SURETY
310 PRISONS
311 PRIVATE ROADS
311H PRIVILEGED COMMUNICATIONS AND CONFIDENTIALITY
313 PROCESS
313A PRODUCTS LIABILITY
314 PROHIBITION
315 PROPERTY
315H PROSTITUTION
315P PROTECTION OF ENDANGERED PERSONS
315T PUBLIC AMUSEMENT AND ENTERTAINMENT
316A PUBLIC CONTRACTS
317 PUBLIC LANDS
317A PUBLIC UTILITIES

Source: Westlaw. 2011. Reprinted with permission of West, a Thomson Reuters business.

possible subjects and subheadings. Second, you can skim the list of subject headings in the right frame and expand those that seem relevant, searching for more specific subheadings.

Regardless of the approach you use, Westlaw will eventually take you to a screen where you must select the jurisdiction for your search and the type of documents you wish to retrieve (e.g., state cases, federal cases, secondary sources). The screen provides a search box where you have the option of entering either a terms-and-connectors search or a natural-language search.

3. *Lexis's Search by Topic or Headnote*

The subject searching function on Lexis is accessed by clicking the "Search" tab pull-down menu and then choosing "Search by Topic or Headnote." As with KeySearch, you have two options: typing terms into a search box or reviewing a list of broad subjects. To use the second option in the prisoner example, you would need to start with the larger topic of "Civil Rights Law" and use the expanders to find the more specific topics relating to whether a prisoner can avoid being subject to grooming regulations on religious grounds. See Figure 4-8. As with Westlaw, you will be directed to a search screen. The results will be documents from the selected jurisdiction that address the selected topic.

After you find a relevant case on Lexis, you can find more cases on point through three additional features. First, click on "Show" next to the LexisNexis Headnotes field to display all headnotes. Then read the relevant headnotes as you view the case on Lexis, and click on "All" at the end of the headnote heading. You will be directed to a search screen where you can select a jurisdiction. The results will be headnotes and cases containing the same point of law as the headnote. (Remember that Lexis and Westlaw headnotes are not interchangeable.)

The other two features are "More Like This" and "More Like Selected Text," which appear at the top of a screen displaying a case. Searching for "More Like This" will allow you to search for other cases with similar citation patterns (by using "core cites") or with similar language patterns (using "core terms"). Using the "More Like Selected Text" feature will allow you to highlight a portion of the case and ask Lexis to find similar cases.

Figure 4-8. Lexis Search by Topic Feature

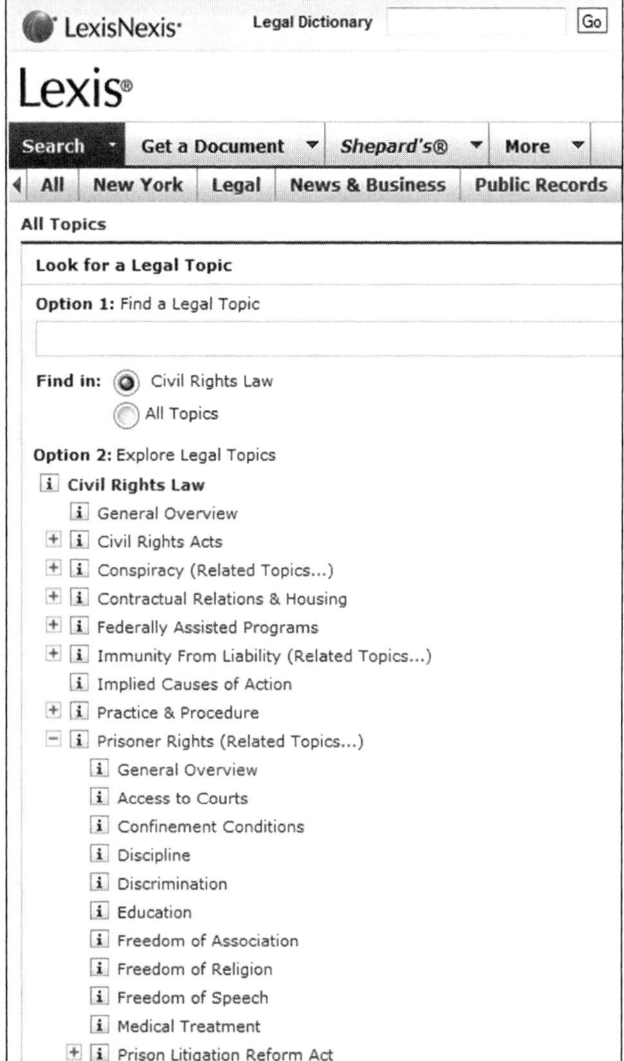

B. Internet Subject Research

Many Internet sites have not yet developed digest features. Both federal and state court sites generally do not yet allow searching by topic. Instead, you must know the case name or docket number to access an opinion. This capability is likely to become available in the near future, and the techniques above may be useful.

Even now, a subject search in a general search engine can produce useful results. A law firm may have posted links to recent judicial opinions or an attorney may have posted links to an outline of research on your very topic.

V. Reading and Analyzing Cases

After locating a possibly relevant case, you must read it, understand it, and analyze its potential relevance to the problem you are researching. This is often challenging, time-consuming work. It is not unusual for a lawyer to spend hours reading (and rereading) cases, especially in unfamiliar areas of law. This reading may be interrupted by references to a law dictionary to try to understand the terms used. The following strategies should make reading and analyzing cases more effective.

A. Reading Cases Effectively

Review the synopsis quickly to determine whether the case seems to be on point. If so, skim the headnotes to find the particular portion of the case that is relevant. Remember that one case may discuss several issues of law, only one or two of which may interest you. Go to the portion of the case identified by the relevant headnote and decide whether it is important for your project. If so, skim the entire case to get a feeling for what happened and why, focusing on the portion of the case identified by the relevant headnote.

After determining that a case is relevant, read the case slowly and carefully. Skip the parts that are obviously not pertinent to your problem. At the end of each paragraph or page, consider what you have read. If you cannot summarize it, try reading the material again.

Read the case again, this time taking notes. The notes may be in the form of a formal "case brief" or they may be scribbles that only you can understand. Regardless of the form, the process of taking notes will help you parse through, identify, and comprehend the essential concepts of the case. When preparing to write a legal document, the notes will assist you in organizing your analysis into an outline. Note that skimming text online or highlighting a printed page is often insufficient to achieve thorough comprehension of judicial opinions.

B. Analyzing the Substance of Cases

If a case concerns the same legally significant facts as your client's situation and the court applies law on point for your problem, then the case is relevant and should be considered carefully as you analyze your problem. Legally significant facts are those that affect the court's decision. Some attorneys call these outcome-determinative facts or key facts. Which facts are legally significant depends on the case. The height of the defendant in a contract dispute is unlikely to be legally significant, but that fact may be critical in a criminal case in which the only eyewitness testified that the thief was about five feet tall.

Rarely will research reveal a case with facts that are exactly the same as your client's situation. Rather, several cases may involve facts that are similar to your client's situation but not exactly the same. Your job is to determine whether the facts are similar enough for a court to apply the law in the same way and reach the same outcome. If the court reached a decision favorable to your client, you will highlight the similarities. If, on the other hand, the court reached an unfavorable decision from your client's perspective, you may argue that the case is distinguishable from yours based on its facts or that the court's reasoning is faulty. Note that you have an ethical duty to ensure that the court knows about a case directly on point, even if the outcome of that case is adverse to your client.

It is also unlikely that one case will address all aspects of your client's situation. Most legal claims have several elements or factors. *Elements* are required subparts of a claim, while *factors* are important aspects but are not required for a claim to succeed. If a court decides that one element is not met, the court might not discuss others. In a different case, the court may decide that two factors are so overwhelming that others have no impact on the outcome. In these circumstances, you would have to find other cases that analyze the other elements or factors.

After determining that a case is relevant to some portion of your analysis, you must decide how heavily it will weigh in your analysis. Two important points need to be considered here. One is the concept of *stare decisis*; the other is the difference between the holding of the case and dicta within that case.

Stare decisis means "to stand by things decided."[28] This concept means that courts must follow prior opinions, ensuring consistency in the application of the law. *Stare decisis*, however, is limited to the courts within one jurisdiction. The lower courts in New York must follow the decisions of the New York Court of Appeals but not those of the courts of any other state.[29] The concept of *stare decisis* also refers to a court with respect to its own opinions. The Court of Appeals, thus, should follow its own earlier cases in deciding new matters. If a court decides not to continue following its earlier cases, it is usually because of changes in society that have outdated the law of the earlier case, or because a new statute has been enacted that changes the legal landscape.

Under *stare decisis*, courts are required to follow the holding of prior cases. The *holding* is the court's ultimate decision on the matter of law at issue in the case. Other statements or observations in-

---

28. *Black's Law Dictionary* 1537 (9th ed. 2009).

29. Cases of the Appellate Division are also binding on trial courts. If neither the Court of Appeals nor a particular department of the Appellate Division has spoken on an issue, trial courts in that department must follow the precedents set by other departments until the Court of Appeals or that department announces a rule. *Mountain View Coach Lines, Inc. v. Storms*, 102 A.D.2d 663, 664–65, 476 N.Y.S.2d 918, 919–20 (1984).

cluded in the opinion are not binding; they are referred to as *dicta*. For example, in deciding whether passing a bad check through the window at a bank's drive-through facility was burglary, a court observed that a person putting his arm through a library chute to remove books would commit burglary. That observation based on hypothetical facts was not the basis of the court's decision. The observation is therefore dicta and is not binding on future courts, though it may be cited as persuasive authority.

After finding a number of relevant cases, you must synthesize them to state and explain the legal rule. Sometimes a court states the rule fully, but if the court does not, piece together the information from the relevant cases. Then use the analysis and facts of various cases to explain the law. Decide how the rule applies to the client's facts, and determine your conclusion. Note that this method of synthesis is much more than mere summaries of all the various cases. Legal analysis texts in Appendix B of this book explain synthesis in detail.

Appendix 4-A. Case Excerpt from Official Reporter *People v. Lewis*, 68 N.Y.2d 923 (1986)

MEMORANDA 923

DER, TITONE and HANCOCK, JR., concur; Judge SIMONS taking no part.

Order affirmed in a memorandum.

THE PEOPLE OF THE STATE OF NEW YORK, Plaintiff, v ALFREDO LEWIS, Defendant.

ALFREDO LEWIS, Respondent, v COMMISSIONER OF DEPARTMENT OF CORRECTIONAL SERVICES OF THE STATE OF NEW YORK, Appellant.

Argued October 6, 1986; decided November 11, 1986

SUMMARY

APPEAL, on constitutional grounds, from an order of the Appellate Division of the Supreme Court in the Second Judicial Department, entered December 16, 1985, which unanimously affirmed a judgment of the Supreme Court (Sol R. Dunkin, J.), entered in Queens County, declaring, *inter alia,* that the initial haircut requirement of the State Department of Correctional Services was unconstitutional as applied to plaintiff Alfredo Lewis, and that Lewis may retain his dreadlocks in accordance with his religious beliefs.

Lewis v Commissioner of Dept. of Correctional Servs., 115 AD2d 597, affirmed.

HEADNOTE

Prisons and Prisoners — Freedom of Worship — Initial Haircut

Plaintiff, an avowed Rastafarian who has not cut his hair, which he wears in dreadlocks, for over 20 years owing to his sincere religious beliefs, shall not have to comply with a directive of the State Department of Correctional Services mandating that all newly received inmates have a haircut for reasons of health and sanitation as well as to permit the taking of initial identification photographs, where there has been an affirmed finding that the identification photographs could be successfully taken if plaintiff simply pulls his hair back; moreover, following the initial haircut, there is no restriction on the length of an inmate's hair. Inasmuch as the Department's legitimate penological interests can be readily satisfied without any interference with plaintiff's beliefs, the Department's directive, as applied to plaintiff, needlessly infringes on those beliefs.

APPEARANCES OF COUNSEL

Robert Abrams, Attorney-General (Esther Furman, O. Peter Sherwood and *Howard L. Zwickel* of counsel), for appellant.

Alan E. Kudisch for respondent.

Appendix 4-A. Case Excerpt from Official Reporter *People v. Lewis*, 68 N.Y.2d 923 (1986), *continued*

Arnold S. Cohen and *Caesar D. Cirigliano* for Legal Aid Society and another, *amici curiae.*

Janet Packard, Michael Raskin, Robert Selcov, Stephen M. Latimer and *David C. Leven* for Prisoners' Legal Services of New York, *amicus curiae.*

OPINION OF THE COURT

MEMORANDUM.

The order of the Appellate Division should be affirmed.

Plaintiff, a convicted felon, challenges as a violation of his First Amendment rights the application to him of defendant's directive requiring that male prisoners receive an initial haircut. Plaintiff is an avowed Rastafarian, wears his hair in dreadlocks, and has not cut his hair for 20 or more years. It is undisputed that he is sincere in his beliefs, that they are of religious nature, and that a haircut would impinge on those beliefs. The challenged directive provides that males received as new commitments have an initial haircut and shave for reasons of health and sanitation as well as to permit the taking of the initial identification photographs; following the initial haircut, there is no restriction on the length of an inmate's hair. On this appeal, defendant urges only that the initial haircut is essential to prison security in that photographs taken at that time facilitate quick identification of inmates and escapees.*

A prisoner retains First Amendment rights "not inconsistent with his status as a prisoner or with legitimate penological objectives of the corrections system." *(Pell v Procunier,* 417 US 817, 822.) A regulation challenged on the ground that it impinges on First Amendment rights will be upheld if—giving due deference to the discretion and expertise of prison authorities—the regulation furthers substantial governmental interests of security, order or rehabilitation, and its encroachment on First Amendment freedoms is no greater than necessary to protect the interest involved *(Wali v Coughlin,* 754 F2d 1015, 1029; *Phillips v Coughlin,* 586 F Supp 1281, 1283).

Plaintiff urges that the regulation must be stricken because it does not constitute the "least intrusive means" of satisfying

* The following issues are not reached on this appeal. First, no State constitutional argument is properly presented. Second, plaintiff has agreed to comply with the shave requirement. Third, we do not consider whether Rastafarianism is a religion entitled to First Amendment protection. *(See, Overton v Department of Correctional Servs.,* 131 Misc 2d 295.)

Appendix 4-A. Case Excerpt from Official Reporter *People v. Lewis*, 68 N.Y.2d 923 (1986), *continued*

defendant's administrative concern; defendant contends that the regulation should be upheld because it does not represent an "exaggerated response" to his legitimate penological interests. Both lower courts found that, as to plaintiff, the asserted objective of the regulation in issue could be fully achieved simply by pulling his hair back when the initial identification photographs are taken. This affirmed finding is supported by the testimony of a deputy commissioner in the Department of Correctional Services; and a sufficient showing was not made here of administrative burden. In this instance, therefore, defendant's interest can be readily satisfied without any interference with plaintiff's beliefs. Thus, whichever test is adopted, on this record the regulation as applied to plaintiff needlessly infringes on his beliefs, and cannot stand.

Chief Judge WACHTLER and Judges MEYER, SIMONS, KAYE, ALEXANDER, TITONE and HANCOCK, JR., concur.

Order affirmed, without costs, in a memorandum.

In the Matter of the Arbitration between ITOMAN (U.S.A.), INC., Respondent, and DAEWOO CORPORATION, Appellant.

Submitted October 7, 1986; decided November 11, 1986

SUMMARY

APPEAL, by permission of the Court of Appeals, from an order of the Appellate Division of the Supreme Court in the First Judicial Department, entered December 3, 1985, which unanimously affirmed an order and judgment (one paper) of the Supreme Court at Special Term (Robert E. White, J.), entered in New York County, *inter alia,* granting the motion of petitioner Itoman (U.S.A.), Inc. to compel respondent Daewoo Corporation to proceed to arbitration before the General Arbitration Council of the Textile Industry in the City of New York, and denying the cross motion of respondent for an order directing the arbitration to take place in South Korea under the Rules of the Korean Commercial Arbitration Association.

Matter of Itoman (U.S.A.), Inc. v Daewoo Corp., 115 AD2d 1023, reversed.

HEADNOTE

Arbitration — Agreement to Arbitrate — Place of Arbitration

In a proceeding to compel arbitration of a commercial controversy, an order of the Appellate Division, which affirmed an order and judgment

Chapter 5

Statutes, Constitutions, Local Law, and Court Rules

One of the largest areas of law is *enacted law*. Enacted law is promulgated by a branch of the government in rule format for general application; in contrast, case law is issued by the courts in narrative form to resolve a particular dispute between specific parties. Enacted law includes statutes, constitutions, local law, court rules, and administrative regulations. This chapter covers each of these types of enacted law except administrative regulations, which are covered in Chapter 7.

How you begin to research enacted law depends on the information you have as you begin your work. Sometimes, especially early in your career, an attorney may tell you exactly which law controls your client's situation. Your supervising attorney, for example, may know from experience that N.Y. Correction Law § 112 addresses the powers and duties of a commissioner of correction relating to correctional facilities. In that case, review the spines of one of the New York codes such as *McKinney's Consolidated Laws of New York Annotated* (called simply "McKinney's") to find the volume that contains the chapter "Correction Law," and then look through the volume to find the statute. Alternatively, use an online database to retrieve the statute.

Often, though, you will begin your research with just the facts of the client's situation. In those instances, follow the general outline provided in Table 5-1. The remainder of this chapter covers each type of enacted law in turn—statutes, constitutions, local law, and court rules.

Table 5-1. Researching Enacted Law

1. Develop a list of research terms.
2. Search the index or conduct a full-text search online.
3. Find and read the language of the provision.
4. Update the provision (if using print sources).
5. Find cases that interpret or apply the provision.

I. New York Statutes

Statutory laws are classified—that is, codified—by subject in volumes called codes. These codes group the laws by subject and show all subsequent amendments. You will use an annotated code (discussed in Part II) when you want to locate statutes with all of their amendments and deletions, along with summaries of judicial decisions applying the statute.

To locate laws efficiently, you need a basic understanding of how the codes are organized. Statutory laws are organized by subject matter into chapters and section numbers. The subject matter of a chapter is a word or phrase like "Banking," "Civil Practice Law and Rules," "General Obligations Law," or "Social Services." The section numbers reference both an article and a specific statute in that article; however, the numbering of the codified statutes is not consistent throughout.

Using the example of a prisoner's grooming rights, N.Y. Correction Law § 112, the chapter is Correction Law and section number 112 is part of Article 6 (*Management of Correctional Facilities*).[1] Another example is the numbering scheme of New York General Oblig-

1. Note that this statute appears in different volumes in the two annotated codifications of New York statutes. In *McKinney's Consolidated Laws of New York Annotated*, this statute is located in volume 10B, while in *New York Consolidated Laws Service* (CLS) it appears in volume 5B. Although standard legal citation format generally integrates the volume number into the citation, the numeric book or volume number is not included in the citation for New York statutes.

ations Law, in which each section number of the code numerically represents an article, title, and section. Using the example N.Y. General Obligations Law § 3-101, General Obligations Law is the name of the chapter, the 3 represents Article 3 (*Capacity*), the 1 represents Title 1 (*Infancy*), and the 01 represents Section 1 (*When contracts may not be disaffirmed on ground of infancy*).

A. Consolidated and Unconsolidated Laws Defined

New York's laws are either "consolidated" or "unconsolidated." Both consolidated and unconsolidated laws are passed by the New York State legislature and, therefore, have equal force of law. The bulk of New York's current laws are consolidated laws, enacted as the *Consolidated Laws of 1909*. This consolidation was an alleged re-enactment of all of "the general substantive statutes of the state since its organization."[2] Unconsolidated laws are any laws in existence in 1909 that were not re-enacted as part of the *Consolidated Laws of 1909* or any laws subsequently passed that do not fit into the substantive architecture of the consolidated laws. The examples below will help clarify the status of laws passed after the 1909 consolidation.

An example of an unconsolidated law passed after 1909 is N.Y. Unconsolidated Laws § 8926 (McKinney 2002). Originally passed in 1920, this law requires a physician to be present at boxing matches and vests power in the physician to make determinations to end boxing matches that result in extensive boxing injuries. All laws pertain-

---

2. Robert A. Emery, *Statutory Codification and Legislative Failure of Nerve: A Brief Note on the New York Consolidated Laws of 1909*, 15 Legal Reference Services Q. 49 (1996) (citing the *Report of the Board of Statutory Consolidation* (1908), reprinted in McKinney's Statutes at VII). Despite this re-enactment, researchers may have to research laws prior to the *Consolidated Laws of 1909* as a result of the subsequent passage of 1909 N.Y. Laws ch. 596, which raises doubt about the purpose and effect of the 1909 consolidation. An excellent historical explanation of the *Consolidated Laws of 1909* and its impact on New York statutory law research can also be found in Chapters 3 and 4 of William H. Manz's *Gibson's New York Legal Research Guide* (3d ed. 2004).

ing to the New York State Athletic Commission were passed beginning in 1920. They are part of the unconsolidated laws because they did not exist when the *Consolidated Laws of 1909* were re-enacted and the subject matter does not fit into the original scheme comprising the compiled general substantive statutes.

An example of a consolidated law that went into effect after the *Consolidated Laws of 1909* is N.Y. Environmental Conservation Law § 11-0317,[3] *Seasons and limits for taking fish in certain border waters.* This law, initially enacted in 1972, empowers the Department of Environmental Conservation, after consultation with neighboring states and provinces, to promulgate regulations establishing open seasons for fishing, the size of the fish, the method of fishing, and other related issues. Although it went into effect after 1909, this law is part of the consolidated laws because it fits into the scheme already in place at the time this law was passed.

Consolidated laws are shelved, for the most part, in alphabetical order according to the name of the law. *New York Consolidated Laws Service* (CLS) assigns volume numbers and McKinney's assigns book numbers to each area of the law. The examples below exemplify how three different areas of law are numerically represented. Note that a CLS volume and a McKinney's book can fill more than one volume. This is a common source of confusion for novices.

EXAMPLES:

Abandoned Property Law
- CLS: in volume 1 (a portion of one volume)
- McKinney's: in book 2½ (one volume)

Alcoholic Beverage Control Law
- CLS: in volumes 1A and 1B (comprising the second half of volume 1A and the first half of volume 1B)
- McKinney's: in book 3A (one volume)

Banking Law
- CLS: in volumes 2, 2A, and 2B (comprising 3 volumes)
- McKinney's: in book 4 (comprising 2 volumes)

---

3. The history line of this law in an annotated code appears as follows: (L.1972, c. 664, § 2; amended L.1990, c. 911, § 11).

B. Sources of Consolidated Laws

New York does not have an official, legislatively sanctioned current code. There are three unofficial, print consolidated codes: the *New York Consolidated Laws Service*, published by LexisNexis; *McKinney's Consolidated Laws of New York Annotated*, published by West; and *Consolidated Laws of New York*,[4] also published by LexisNexis. CLS and McKinney's contain similar editorial enhancements and will be discussed together in the next section of this chapter. *Consolidated Laws of New York*, on the other hand, does not include editorial enhancements and will be discussed separately later.

1. New York Consolidated Laws Service *and* McKinney's Consolidated Laws of New York Annotated

New York Consolidated Laws Service (CLS), published by LexisNexis, and *McKinney's Consolidated Laws of New York Annotated* (McKinney's), published by West, are arranged by chapter—represented by subject matter—and section numbers. The citation format for CLS and McKinney's citations is exactly the same when following Bluebook and ALWD citation rules. Examples of how to cite CLS and McKinney's are in Table 5-2.

New York Consolidated Laws Service is available on Lexis. *McKinney's Consolidated Laws of New York Annotated* is available on Westlaw. These online resources are updated regularly, reflecting the most current editorial enhancements and the most current text of each law. Refer to Section I.F later in this chapter for more information about these online resources.

If working with the statutes in print, please be aware that CLS has recently changed its published format. McKinney's is bound in a black hardcover with gold writing, and CLS had always been quickly distinguishable in its blue hardcover with dark blue writing. How-

4. Until recently, this unannotated version of the statutes was known as *Gould's New York Consolidated Laws Unannotated*.

Table 5-2. Example of Citation Formats for McKinney's and CLS

N.Y. General Obligations Law § 3-101								
Statutory Compilation	**Jurisdiction**	**Subject Matter**	**§**	**Article**	**-**	**Title**	**Section**	**Vendor Designation & Year**
McKinney's Consolidated Laws of New York Annotated	N.Y.	General Obligations Law	§	3	-	1	01	(McKinney 2001)
New York Consolidated Laws Service	N.Y.	General Obligations Law	§	3	-	1	01	(Consol. 2006)
N.Y. Civil Practice Law and Rules § 112								
Statutory Compilation	**Jurisdiction**	**Subject Matter**	**§**	**Article**			**Section**	**Vendor Designation & Year**
McKinney's Consolidated Laws of New York Annotated	N.Y.	Correction Law	§	6			112	(McKinney 2003)
New York Consolidated Laws Service	N.Y.	Correction Law	§	6			112	(Consol. 2005)

ever, CLS has changed its published format to a black hardcover with gold writing.

CLS and McKinney's are annotated. This means the publisher's editorial staff provides additional information about each code section. Both resources provide short summaries of cases. Case summaries are called "Case Notes" in CLS and "Notes of Decisions" in McKinney's. Case summaries are like digests because they are categorized by topic and each provides the citation to the case it is summarizing. In addition to case summaries, CLS and McKinney's provide some legislative history of the code section and cross-references to related primary and secondary sources, such as administrative regulations or sections in a legal encyclopedia. The entry point to both CLS and McKinney's is the general index, which is a softbound, multi-volume grouping of volumes replaced annually. (New York's other code, *Consolidated Laws of New York*, discussed below under subheading 2, does not have a general index.)

CLS and McKinney's each has it strengths. CLS is an excellent resource for the most commonly used legal forms associated with a code section and has recently added "Practice Insights" to its entries. The text of a standard form, if relevant to a code section, will appear immediately following the Case Notes. McKinney's boasts "Practice Commentaries." Written by legal experts, Practice Commentaries, where available, typically provide realistic implications of each provision of a code section. Practice Commentaries vary in length and can be found below the text of a code section among the other editorial enhancements. An appendix to this chapter includes a detailed comparison of these two sources for New York law.

Researchers using print codes must consult the annual pocket part of each relevant volume. Pocket parts fit into pockets in the back cover of each volume and update the statutory provisions and annotations contained in that volume. The pocket parts are organized with the same numbering scheme as the bound volumes.

To locate recently enacted or amended laws after the publication of the annual pocket part, consult the *Interim Update* pamphlets that accompany McKinney's, the CLS cumulative *Quarterly Service Updates*, or *McKinney's Session Laws of New York*. These sources can also be used to locate annotations created since the printing of the annual pocket parts. The statutory tables in the case reporters *West's New York Supplement, 2d* and *New York Reports* also contain new annotations. Legislation from the current legislative session can be found in the *Advance Legislative Service for the New York Consolidated Laws Service* or *McKinney's Session Law News of New York*. Consult Chapter 6 for online sources of recently enacted legislation.

To trace the successive changes in the text of a code section, refer to the history line directly under the text. The history line contains the year the code section was enacted as well as the session law citations to subsequent changes in the code section. The citations included in the history line are to the *Laws of the State of New York* (called simply "*Laws of New York*").

2. Consolidated Laws of New York *(formerly* Gould's*)*

Consolidated Laws of New York is published by LexisNexis. Unlike CLS and McKinney's, *Consolidated Laws of New York* is unannotated and has no general index. Instead, it provides a separate index for each consolidated law. It contains the full text of the consolidated laws, the New York Constitution, and the court acts.[5] The volumes are replaced in their entirety every year instead of issuing pocket parts or interim pamphlets.

Consolidated Laws of New York is not available as an online resource. However, an unannotated version of the consolidated laws is available on Lexis, Westlaw, and Legislative Retrieval System (LRS), a resource that is maintained by New York's Legislative Bill Drafting Commission. Refer to Table 5-4 later in this chapter for more information about the online availability of consolidated laws generally. Additional comparisons of the three sources of consolidated laws are outlined in an appendix at the end of this chapter.

C. Sources of Unconsolidated Laws

1. Current Sources of Unconsolidated Laws

There are many sources of unconsolidated laws in print. The most comprehensive source of unconsolidated laws can be found in the *Laws of New York*. Two major annotated sources are *CLS Unconsoli-*

5. The court acts are unconsolidated laws enacted for specialized courts. They are the Court of Claims Act, the Family Court Act, the New York City Civil Court Act, the New York City Criminal Court Act, the Uniform City Court Act, the Uniform District Court Act, and the Uniform Justice Court Act.

dated Laws and *McKinney's Unconsolidated Laws*. Both of these resources are part of their larger consolidated counterparts, *New York Consolidated Laws Service* and *McKinney's Consolidated Laws of New York Annotated*, respectively. The editorial staffs of these publications include only select unconsolidated laws. They are integrated into the scheme of the consolidated laws by having editorially assigned (unofficial) chapter and section numbers.

2. Historical Source of Unconsolidated Laws

The *Statutory Record of the Unconsolidated Laws* is a compilation of unconsolidated laws from 1777 to 1928. It includes all laws not included in the *Consolidated Laws of 1909*. In addition, unconsolidated laws passed or amended through the end of 1928 were added later.

D. The Research Process Using Print Codes

This section explains the process of using the print codes when you do not know the citation of relevant statutes. The steps are outlined in Table 5-3. The explanation of research steps in this section corresponds with both McKinney's and CLS.

Table 5-3. Researching New York Statutes in Print

1. Develop a list of research terms.
2. Search the index.
3. Find and read the statutory language.
4. Update the section of the code.
5. Find cases that interpret or apply relevant code sections.

1. Develop a List of Research Terms

To find all the statutes that may relate to your issue, develop a list of research terms. Using the hypothetical from Chapter 1, you might list some of the research terms generated in Table 1-3, such as prisoner, personal hygiene, or religious freedom.

2. *Search the Index*

Take these research terms to the index volumes shelved at the end of the code. As you find the terms in the index volumes, write down any statutory references given. Do not stop reviewing the index after finding just one statutory reference, as several statutes may address your issue. Sometimes a research term will be included in the index but will be followed by a cross-reference to another index term. For example, the term "Prisoner" redirects you to the index heading "Correctional Institutions." Review the entry for "Correctional Institutions" and its neighboring entries, such as "Correctional Services Commissioner." Both of those entries refer to the statutory chapter "Correction Law." You might continue your search in the index using other research terms from Table 1-3. In this case, however, you realize that Correction Law is on point generally. Go to the volume labeled Correction Law and browse its table of contents for further detail.

3. *Find and Read the Statutory Language*

Use the tables at the beginning of the index to translate the chapter abbreviation if necessary. Review the spines of CLS or McKinney's to find the volume that contains this chapter topic. Note your section number and pull the volume that contains the relevant section. Look up the section number to find your statute.

This next step is the most important: *Read* the statute very carefully. Too many researchers fail to take the time necessary to read the language of the statute and consider all its implications before deciding whether it is relevant to the research problem. Moreover, because few statutes are so clear that they can be understood on one reading, careful research may require you to read a statute several times before you understand its meaning and relevance.

To understand a single statute you may have to read other, related statutes. One statute may contain general provisions while another contains definitions. Yet another statute may contain exceptions to the general rule.

To guarantee that you understand the statute, break it into elements. Using bullet points or an outline format is helpful for identifying key ideas. Connecting words and punctuation provide guidance for the relationships between the different requirements of the statute. Small words like "and" and "or" can drastically change the meaning of the statute. With "and," all statutory requirements must be present for the statute to apply. With "or," only one part is needed. Note, too, the difference between "shall," which requires action, and "may," which is permissive. As an example, consider Figure 5-1, which includes an excerpt from McKinney's Correction Law § 112 on Westlaw. Note the use of "shall" and "and."

4. *Update the Section of the Code*

The constant possibility of change in legislation means that you must always check a law for recent changes. Look at the publication date (the copyright date on the back of the title page) of the hardbound volume of the code to determine whether a law needs updating.

To check for amendments and deletions that have appeared since the bound volume was published, refer to the pocket parts inserted in the back of each volume. The pocket parts are arranged by the same section numbers as the bound volumes. Also, check any supplementary pamphlets shelved at the end of the set.

5. *Find Cases that Interpret or Apply Statutes*

It is rare to locate a relevant statute and apply it immediately to your client's facts without having to research case law. Legislatures write broad statutes to apply to a wide array of circumstances. To be able to predict how a court may apply a statute to your client's specific facts, you must know how the courts have interpreted the statute and applied it in the past.

Listed under "Notes of Decisions" in McKinney's or "Case Notes" in CLS are short summaries of cases that have interpreted and applied that statute. Usually, the summaries are organized by subject areas. Each summary concludes with the name of the case, followed by a citation. The citation indicates which court decided the case and where it can be found. You must record the citation information accurately to enable you to find the cases in the reporters. To find the most re-

Figure 5-1. Excerpts from the Act

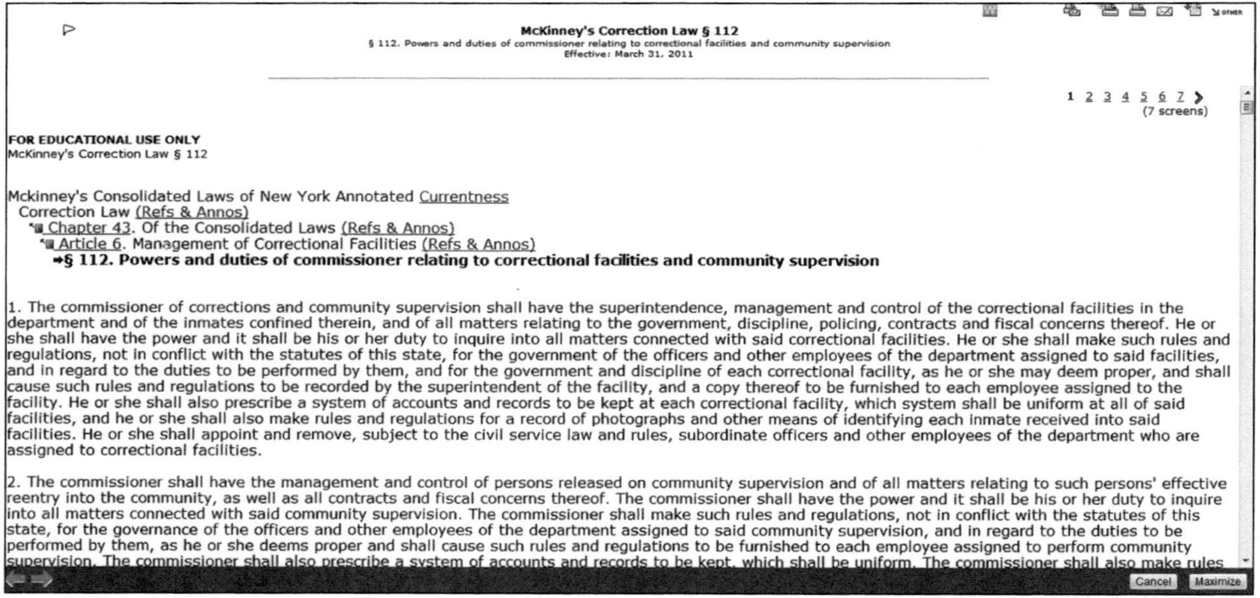

McKinney's Correction Law § 112
§ 112. Powers and duties of commissioner relating to correctional facilities and community supervision
Effective: March 31, 2011

1 2 3 4 5 6 7 (7 screens)

FOR EDUCATIONAL USE ONLY
McKinney's Correction Law § 112

Mckinney's Consolidated Laws of New York Annotated Currentness
Correction Law (Refs & Annos)
Chapter 43. Of the Consolidated Laws (Refs & Annos)
Article 6. Management of Correctional Facilities (Refs & Annos)
§ 112. Powers and duties of commissioner relating to correctional facilities and community supervision

1. The commissioner of corrections and community supervision shall have the superintendence, management and control of the correctional facilities in the department and of the inmates confined therein, and of all matters relating to the government, discipline, policing, contracts and fiscal concerns thereof. He or she shall have the power and it shall be his or her duty to inquire into all matters connected with said correctional facilities. He or she shall make such rules and regulations, not in conflict with the statutes of this state, for the government of the officers and other employees of the department assigned to said facilities, and in regard to the duties to be performed by them, and for the government and discipline of each correctional facility, as he or she may deem proper, and shall cause such rules and regulations to be recorded by the superintendent of the facility, and a copy thereof to be furnished to each employee assigned to the facility. He or she shall also prescribe a system of accounts and records to be kept at each correctional facility, which system shall be uniform at all of said facilities, and he or she shall also make rules and regulations for a record of photographs and other means of identifying each inmate received into said facilities. He or she shall appoint and remove, subject to the civil service law and rules, subordinate officers and other employees of the department who are assigned to correctional facilities.

2. The commissioner shall have the management and control of persons released on community supervision and of all matters relating to such persons' effective reentry into the community, as well as all contracts and fiscal concerns thereof. The commissioner shall have the power and it shall be his or her duty to inquire into all matters connected with said community supervision. The commissioner shall make such rules and regulations, not in conflict with the statutes of this state, for the governance of the officers and other employees of the department assigned to said community supervision, and in regard to the duties to be performed by them, as he or she deems proper and shall cause such rules and regulations to be furnished to each employee assigned to perform community supervision. The commissioner shall also prescribe a system of accounts and records to be kept, which shall be uniform. The commissioner shall also make rules

Cancel Maximize

Source: Reprinted with permission of West, a Thomson Reuters business.

cent annotations, remember to check pocket parts and supplementary pamphlets.

E. Chapter Laws and Session Laws

Occasionally, research requires review of the original statutory language as initially passed by the New York legislature. In addition, research may involve a repealed law that has been deleted from the code. Both of these research problems require reference to chapter laws or session laws. A *chapter law* is a copy of the text of the act as passed.[6] *Session laws* are chapter laws compiled chronologically by chapter law number and published annually at the end of the legislative year.

Chapter laws are not distributed by the State of New York. However, they are available in *Advance Legislative Service for the New York Consolidated Laws Service* in print and online in Lexis, and *McKinney's Session Law News of New York* in print and on Westlaw. In addition, subscription services for chapter laws are available from many vendors, such as New York Legislative Service, Inc.[7]

Session laws are printed in the official *Laws of New York* and the unofficial *New York Consolidated Laws Service Session Laws* (LexisNexis) and the *McKinney's Session Laws of New York* (West).

F. Using Online Codes and Session Laws

The code and session laws are available online in various sources. Note that the Legislative Retrieval System (LRS) is the most up-to-date online source of the text of consolidated laws, providing updates to the LRS service in real-time. Table 5-4 lists online sources of the New York code and session laws.

---

6. Chapter laws are New York's equivalent of the federal slip laws.
7. The address is www.nyls.org.

Table 5-4. Online Sources of New York's Consolidated Laws

Source Name	Annotated Code	Unannotated Code	Chapter Laws	Session Laws	Web Address	Paid Service?
Legislative Retrieval System (LRS)	Not included	Included	Included	Included	http://nyslrs.state.ny.us	Yes
Lexis	NYCODE	Open code section in Lexis. Below FOCUS Terms on left side, under "View," click on "Custom." Click "Clear All," then check "Unanno" and "Ok"	NYALS		www.lexis.com	Yes
Westlaw	NY-ST-ANN	NY-ST	NY-LEGIS	NY-LEGIS	www.westlaw.com	Yes
New York State Legislature	Not included	Included	Included	Not included	http://public.leginfo.state.ny.us	No

1. Using the Online Codes and Chapter Laws on Lexis and Westlaw

CLS is available on Lexis. McKinney's is available on Westlaw. You may search both codes online by using search terms, the code citation, the Statutes Index, or the Table of Contents. Both Lexis and Westlaw include the full text of chapter laws.

You can use search terms by performing a terms-and-connectors or natural-language search. However, when searching for statutes online, you have to anticipate the language used by the legislature in writing the law. Searching the online Table of Contents is often more productive than searching the entire database with your search terms.

On Lexis and Westlaw, the New York Statutory Table of Contents provides the best option for online statutory research. The file allows you to retrieve code sections by navigating through the titles of the code. The Table of Contents also allows you to scroll through related sections of the code. Because statutory sections are part of a large code section, there can be many related sections.

When you access the Table of Contents file, the first level of the outline automatically appears. Each document contains a hierarchical outline with descriptive headings for the code sections. You can also use the file to find terms specific to the New York statutes and then use those terms to develop a full-text search. To browse the Table of Contents, click the plus (+) and the minus (–) symbols. To retrieve a specific section, click its hypertext link.

Both the Table of Contents file and the Statutes Index are particularly useful when you are searching for a very common legal term, for example, "Contracts—statute of frauds." If you search the entire code using natural language, your search will retrieve too many hits.

As an added enhancement on Lexis, information enclosed in asterisks regarding the date of a section indicates the most recent update to the statutes. On Westlaw, the current date is indicated at the end of the code section.

You may need to update a statute if the legislature is in session, or if the session laws have not yet been incorporated into the code. Once you are in the code database, you can Shepardize the law on Lexis or

KeyCite the law on Westlaw.[8] The code is updated continually during the legislative session.

2. *Using LRS Online to Retrieve Current Codes and Session Laws*

The Legislative Retrieval System (LRS)[9] is a full-text, fee-based service that provides access to New York State legislative information. LRS is an excellent resource for legislative history research and includes access to the New York chapter, session, and consolidated laws. The chapter laws are searchable by chapter number or browsable by year. The *Laws of New York* are searchable by document number or keyword, and browsable through the table of contents. The consolidated and unconsolidated laws are also searchable by keyword, document number, or browsing. Figure 5-2 is an image of the main LRS search interface.

G. *Uniform Laws Annotated*

New York has adopted several uniform laws promulgated by the National Conference of Commissioners on Uniform State Laws. Interpretations from other state courts that have adopted the uniform law may be valuable as persuasive authority. The *Uniform Laws Annotated* (ULA), published by West, contains this information.

The ULA includes the text of each uniform law approved by the Commissioners, with each section of the act followed by the Commissioners' comments, citations to secondary sources, and digests of decisions. A table immediately precedes the text of each uniform act, showing the states that have adopted the act and the citation to the state law. You can identify the uniform laws by looking under the

8. Shepard's and KeyCite are discussed in detail in Chapter 8.
9. The Legislative Retrieval System is available at http://nyslrs.state.ny.us.

Figure 5-2. Image of Legislative Retrieval System Search Interface

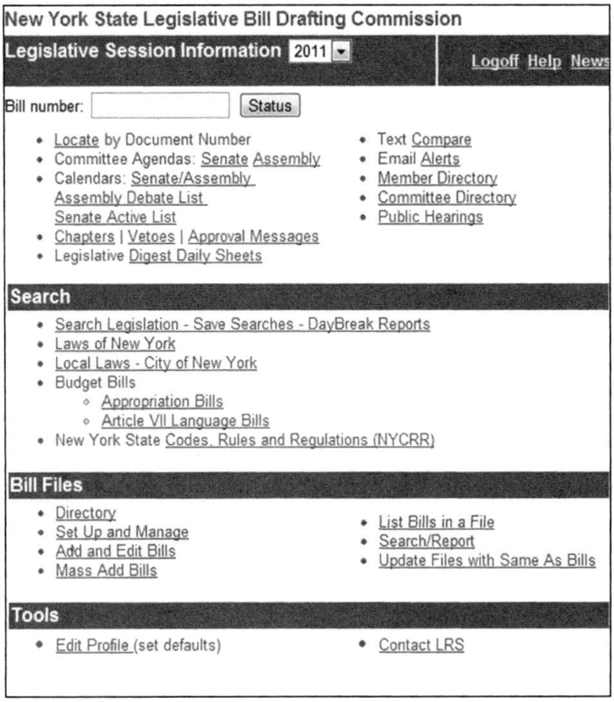

New York State Legislative Bill Drafting Commission

Legislative Session Information 2011

Logoff Help News

Bill number: Status

- Locate by Document Number
- Committee Agendas: Senate Assembly
- Calendars: Senate/Assembly
  Assembly Debate List
  Senate Active List
- Chapters | Vetoes | Approval Messages
- Legislative Digest Daily Sheets
- Text Compare
- Email Alerts
- Member Directory
- Committee Directory
- Public Hearings

Search

- Search Legislation - Save Searches - DayBreak Reports
- Laws of New York
- Local Laws - City of New York
- Budget Bills
  - Appropriation Bills
  - Article VII Language Bills
- New York State Codes, Rules and Regulations (NYCRR)

Bill Files

- Directory
- Set Up and Manage
- Add and Edit Bills
- Mass Add Bills
- List Bills in a File
- Search/Report
- Update Files with Same As Bills

Tools

- Edit Profile (set defaults)
- Contact LRS

Source: http://nyslrs.state.ny.us.

heading "Uniform Laws" in the McKinney's index. An alternative is to look in the *Directory of Acts and Tables of Adopting Jurisdictions*, a pamphlet published by the ULA.

II. New York Constitutions

New York's first constitution was adopted in 1777. Major amendments were adopted in 1801, 1821, 1846, and 1894. The Constitution of 1894, along with many subsequent amendments, is the current constitution.

The constitution is cited by article and section. The citation format is N.Y. Const. art. [x], § [x].

A. Researching in Print

The current text of the New York Constitution is available in McKinney's (in book 2, which fills seven volumes) and CLS (in volumes 41E, 42, and 42A). The annotated versions of the constitution, available in both McKinney's[10] and CLS, provide citations to court decisions interpreting the New York Constitution. You may also find New York and federal cases and other sources citing the New York Constitution by using Shepard's and KeyCite.

In addition to providing annotations to judicial decisions, McKinney's and CLS include the "Historical Notes" or "History" of the code section, respectively. Historical notes that refer to the presence or absence of similar provisions in earlier documents may be useful for research purposes. "Notes of Decisions" or "Case Notes" are summaries of judicial opinions interpreting the law. Citations to law review articles and other related research references are also included.

Article XIX of the New York Constitution outlines amendment procedures. Use the McKinney's Historical Notes or the CLS History portion of the editorial analysis to trace the text of constitutional amendments.

B. Researching Online

The New York Constitution is available online through a number of sources. Lexis and Westlaw provide annotated versions of the current constitution, and the services update their annotated versions frequently. The New York State Legislature's website provides the cur-

10. Although McKinney's is annotated, it also includes the full text of the constitution without annotations, making it easier to browse just the text.

rent version of the constitution.[11] Click on "Laws of New York," scroll down to "Constitution," and click on "CNS."

III. Local Laws, Special Laws, and Ordinances

The New York Constitution[12] and the state legislature[13] provide self-governing power to some cities and counties in New York, allowing them to exercise legislative functions.

A. New York City

The State of New York comprises sixty-two counties. New York City's five counties—Bronx, Kings, New York, Queens, and Richmond—are governed by the Charter of the City of New York. The current Charter of the City of New York is available on the New York City Charter Revision Commission's website[14] and the New York State Legislature's website.[15] The Charter is also available on commercial sources, such as LRS.

B. Other Jurisdictions in New York

The other fifty-seven counties and the towns, villages, and cities within them are governed by "home rule," meaning they are constitutionally[16] and statutorily[17] sanctioned to govern at the local level.

---

11. The address is http://public.leginfo.state.ny.us.
12. N.Y. Const. art. IV, § 2.
13. N.Y. Mun. Home Rule Law § 10 (McKinney 1994 & Supp. 2010).
14. The address is www.nyc.gov/html/charter/html.
15. The address is http://public.leginfo.state.ny.us (click on "Laws of New York," scroll down to the miscellaneous section, and click on "NYC").
16. N.Y. Const. art. IX (passed 1963; effective Jan. 1, 1964).
17. Municipal Home Rule Law of 1963 (effective Jan. 1, 1964); Statute of Local Governments of 1964 (effective July 1, 1965).

Governance at each municipal level varies. In New York, all cities and many counties are governed by charters.[18] Counties not governed by charters are governed by a combination of county laws, local laws,[19] special laws,[20] ordinances,[21] and resolutions.[22]

C. Sources of Local Laws, Special Laws, and Ordinances

New York's municipal charters, codes, and ordinances are widely available online for most local jurisdictions through the General Code Corporation's website.[23] Eight New York jurisdictions provide access to their charters, codes, and ordinances through the Municipal Code Corporation.[24] Charters, codes, and ordinances not available in print or online through these publishers must be accessed by contacting the clerk's office of the municipality. Table 5-5 lists free online sources of New York ordinances.

---

18. A charter is "[a]n alternative form of county government provided in accordance with the constitution by act of the legislature or local law." N.Y. Mun. Home Rule Law § 32(4) (McKinney 1994).

19. Local laws are laws "(a) adopted pursuant to [Home Rule] or to other authorization of a state statute or charter by the legislative body of a local government, or (b) proposed by a charter commission or by petition, and ratified by popular vote ... but shall not mean or include an ordinance, resolution or other similar act of the legislative body or of any other board or body." N.Y. Mun. Home Rule Law § 2(9) (McKinney 1994).

20. A special law is defined as a "state statute which in terms and in effect applies to one or more, but not all, counties, counties other than those wholly included within a city, cities, towns or villages." N.Y. Mun. Home Rule Law § 1(12) (McKinney 1994).

21. Ordinances are laws passed by local governments with legislatively enacted limitations. N.Y. Town Law § 130 (McKinney 2004 & Supp. 2010).

22. Resolutions are created by local municipalities to address administrative needs of a temporary nature or special issues specific to the municipality. N.Y. Mun. Home Rule Law § 10(2) (McKinney 1994 & Supp. 2010).

23. The address is www.generalcode.com/webcode2.html (scroll down for "New York").

24. The address is www.municode.com/library/library.aspx (click on "New York").

Table 5-5. Online Sources of New York Ordinances

Publisher or Resource	Website	Commercial or Free
General Code Corporation	www.generalcode.com	Free
Municipal Code Corporation (publishes ordinances for many cities and counties within New York state)	www.municode.com	Free
New York State Government list of contact information for counties and cities	www.ny.gov (click on "Counties" or "Cities and Towns")	Free
Lexis	www.lexis.com (click on "New York," "Find Statutes...," "New York Municipal Codes"	Commercial

IV. Court Rules

New York court rules are procedural regulations that are mandatory on the parties and their lawyers in front of a particular court. Some court rules apply to all New York courts. These rules can be found in the New York Judiciary Law. Local court rules are rules that apply to a specific court or courts. Courts are empowered with rule-making authority by Article VI of the New York Constitution. Court rules often include court-approved forms that apply to specific rules. The official version of these court rules, including rules that apply to specific courts sitting in New York, can be found in *Official Compilation of Codes, Rules and Regulations of the State of New York* (NYCRR), which is the compilation of New York's administrative rules.

Table 5-6 provides selected print and online sources of New York court rules. New York court rules are available on court websites, LRS, Lexis, and Westlaw. Westlaw's NY-RULESUPDATES database reports court orders updating court rules governing state and federal practice in New York. New York court websites also report changes to court rules.

Table 5-6. Selected Print and Online Sources of New York Court Rules

	Title	Publisher	Print	Online	Free or Commercial
State Courts—General	*McKinney's New York Rules of Court—State*	West	Yes	www.westlaw.com	Commercial
	New York Court Rules from the Consolidated Law Service	LexisNexis		www.lexis.com	Commercial
	New York Law Journal *Judges' Part Rules*	New York Law Journal	Yes	http://judges.newyorklawjournal.com/partrule.aspx	Free, requires registration
State Courts—Civil	*New York Civil Practice Law & Rules Handbook*	LexisNexis	Yes		Commercial
	McKinney's New York Civil Practice Law and Rules: CPLR	West	Yes	www.westlaw.com	Commercial
State Courts—Criminal	*New York Criminal Statutes and Rules* (Graybook)	LexisNexis	Yes		Commercial
Trial Courts	*New York Surrogate's Court* (Greenbook)	LexisNexis	Yes		Commercial
	New York State Unified Court System			www.courts.state.ny.us/rules/trialcourts/index.shtml	Free
Appellate Division—General	*New York Appellate Practice* by Thomas R. Newman	LexisNexis	Yes	www.lexis.com	Commercial
	NY Court of Appeals Rules of Practice		Available in NYCRR	www.nycourts.gov/ctapps/500rules10.htm	Free

Table 5-6. Selected Print and Online Sources of New York Court Rules, *continued*

	Title	Publisher	Print	Online	Free or Commercial
Appellate Division—Specific	New York Supreme Court Appellate Division—1st Department			www.courts.state.ny.us/courts/ad1/Practice&Procedures/rules.shtml	Free
	New York Supreme Court Appellate Division—2d Department			www.courts.state.ny.us/courts/ad2/pdf/rulesofprocedure.pdf	Free
	New York Supreme Court Appellate Division—3d Department			www.nycourts.gov/ad3/Rulesofthecourt.html	Free
	New York Supreme Court Appellate Division—4th Department			www.nycourts.gov/courts/ad4/Clerk/AD4-RuleBook-05-08.pdf	Free
Federal Courts in NY	*Civil Practice in the Southern District of New York* by Michael C. Silberberg	West	Yes		Commercial
	McKinney's New York Rules of Court—Federal	West	Yes	www.westlaw.com	Commercial
	Rules of the US Courts in NY	West	Yes		Commercial
	Local Rules of the United States District Courts for the Southern and Eastern Districts of New York			www.nysd.uscourts.gov/rules/rules.pdf	Free
	Local Rules of the United States District Court for the Northern District of New York			www.nynd.uscourts.gov/documents/2011LocalRules-Final.pdf	Free
	Local Rules for the United States District Court for the Western District of New York (Civil and Criminal)			www.nywd.uscourts.gov/document/Local Rules of Civil Procedure (Revised 2a).pdf www.nywd.uscourts.gov/document/local_rules_criminal_procedure_jan_2011.pdf	Free

V. Federal Research

A. Federal Codes

Similar to the New York codes, the federal codes are organized by subject matter and then numbered by title, chapter, and section.

1. Print Sources of the Federal Codes

The federal code is found in these publications:

- *United States Code* (USC), the official code for federal laws,
- *United States Code Service* (USCS), published by LexisNexis, and
- *United States Code Annotated* (USCA), published by West.

For statutory research, you will probably want to use an annotated code, which contains the same text and numbering as the official USC but also provides research aids. An annotated code includes cross-references to related sections within the code, notes of cases that have construed the statutes, references to regulations and secondary sources, and references to other research tools provided by its publisher.

2. United States Code

The USC is published by the U.S. Government Printing Office. The set is recompiled every six years, using the same fifty-one subject categories or titles. Congress has deemed the USC to be prima facie evidence of the law. While the USC has the advantage of being official, the unofficial *United States Code Annotated* (USCA) and the *United States Code Service* (USCS) are more helpful research tools because the USC does not give citations to cases that have interpreted the statutes. Moreover, the USC will not be as current as you need. In theory, the USC is reissued every six years with cumulative annual supplements published between the new editions. In reality, the annual cumulative supplements do not appear in the library until eight months to two years have passed. Therefore, if you rely only on the USC, you will miss current laws, amendments, and deletions.

Note that both the Bluebook and the ALWD Manual recommend citing the official code when possible. See Appendix A at the end of this book for additional information on legal citation format.

3. USCA and USCS

The two annotated codes, USCA and USCS, are quite similar. A small library may have just one of these series, and using either one is appropriate.

USCA is an example of the West publishing philosophy. West believes in providing as much information as possible and giving researchers tools that help them use that information efficiently and effectively. USCA fills more than 300 volumes and provides researchers with citations to cases and a wide variety of other references. Because each statute is followed by editorially enhanced notes and references to other research materials, case references are easily found in USCA. USCA is available online on Westlaw.

USCS, published by LexisNexis, also includes annotations to cases and other useful materials. USCS fills 235 volumes and has numerous cross-references to the *Code of Federal Regulations*, treatises, and law review articles. USCS has better coverage of citations to administrative decisions than USCA. USCS is available online on Lexis.

4. Finding Statutes in USCA and USCS

The following tips will help you use USCA and USCS in print. When you need a specific statute but know only the subject of the law, you will need to use the multi-volume General Index. It is important to consider alternative research terms when using the index. The index includes many cross-references that can lead you to the correct statutory title and section.

If you know the popular name of an act or its acronym, you can check the Popular Name Table located at the end of the General Index. The popular name of an act is the name by which it is commonly known. Sometimes, an act is commonly known by the name of its author. For example, the Sarbanes-Oxley Act of 2002 (aka, SOX or Sarbox) is named after its congressional authors, Paul Sarbanes and Michael Oxley.

B. Session Laws

At the end of each session of Congress, the laws for that session are compiled and published in numerical order in bound volumes. These laws are referred to as session laws. Session laws include preambles and other information that may be evidence of legislative intent, but these preambles are not codified.

Session laws are useful when you are looking for the original version of an act as it existed prior to its codification by subject in USC or before amendment, or when you require the language of a particular amendment.

You will also use session laws when you need to find laws that have been repealed and deleted from the current code. For example, assume that your client has been charged with committing a federal crime based on conduct that occurred several years ago. Assume further that the law applying to that conduct has changed since the conduct occurred. You will have to look for the law that applied at the time of the conduct.

You can locate federal session laws in these print sources:

- *United States Statutes at Large* (Stat.), the official session laws publication produced by the U.S. Government Printing Office. It is found in every law library, but—as is frequently true of government publications—it is slow to arrive, lagging several years behind the end of the session covered.
- Advance pamphlets to USCS and advance pamphlets to USCA.
- *U.S. Code Congressional and Administrative News* (USCCAN), published by West. In addition to reprinting *Statutes at Large*, USCCAN includes selected legislative history material. It lists citations for House, Senate, and conference committee reports and reprints the report or reports that West attorney-editors determine to be the most closely related to the law. USCCAN

is available on Westlaw in the U.S. Code Congressional & Administrative News database (USCCAN).

A word of caution: You cannot safely use a session-law version of an act to determine present law after that act has been codified since the original (session) law may have been subsequently repealed or amended. You will find the present text of a law in a code, as explained in the section above.

C. United States Constitution

The Federal Constitution is published in both McKinney's and CLS. It is also available in print in the first few volumes of USCA and USCS. Additionally, publications of other states' codes may include the U.S. Constitution, just as the New York codes do. The Federal Constitution is widely available online.

D. Federal Court Rules

Rules similar to New York's court rules exist on the federal level. They are published in *McKinney's New York Rules of Court—Federal* (called a deskbook) and in USC, USCA, and USCS. Placement of the rules varies among the statutory publications. In USC and USCA, for example, the Federal Rules of Appellate Procedure appear at the end of Title 28. In USCS, those rules are found at the end of all fifty-one titles in separate volumes devoted to rules.

As at the state level, each court may have its own "local rules" with specific practices required by that court. Check the annotated codes and West deskbooks or look on the court's website to learn about local rules. The U.S. Supreme Court's rules are on its website.[25]

25. The address is www.supremecourt.gov.

Appendix 5-A. Comparison of the Three Current Sources of Consolidated Laws

	McKinney's	CLS	*Consolidated Laws of New York*
Official/Unofficial	Unofficial but text certified accurate by the Temporary President of the Senate and the Speaker of the Assembly	Unofficial but text certified accurate by the Temporary President of the Senate and the Speaker of the Assembly	Unofficial but text certified accurate by the Temporary President of the Senate and the Speaker of the Assembly
Number of Volumes	304	204	9
Arrangement of Subject Areas	Alphabetical	Alphabetical	Grouped roughly by subject
ALWD Citation	N.Y. [Subject] Law §X (McKinney [year])	N.Y. [Subject] Law §X (Consol. [year])	
Bluebook Citation*	N.Y. [Subject] Law §X (McKinney [year])	N.Y. [Subject] Law §X (Consol. [year])	
Supplementation	Annual pocket parts *Cumulative Supplementary Pamphlets* for selected individual volumes *Interim Update* pamphlets Replacement volumes	Annual pocket parts *Cumulative Supplements* for selected individual volumes *Quarterly Update Service* pamphlets Replacement volumes *Advance Legislative Service for the New York Consolidated Laws Service*	All volumes replaced annually
Annotations	Annotations of New York state and federal cases arising in New York Attorney General & State Comptroller opinions	Annotations of New York state and federal cases arising in New York Attorney General & State Comptroller opinions	Not included

* The examples here are for practice documents like memoranda and court briefs. In law review footnotes, the Bluebook uses large and small capital letters for the subject abbreviation. For example, a citation to a statute in McKinney's would appear in this format: N.Y. [SUBJECT] LAW §X (McKinney [year]).

Appendix 5-A. Comparison of the Three Current Sources of Consolidated Laws, *continued*

	McKinney's	CLS	*Consolidated Laws of New York*
Unconsolidated Laws	Selected unconsolidated laws included Indexed separately at the end of the unconsolidated laws volumes and in general index	Selected unconsolidated laws included Indexed separately at the end of the unconsolidated laws volumes and in general index	Not included
History Line to New York Laws	Included	Included	Not included
Historical Notes	Included	Included	Not included
New York Constitution	Included	Included	Included
U.S. Constitution	Included	Included	Not included
Cross-references to Related New York and Federal Constitutional and Statutory Provisions	Included	Included	Not included
Cross-references to the Administrative Code (NYCRR)	Included	Extensive references to New York rules and regulations included	Not included
Forms	Not included but provides cross-references to *McKinney's Forms*	Included	Not included
Law Review Citations from New York Law Reviews	Included	Included	Not included

Appendix 5-A. Comparison of the Three Current Sources of Consolidated Laws, *continued*

	McKinney's	CLS	*Consolidated Laws of New York*
Other Resources	References to: West's Key Numbers CJS New York Jur Signed practice commentaries	References to: New York Jur Carmody-Wait Am Jur Practice Insights References to legal treatises published by LexisNexis Jury instructions	Not included
Research Guides	*McKinney's Consolidated Laws of NY Research Guide*	*New York Consolidated Laws Service Research Guide*	Not included
Federal Laws	Not included	Not included	Not included
U.S. Supreme Court References	Included	Included	Not included
Indexes	General Index (replaced annually) Popular Name Table Index	Subject Index Popular Name Table Each title has own index	No general index Separate indexes for each consolidated law
Online Availability	Westlaw	Lexis	Not available online

Chapter 6

Legislative History

"New York State legislative procedures remain an arcane mystery to many of even the most sophisticated counsel."[1]

This chapter covers the process by which the New York State Legislature enacts laws. It begins with an overview of the legislative process in New York; through that process, the statutory laws of New York are enacted and amended. This chapter then describes the process of bill tracking or monitoring the status of a current bill that may or may not ultimately be enacted. Lawyers track bills that may affect a client's interests when they are acting in an advisory role. Next, this chapter explains how to research the legislative history of a statute that has already been enacted.

I. Introduction to the Legislative Process

The New York State Legislature consists of an Assembly and a Senate. The Assembly is the larger of the two chambers with 150 members and is presided over by the Speaker of the Assembly. The Lieutenant Governor is the President of the Senate, which has 62 members. New York's annual legislative session begins in January and adjourns in mid-June. Each legislative term is two years. Each term includes two legislative sessions lasting a year.

---

1. Richard A. Givens, *A Primer on the New York State Legislative Process: And How It Differs from Federal Procedure*, New York Legislative Law, Practice Commentary, Book 31 at Supp. 80 (McKinney 1991 & Supp. 2011).

Reviewing the legislature's structure, the legislative process, and the documents produced directly and peripherally from the legislative process provides an overview of how a bill becomes a law. Figure 6-1 shows the typical pattern of how a bill becomes a law in New York.

A. Overview of the New York Legislative Process

A bill must have a sponsor—a legislator or the Governor[2]—to be introduced. Bills that receive the most serious consideration are uni-bills, or bills introduced simultaneously into both houses. Bills introduced in one house often receive less consideration because it is likely that a concession or compromise is necessary for passage in both houses.[3] For this explanation, assume that a uni-bill is introduced.

The Legislative Bill Drafting Commission (LBDC) is charged with assisting in the legislative drafting process.[4] The LBDC may be asked to draft, review, proofread, or examine bills for constitutionality and impact of the legislation. LBDC assigns new legislation a bill number and the official date of introduction. The bill is then printed. This printing is the first of the three readings required by the rules of both houses. The bill is entered into the LBDC's legislative database called Legislative Retrieval System (LRS).[5]

Next, the bill is introduced by the sponsor, who prepares a sponsor's memorandum explaining the purpose of the bill, and is sent to

---

2. The Governor can introduce budget bills pursuant to Article VII of the New York Constitution.

3. Givens, *supra* n.1, Book 31 at Supp. 84.

4. The Legislative Bill Drafting Commission should not be confused with the Law Revision Commission (LRC). The LRC is charged with examining state law to identify laws that need to be developed or existing laws that need reform. The LRC reports its recommendations to the legislature for consideration.

5. The Legislative Retrieval System is available at http://nyslrs.state.ny.us.

Figure 6-1. How a Bill Becomes a Law in New York

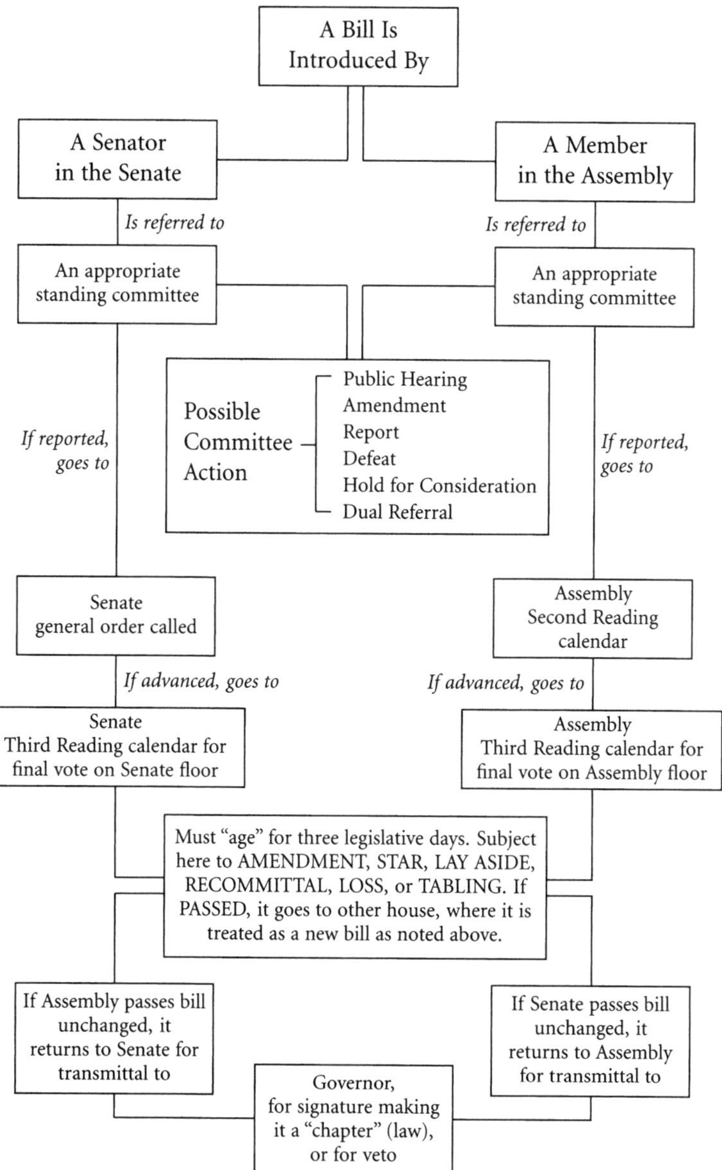

Source: www.acog.org/acog_districts/dist_notice.cfm?recno=1&bulletin=2158.

a standing committee for examination and possibly for amendments. This is considered the Second Reading. If the committee rejects the bill, it "dies." The committee may hold the bill for further consideration or approve the bill. If amendments are proposed, a bill's passage may depend on coordination of the amended language in both houses. If the committee approves the bill, the committee orally reports the bill to the full Senate. The bill is then placed on the Daily Calendar and assigned a Calendar Number.

Each time there are amendments, the bill sponsor sends the bill to the LBDC for review throughout this process. Amended versions are denoted with an alphabetical suffix A, B, C, D, and so on.

EXAMPLE:

S2011-A—example of a Senate Bill S2011 amended once

S2011-B—example of a Senate Bill S2011 amended twice

S2011-C—example of a Senate Bill S2011 amended three times

Next, the bill is brought to the floor for debate and suggested amendments prior to a final vote. Support of house leadership is important at this stage.[6] Sometimes, the bill is "starred" by the Senate Majority Leader, suspending action by placing the bill in an inactive file. In some cases, the bill is sent back to committee to address a defect before the vote.

A bill must age for three days prior to a final vote. This aging period is considered the Third Reading. The exception to this three-day rule is a Governor's Message of Necessity which justifies why the Governor wants an immediate vote on the bill.[7]

If the two houses do not agree on the language of the bill, differences are often resolved through negotiation of bill sponsors or house leaders. Ultimately, the two houses have to decide whether the As-

6. Givens, *supra* n.1, Book 31 at Supp. 86.
7. N.Y. Const. art. 3 § 14 (McKinney 2006).

sembly or the Senate version will be adopted in both houses. This decision dictates which house receives credit for the legislation.[8]

If an identical bill is passed by a majority of each house,[9] the bill is sent to the Governor who has a ten-day period in which to act. This period is extended to thirty days if the bill reaches the Governor within the last ten days of the legislative session or after the legislative sessions has ended. The Governor may choose to sign the bill into law. Often, a signed bill is accompanied by a memorandum. If the Governor does nothing, the bill becomes law after the ten-day period. The Governor may also veto the bill. A gubernatorial veto triggers a disapproval message that explains the reasons for the veto and suggests a cure in order to win gubernatorial acceptance. A veto can be overridden by a vote of two-thirds of both houses.

Documents produced up through this point in the legislative process become part of the file or "bill jacket" in the Governor's counsel's office. The bill jacket—often including the sponsor's memorandum, the approval memorandum, and the disapproval message—is the central source of New York legislative history.

An enacted bill is assigned an act number, also known as the chapter number. The act becomes effective on the date specified in the law;[10] if not specified, the default effective date is twenty days after the date of certification by the Governor or the Secretary of State.[11] The act is deposited with the Secretary of State and distributed to the LBDC and the leaders of both houses in slip law form. Later the act is published in the *Laws of New York* in session law form. The act is also codified, meaning that it is arranged by subject in the code. The codes are discussed in more detail in Chapter 5.[12]

---

8. Givens, *supra* n.1, Book 31 at Supp. 85.
9. N.Y. Const. art. 3 § 14 (McKinney 2006).
10. N.Y. Legis. Law § 41 (McKinney 1991).
11. N.Y. Legis. Law § 43 (McKinney 1991).
12. The three unofficial, print consolidated codes for New York are the *New York Consolidated Laws Service* (CLS), published by LexisNexis; *McKinney's Consolidated Laws of New York Annotated*, published by West; and *Con-*

B. Categories of Bills

The New York State Legislature considers a variety of bills. Knowing the categories of bills can make research less confusing.

Public bills are bills that have uniform operation throughout the state. A standard bill number for an Assembly bill and Senate bill may take the following form.

EXAMPLES: A391 is Assembly Bill 391
S2011 is Senate Bill 2011

Private bills are introduced on behalf of a citizen or a small group of citizens. A private bill passed into law does not have uniform operation throughout the state. Instead, the law is binding only on a specific person or group.

Budget bills deal specifically with the state budget. They are the only bills that can be submitted by the Governor. After approval by both houses, budget bills become law without being sent to the Governor for approval.

Carryover bills are bills not reported from committee or bills that never made it through both houses prior to the end of the first session of the two-year term. They are carried over to the next session and maintain the same bill number. Bills that are not passed into law by the end of the two-year term have died and can be reintroduced during the next term.

Departmental bills are bills desired by an executive branch department. Departmental bills must be introduced into both houses by a legislator or standing committee.

Governor's program bills are those desired by the Governor as set forth in the annual State of the State message. These bills must be introduced into both houses by a legislator or standing committee.

---

solidated Laws of New York (formerly known as *Gould's New York Consolidated Laws Unannotated*), also published by LexisNexis.

Special bills propose legislation that, if passed, would have applicability to one or more counties or municipalities.

Uni-bills are bills introduced simultaneously by a member of each house. Uni-bills are discussed in detail above.

C. Resolutions

Resolutions are different from bills because they do not require gubernatorial approval. Resolutions are typically less controversial in nature and are swiftly passed by both houses because they honor or memorialize people, events, or movements. Examples of resolutions passed by both houses in 2011 are listed below.

- Assembly Resolution 288/Senate Resolution 953: Memorializing Governor Andrew M. Cuomo to proclaim April 6, 2011, as Missing Persons Day in the State of New York.
- Assembly Resolution 252/Senate Resolution 850: Mourning the death of Anthony DeTomaso, distinguished citizen and devoted member of his community.

Concurrent resolutions typically address constitutional amendments and, if passed by both houses, are published in the *Laws of New York*. They are also available online in the LRS[13] and on the New York State Legislature's website.[14]

II. Bill Tracking

Of the many bills that are introduced in each legislative session, some may affect the rights of your client by proposing new laws or amending existing laws. In advising a client, an attorney needs to learn of any bills on topics relevant to the client's interests and follow their progress through the process outlined above.

---

13. The LRS address is http://nyslrs.state.ny.us.

14. The New York State Legislature's website is http://public.leginfo.state.ny.us.

Table 6-1. Outline for Online Bill Tracking

1. Go the legislature's website at http://public.leginfo.state.ny.us.
2. When you know the bill number, type the bill number into the box and click on "Status" (see Figure 6-2 for an example).
3. When you do not know the bill number, click on "NYS Legislative Bills" (also shown in Figure 6-2). Search boxes will appear on the next screen. The next screen is not shown in Figure 6-2 but looks exactly like the search boxes in the top frame of Figure 6-3. Perform a text search by typing a keyword or a code citation in the search box and then clicking on "Search."
4. You will be sent to the status page (see lower frame of Figure 6-3 for an example).

A. Bill Tracking Online

Bill tracking online, rather than with print materials, is the norm because of timeliness. Table 6-1 gives an outline of the process for bill tracking online.

The New York State Legislature website[15] is available to the public at no charge. This website provides the full text of bills and their proposed amendments, bill status, sponsor's memoranda, and voting records. You can search for bills by topic, bill number, calendar number, chapter number, veto number, or approval number. Figure 6-2 displays the main search page on the New York legislature's website. Figure 6-3 is a sample bill status page.

In addition to the New York State Legislature's website, there are several excellent commercial websites for bill tracking. The Legislative Retrieval System (LRS)[16] includes the same information as the New York legislature's website but includes tracking back to 1995. The LRS is a more robust service. It includes additional information, such

15. The address is http://public.leginfo.state.ny.us.
16. The address is http://nyslrs.state.ny.us.

Figure 6-2. Bill Status Search by Bill Number

New York State
Legislature

Legislative Session Information for Year 2008

Bill Text, Status, Summaries, Sponsor Memos, Floor Votes

Bill number: S01971 Status

- Locate by Document Number
- Floor Calendars: Senate/Assembly
- Committee Agenda: Senate | Assembly
- Chapters | Vetoes | Approval Messages
- Budget Bills

Search

- NYS Legislative Bills
- NYS Legislative Resolutions
- Laws of New York

Source: http://public.leginfo.state.ny.us.

as the Daily Digest Sheets that allow a researcher to gather a list of legislative action on a particular legislative day, including bills introduced, bills amended, bills passed, and bills vetoed. The LRS offers services such as alerts for changes in bill status in addition to bill text comparison capabilities. See Figure 6-4. It also includes a Member Directory, a Committee Directory, and a Public Hearings list. LRS is run by the Legislative Bill Drafting Commission (LBDC). Once a bill is introduced, it is available in the LRS. Each time a bill is amended, it must go back to LBDC for review. Because the LRS is an organ of the LBDC, its real-time updating makes it *the* resource for anyone whose livelihood depends on the most up-to-date bill-tracking information available.

Lexis has a current bill-tracking database (NYTRCK). Westlaw also has a current bill-tracking database (NY-BILLTRK) and an historical

Figure 6-3. Bill Status

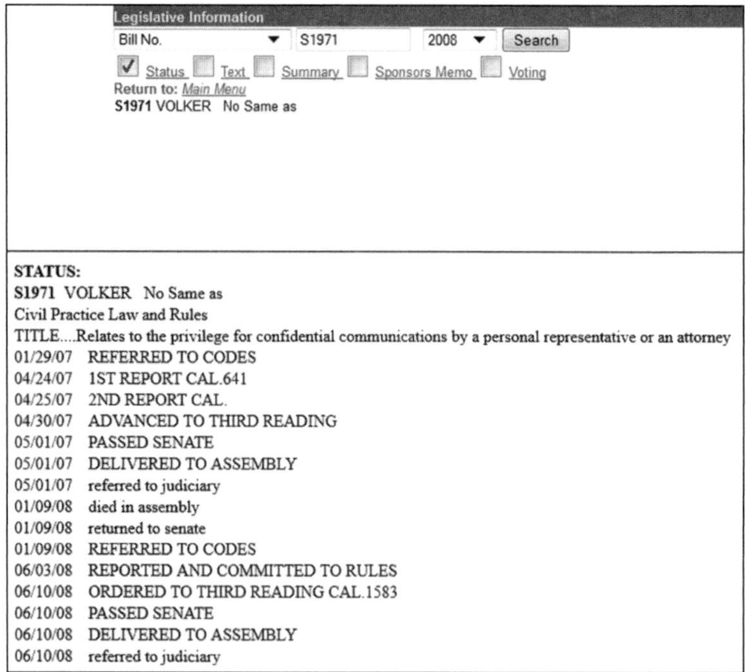

Legislative Information
Bill No. S1971 2008 Search
Status Text Summary Sponsors Memo Voting
Return to: Main Menu
S1971 VOLKER No Same as

STATUS:
S1971 VOLKER No Same as
Civil Practice Law and Rules
TITLE....Relates to the privilege for confidential communications by a personal representative or an attorney

01/29/07	REFERRED TO CODES
04/24/07	1ST REPORT CAL.641
04/25/07	2ND REPORT CAL.
04/30/07	ADVANCED TO THIRD READING
05/01/07	PASSED SENATE
05/01/07	DELIVERED TO ASSEMBLY
05/01/07	referred to judiciary
01/09/08	died in assembly
01/09/08	returned to senate
01/09/08	REFERRED TO CODES
06/03/08	REPORTED AND COMMITTED TO RULES
06/10/08	ORDERED TO THIRD READING CAL.1583
06/10/08	PASSED SENATE
06/10/08	DELIVERED TO ASSEMBLY
06/10/08	referred to judiciary

Source: http://public.leginfo.state.ny.us.

bill-tracking database (NY-BILLTRK-OLD) with tracking information dating back to 1991. All online sources of bill tracking allow keyword and number searching. Your approach to searching for bill-tracking information will vary depending on the information you already have.

B. Bill Tracking Using Print Materials

Very few print materials are available to the public during legislative sessions. Copies of current bills are available from the Assembly Information Office or the Secretary of the Senate, from Senators or Assembly members in your home district, or from the LRS or the

Figure 6-4. Bill Text Comparison on Legislative Retrieval System

Document Compare: S3015A to S1987	
S3015A	S1987
Page 1 3015—A 2003–2004 Regular Sessions IN SENATE March 14, 2003 ——— Introduced by Sens. MAZIARZ, ALESI, BALBONI, DeFRANCISCO, FARLEY, FLANAGAN, FUSCHILLO, HOFFMAN, LARKIN, LITTLE, MALTESE, MARCHI, McGEE, MENDEZ, MORAHAN, PADAVAN, SALAND, TRUNZO, WRIGHT—read	Page 1 1987 2005–2006 Regular Sessions IN SENATE February 8, 2005 ——— Introduced by Sens. MAZIARZ, ALESI, DeFRANCISCO, FARLEY, FUSCHILLO, LARKIN, LITTLE, MALTESE, MARCHI, McGEE, MORAHAN, PADAVAN, SALAND,
Page 1 Committee on Insurance—recommitted to the Committee on Insurance in accordance with Senate Rule 6, sec. 8—committee discharged, bill amended, ordered reprinted as amended and recommitted to said committee	Page 1 Be committed to the Committee on Insurance
Page 2 5 agreement executed on or before such date.	Page 1 22 agreement executed on or before such date.

Source: http://nyslrs.state.ny.us.

New York Legislative Bill Service via subscription service.[17] Bill status is available from the weekly *Legislative Digest*.[18]

C. Broadcasts of Current Legislative Sessions

SenNet TV, a service provided by the New York Senate, provides live audio and video access to legislative sessions on its website.[19] The Assembly also provides live audio and video coverage of Assembly sessions and other legislative proceedings.[20]

III. New York Legislative History Research

Legislative history research is the reverse of bill tracking. Bill tracking follows the legislative process forward, from the introduction of a bill to its possible enactment. In contrast, legislative history research works backwards, beginning with an enacted statute.

New York legislative history research is a notoriously daunting task. There are often multiple sources available for some documents, yet few or no sources available for other documents. In addition, there is no person or group charged with preserving, organizing, compiling, or cataloging the documents. Part III of this chapter is by no means a comprehensive documentation of available resources. Instead, it is an overview of the legislative process, the documents produced, and the sources and process of locating them.[21]

---

17. Contact information for these offices and services is available in an appendix to this chapter.

18. The *Legislative Digest* cumulates in an annual bound volume that is very useful when performing legislative history research using print resources.

19. The address is http://63.118.56.3/senatehomepage.nsf/SenNetTV?OpenForm.

20. The address is http://assembly.state.ny.us/av.

21. More detailed legislative history sources are available, including Chapter 5 of William H. Manz, *Gibson's New York Legal Research Guide* (3d ed. 2004); Kevin P. Gray, *New York Legislative History Sourcebook* (2004); Richard A. Givens, *A Primer on the New York State Legislative Process: And*

A. Sources of New York Legislative History

The legislative process described in Part I of this chapter yields documents that may provide valuable insight into the origins and intent of a law. Many of the documents produced on a bill's journey from idea to codification are listed in Table 6-2. Selected print and online sources are also provided.

B. Process of New York Legislative History Research

Legislative history research begins with the year of enactment and the chapter number of the law. If the chapter number is unknown, consult the history line[23] beneath the text of the current statute in CLS or McKinney's or their online counterparts, Lexis and Westlaw, respectively. The history line references the chapter law citation to the original enactment in addition to the date of enactment. In Table 6-3, the history line is the line beginning with L.1962, c. 308. The history line also includes references to session laws amending the statute.

The year of enactment and the chapter number of the law are needed to obtain the bill jacket, which often serves as the sole or the main source of legislative history information available. Bill jackets are available for 1905 and the years from 1921 to the present. Although the contents of a bill jacket vary, it typically includes the introducer's memoranda, the bill, and letters of interest from stakeholders regarding the impact of the law.[24] "Approval jackets" are bill jackets that contain the approved bills. "Veto jackets" are bill jackets that have been vetoed by the Governor. As implied by the name, a veto jacket includes the veto memoranda and can be accessed by year and introductory number (1921–1963) or veto number (1964–present). A third category of bill jackets is called "recall jackets." Recall

---

How It Differs from Federal Procedure, New York Legislative Law, Practice Commentary, Book 31 at Supp. 80 (McKinney 1991 & Supp. 2011).

23. The history line is a vendor-neutral term used to refer to the "History" in CLS and the "Credits" in McKinney's.

24. There are additional sources to locate memoranda and the bill. These are outlined in Table 6-8.

Table 6-2. Summary of How a Bill Becomes a Law and Documents Associated with the Process

Legislative Action	Documents Produced	Selected Print Sources	Selected Online Sources
An idea for legislation is drafted into a bill.			
Legislative Bill Drafting Commission (LBDC) proofreads, assigns bill number, and prints the bill.	**First Reading** is noted in Senate or Assembly Journal.	Print copies of Assembly and Senate Journals are not distributed widely. Annual bound copies are deposited at the NY State Library and the Legislative Library.	Journals are available in the NY State Library's Digital Collection at http://nysl.nysed.gov. Currently, holdings for the Journals are 1994 through the present with a time lag for the most recent few years.
	Bill is printed with bill number, sponsors, title, and text. If the bill is an amendment to an existing act, it will be visible in the bill. Added text is underlined and deleted text is enclosed in brackets.	• Assembly and Senate Document Rooms • NY State Legislative Service (subscription) • LRS (subscription)	• LRS ($) • Lexis ($) • Westlaw ($) • NY State Assembly http://assembly.state.ny.us/leg • NY State Senate www.nysenate.gov/legislation
Bill introduced by legislator(s) or by standing committee of the Senate or Assembly; Governor may only introduce budget bills.	**Bill sponsor's memoranda** articulating the legislative intent must be submitted when bill is introduced.	Current: • *McKinney's Session Laws News*	Current: • LRS ($) • Lexis ($) • Westlaw ($) • NY State Legislature http://public.leginfo.state.ny.us
		Historical: • New York State Legislative Annual • Bill jackets • *McKinney's Session Laws of New York*	Historical: • LRS ($), 1995–present • Westlaw ($), 1996–present • New York State Archives http://iarchives.nysed.gov/dmsBlue/listCollections.jsp?id=68007

Table 6-2. Summary of How a Bill Becomes a Law and Documents Associated with the Process, *continued*

Legislative Action	Documents Produced	Selected Print Sources	Selected Online Sources
Bill sent to Standing Committee for Second Reading.	**Second Reading** is noted in Senate or Assembly Journal. Transcripts of **Committee Hearings** are produced.	Documentation of the Second reading is the same as above for First Reading. Hearings are available in the Legislative Library, the New York State Library, and the New York State Archives. Also available on microfiche: New York State Legislative and Executive Department Hearings Transcripts on Microfiche.	Documentation of the Second Reading is the same as above for First Reading.
Committee reports bill to full house.	After bill is out of committee, it is placed on the agenda for the house. This agenda is called the **Daily Calendar**.		New York State Legislature http://public.leginfo.state.ny.us
Bill ages for three days prior to house vote. This is considered the Third Reading.	**Third Reading** is noted in Senate or Assembly Journal.	Same as above for First Reading.	Same as above for First Reading.
Bill brought before house for debate prior to a final vote.	Transcripts of **legislative debates** are produced.	**Current** Available from the Assembly Information Office and the Secretary of the Senate.* **Historical** Senate: Office of Microfilm and Records Assembly: Assembly Information Office.	

* The Secretary of the Senate can be reached at (518) 455-2051.

Table 6-2. Summary of How a Bill Becomes a Law and Documents Associated with the Process, *continued*

Legislative Action	Documents Produced	Selected Print Sources	Selected Online Sources
If bill passed by one house, then it is sent to the other house. Other house sends it to committee.	**Votes** are recorded in Senate or Assembly Journal.	Same as above for First Reading.	Same as above for First Reading. In addition, voting records available on: • LRS ($) • Westlaw ($)
The other house votes. OR The other house modifies the language of the bill and then votes.	**Votes** are recorded in Senate or Assembly Journal.	Same as above for First Reading.	Same as above for First Reading. In addition, voting records available on: • LRS ($) • Westlaw ($)
Governor has a ten-day period to act. Governor may sign the bill or do nothing, and bill becomes law after the ten-day period. Governor may veto bill; two-thirds of members of each house required to override Governor's veto.	**Bill awaiting Governor's signature:** Information gathered by the Governor's office, including the bill, the introducer's memo, and letters from stakeholders concerning the effect of the law are included in bill jackets.	**Bill awaiting Governor's signature:** Current: • N.Y.S. Legislative Secretary (print)	**Bill awaiting Governor's signature:** • LRS ($)
		Historical: • New York State Archives (print) • New York State Library (microform) • New York Legislative Service • Many New York law school libraries have microform holdings.	Historical: • New York State Archives at http://iarchives.nysed.gov/dmsBlue/listCollections.jsp?id=68007
	Bill becomes a law: The official copy of the law signed by the Governor or the official copy with certification of how the billed passed is called the engrossed bill. It is deposited with the Secretary of State. Official copies are distributed to the leaders of both houses and the LBDC, which enters the text into LRS.	**Bill becomes a law:** Official copy of the engrossed bill is printed but not widely distributed by the state. An official copy of the engrossed bill can be obtained from the Secretary of State's Miscellaneous Records Office.**	**Bill becomes a law:** • LRS ($)

** Contact information for these offices and services are available in an appendix to this chapter.

Table 6-2. Summary of How a Bill Becomes a Law and Documents Associated with the Process, *continued*

Legislative Action	Documents Produced	Selected Print Sources	Selected Online Sources
	Bill is vetoed: The Governor is required to draft a veto memorandum explaining the reasons for the veto.	**Bill is vetoed:** • Veto jackets • *Legislative Digest* • *Public Papers of the Governors*	**Bill is vetoed:** • LRS ($) • Lexis ($) • Westlaw ($) • New York State Legislative website at http://public.leginfo.state.ny.us • New York State Archives at http://iarchives.nysed.gov/dmsBlue/listCollections.jsp?id=68007
The enacted bill is assigned an act number. The act becomes effective on the date specified in the law; if not specified, the default is the date of certification by either the Governor or the Secretary of State.	Bills that become acts are called chapter laws. Chapter laws that are printed as individual pamphlets are called slip laws. Chapter laws bound annually in chronological order are generically referred to as **session laws.**	Slip laws are not printed and distributed by the state. Copies of slip laws can be obtained from LRS or the NY Legislative Bill Service. Session Laws: • *Laws of New York* • *New York Consolidated Laws Service Session Laws* • *McKinney's Session Laws of New York*	Session laws: • HeinOnline ($) • LLMC Digital ($) • LRS ($) • Lexis ($) • LoisLaw ($) • Westlaw ($)
The act is codified or arranged by topic.	Act is incorporated into the **code.**	Statutory codes: • CLS • McKinney's • Consolidated Laws of New York	Statutory codes: • LRS ($) • Lexis ($) • LoisLaw ($) • Westlaw ($) • http://public.leginfo.state.ny.us • Findlaw at http://codes.lp.findlaw.com/nycode

Table 6-3. Text of Statute with History Line—CLS and McKinney's

Example from CLS:

NY CPLR §4505 (Consol. 2007)

Unless the person confessing or confiding waives the privilege, a clergyman, or other minister of any religion or duly accredited Christian Science practitioner, shall not be allowed disclose a confession or confidence made to him in his professional character as spiritual advisor.

Legislative History:

History:

(L.1962, c. 308; amended L.1965, c. 520.)

Example from McKinney's:

NY CPLR §4505 (McKinney 2007)

Unless the person confessing or confiding waives the privilege, a clergyman, or other minister of any religion or duly accredited Christian Science practitioner, shall not be allowed disclose a confession or confidence made to him in his professional character as spiritual advisor.

CREDIT(S)

(L.1962, c. 308; amended L.1965, c. 520.)

---

jackets contain bills that were recalled by the Governor and never became law.[25]

Print copies of bill jackets can be obtained at the New York State's Library or Archives, and through the New York Legislative Service. Many libraries subscribe to bill jackets on microfiche. The time lag for the microfiche is about four years.

Westlaw recently upgraded its state and federal legislative history databases. The NY-LH-BILLJACKET database includes bill jackets from 1996 and continues to the present with a time lag.[26] The Digi-

---

25. Recall jackets were declared unconstitutional in *King v. Cuomo*, 81 N.Y.2d 247 (1993).

26. In October 2011, bill jackets on Westlaw were only available through 2009.

Table 6-4. Checklist for New York Legislative History Research

1. Determine the year of enactment and the chapter number by consulting the history line beneath the text of the current statute in CLS or McKinney's.
2. Obtain a copy of the bill jacket, which includes the sponsor's memoranda and other material.
3. Continue research with the following steps, depending on your needs:
   - Use session law citations found in the history line to trace the changes in the text of the statute.
   - Browse the historical notes in CLS and McKinney's to gain insight into the development of the law.
   - Read Case Notes in CLS or Notes of Decisions in McKinney's to find relevant cases.
   - Consult CLS's Practice Insights in McKinney's Practice Commentaries.
   - Consult bill-tracking resources to find other relevant actions and their dates.
   - Locate committee reports, floor debate transcripts, and other legislative documents.
   - Consult Westlaw's New York Legislative History database for additional resources.

tal Collections of the New York State Archives[27] includes digital images of bill jackets for the years 1995 through 2009.

Once the bill jacket is obtained, additional steps can be taken to obtain a complete legislative history. Table 6-4 lists the steps in New York legislative history research. The first two steps are recommended for all New York legislative history research. The third step is a bulleted list of the additional steps in no particular order. Tailor your legislative history research to your needs. Some steps may not be necessary and the order of steps may vary in each research scenario.

CLS and McKinney's and their online counterparts are excellent resources for additional legislative history information. The history

27. The address is www.archives.nysed.gov/a/digital/images/about/about_billveto.shtml.

line provides citations to the chapter laws that created or amended the section in the official *Laws of New York* or their unofficial counterparts.[28] Chapter law citations can be used to locate the text of the chapter laws. Comparing changes in the text of the chapter laws may provide clues in the quest for legislative intent.

The historical notes in CLS and McKinney's may also provide insight into the development of the law. In addition, Case Notes and Notes of Decisions provide summaries of and citations to cases that have interpreted the statute. This is an excellent finding aid for relevant cases. Another source for legislative history, Practice Commentaries,[29] is unique to McKinney's. Authored by attorneys who are considered experts in the area of law, Practice Commentaries are likely to include legislative history information. Although not primary authority, they have been cited by New York courts and, therefore, Practice Commentaries are considered persuasive. CLS recently began adding a competing feature similar to McKinney's Practice Commentaries called Practice Insights.

Bill-tracking resources, as discussed in Part II of this chapter, may provide dates of legislative activity that can be useful in locating additional official and unofficial legislative resources. For example, knowing the dates of legislative action may narrow your search for relevant news articles discussing the action. In addition, legislative action may indicate the existence of a committee report or other documents.

Another source for learning legislative intent is reports of the Law Revision Commission. The Law Revision Commission, a legislatively enabled entity, is charged with examining New York's common law and statutory scheme to discover any defects or omissions and to overhaul archaic laws. Issues to be examined are suggested by the legislature, state agencies, and various associations and groups across the state. The Law Revision Commission makes recommendations for legislative change by introducing bills, via ex-officio members, that address the defects. Selected reports of the Law Revision Commission

---

28. *See* Chapter 5.

29. Practice Commentaries are discussed in Chapter 5, Part I.B.1.

are available on the Law Revision Commission website.[30] The reports are grouped by topic. From 1936 to 1994, the Commission published annual reports. The reports are most accessible in print in *McKinney's Session Laws of New York* and available on Westlaw. Annual reports were not published for the years 1995–2001.

Legislative intent may also be derived from unofficial sources, including treatises and law review articles. Although not primary source material, these resources may provide background knowledge and citations to relevant documents. Research using treatises and law review articles is discussed in Chapter 3.

This section has focused on legislative history resources that you can reasonably expect to find. Knowing what is difficult to find is also important. Committee reports addressing specific legislation are not required, and therefore they are rarely published. In addition, transcripts of debates are typically not available. The Journals of both the Assembly and Senate, resources in which researchers might expect to find such transcripts, contain mere summaries of daily legislative action.

C. Additional New York Legislative History Sources

Much has been written about New York legislative history and many sources of legislative history are available. An appendix at the end of this chapter provides a bibliography and contact information.

IV. Federal Legislative Research

Federal legislative research is rich with lengthy documents, such as committee reports and transcripts of hearings and debates, which provide details about the federal legislative process. In addition, free resources for federal legislative information are plentiful.

---

30. The address is www.lawrevision.state.ny.us (click on "Recent Commission Reports").

A. Brief Overview of the Federal Legislative Process

The United States Congress is made up of the Senate and the House of Representatives (House). The Senate consists of one hundred members. The Vice President of the United States is the presiding officer of the Senate, with the President pro tempore officiating in the presiding officer's absence. The House consists of 435 members apportioned by state population. Its presiding officer is the Speaker of the House. Federal legislative sessions begin on January 3 and last approximately one year. A Congress lasts for two years and spans two legislative sessions.

A bill is introduced by the bill sponsor and given a bill number. Federal bills are numbered sequentially in each chamber of Congress. Generally, an "S." precedes Senate bill numbers, and House of Representatives bill numbers are preceded by "H.R." The First Reading of the bill is when the bill's title is read on the chamber floor. The bill goes to a standing committee and is placed on the committee calendar. The bill is debated and changes may be made to the bill prior to the committee vote. The committee produces a report explaining the provisions in the bill. The bill goes to the chamber floor for debate. After the debate, the Second Reading occurs and amendments may be made. The Third Reading occurs when the debates end and the chamber votes. If passed, the bill is sent to the other chamber for consideration, following roughly the same process. If the other chamber passes the bill with amendments, a conference committee may be formed to reach a consensus on the text. If the text of the bill passed is exactly the same in both chambers, the bill is sent to the President for signature. (The bill is considered enrolled at this point.) The President may sign the bill into law, veto the bill, or do nothing and the bill will become law after ten days. Figure 6-5 is an overview of how a bill becomes a law.

When a federal statute is enacted, it is assigned a public law number. This number is in the form "Pub. L. No. 101-336." The numerals before the hyphen represent the session of the Congress in which the law was enacted, and the numerals after the hyphen are assigned chronologically as bills are enacted. The public law number given

Figure 6-5. How a Bill Becomes a Law

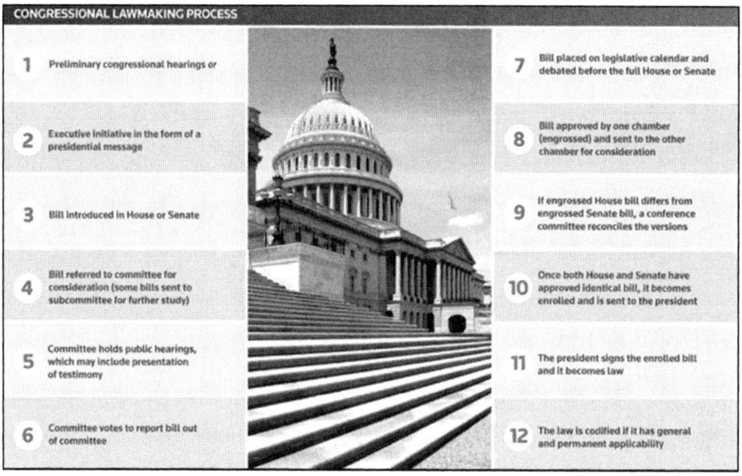

Source: Westlaw. Reprinted with permission of West, a Thomson Reuters business.

above is for the Americans with Disabilities Act (ADA), which was passed in 1990 during the 101st Congress.

The new statute is later published as a session law in *United States Statutes at Large*, which is the federal counterpart of *Laws of New York*. Session laws are designated by volume and page in Statutes at Large (e.g., 104 Stat. 328). Finally, the new statute is assigned a different number when it is codified with statutes on similar topics in the United States Code. The citation for the first section of the ADA is 42 U.S.C. § 12101 (2006).

B. Federal Bill Tracking

Bill tracking for federal legislation is best accomplished using online sources. More congressional material is available daily on the Internet, and using Internet sources for bill tracking is often easier than using print sources. The Library of Congress website[31] provides bill

31. The address is http://thomas.loc.gov.

summaries and status, committee reports, selected hearings, and debates. The U.S. Government Printing Office site, the Federal Digital System (FDsys),[32] contains bills, bill status, reports, selected hearings, and debates. Coverage varies even within a single website, so check carefully. Lexis and Westlaw also have excellent databases for federal bill tracking.

C. Federal Legislative History

As with New York legislative history, you most often begin federal legislative history research with an enacted statute. If you do not know the statute number, use the index of an annotated code to find it as discussed in Chapter 5. With a statute number, you can find the session law citation and public law number, which will lead to the legislative history of the bill as it worked its way through Congress.

1. *Sources of Federal Legislative History*

In conducting federal legislative history research, you are looking for committee reports, materials from committee hearings, and transcripts of floor debates. Committee reports are considered the most persuasive authority. Congressional committee reports are often lengthy documents. These reports contain the committee's analysis of the bill, the reasons for enacting it, and the views of any members who disagree with those reasons. Congressional hearing materials include transcripts from the proceedings as well as documents such as prepared testimony and exhibits.

Floor debates are published in the *Congressional Record.* Floor debates are usually the least persuasive materials; however, debates may be important if the sponsor of the bill is debating the merits of the bill.

2. *Compiled Legislative History*

Compiled legislative histories include documents and other helpful citations to reports, hearings, and debates. A compiled legisla-

---

32. The address is www.gpo.gov/fdsysinfo/aboutfdsys.htm.

tive history can save researchers hours of time hunting for these documents. Check *Sources of Compiled Legislative Histories* either in print or on HeinOnline.[33] This bibliography provides citations to compiled legislative histories. Additionally, HeinOnline includes "The Legislative History Title Collection," which is a collection of full-text legislative histories on some of the most important and historically significant legislation of our time.

3. Print Sources for Federal Legislative History

The *United States Code Congressional and Administrative News* (USCCAN) from 1944 to the present (also available on Westlaw) includes the enacted law, committee reports, and references to other reports and to the *Congressional Record*. Oftentimes, researchers use this set for a quick review of the law and the committee report. The set does not include all the documents necessary for a thorough review of the legislative history, but it does provide the committee report, which is often the best source of legislative intent. A more comprehensive service, ProQuest's Congressional Information Service (CIS) Serial Set, uses a combination of print finding tools and microfiche to make a large number of legislative history documents available. The ProQuest U.S. Serial Set Digital Collection and ProQuest Congressional are the online counterparts.[34]

4. Online Sources for Federal Legislative History

There are several excellent sources for conducting federal legislative history research online. The websites noted earlier in this chapter for tracking federal legislation also provide useful information for legislative history research. THOMAS, the Library of Congress web-

---

33. Nancy P. Johnson, *Sources of Compiled Legislative Histories: A Bibliography of Government Documents, Periodical Articles, and Books* (AALL 1979–present). HeinOnline is available at www.heinonline.org.

34. The ProQuest CIS Serial Set on microfiche has more complete coverage of hearings testimony than the ProQuest U.S. Serial Set Digital Collection.

site,[35] provides bills and bill status, public laws, committee reports, debates, and selected hearings. The U.S. Government Printing Office website[36] also contains bills and bill status, public laws, committee reports, debates, and selected hearings. The years covered vary on the two government sites, so you should check both.

Westlaw and ProQuest also have excellent databases for federal legislative history materials. The ProQuest Congressional database is available through a subscription and its counterpart, the ProQuest U.S. Serial Set Digital Collection, is a digital collection that can be purchased. Both are extensive databases[37] for online federal legislative materials. They are the online counterpart to the ProQuest's CIS Serial Set. The ProQuest CIS Serial Set on microfiche (mentioned above in Part IV.C.3), however, has more complete coverage of hearings testimony than the ProQuest products. Westlaw also has robust federal legislative history resources. Figure 6-5 is an image of the springboard for Westlaw's legislative history databases. This springboard is available by clicking on Westlaw's "Legislative History-Fed" tab.[38] Simply click on a step of the process to search the applicable databases.

---

35. The address is http://thomas.loc.gov.

36. The address is www.access.gpo.gov.

37. ProQuest Congressional (1970–present) and ProQuest U.S. Serial Set Digital Collection (1789–1969) cumulatively provide coverage for the years 1789 to the present.

38. To add the "Legislative History-Fed" tab, click on the "Add a Tab" link on the right side of the Westlaw screen. Next, click on "Add Westlaw Tabs" and scroll down to the "Jurisdictional-Federal" section. Check the box marked "Legislative History-Fed" and click "Add to My Tab Set" at the bottom.

Appendix 6-A. Bibliography and Contact Information for New York Legislative History Research

Article

William H. Manz, *If It's Out There: Researching Legislative Intent in New York*, 77 N.Y. State Bar J. 43 (2006).

Books

Robert Allan Carter, *Legislative Intent in New York State: Materials, Cases and Annotated Bibliography* (2001).

Kevin P. Gray, *New York Legislative History Sourcebook* (2004).

William H. Manz, *Gibson's New York Legal Research Guide* (3d ed. 2004).

Legislative Documents (Digital Format)

Selected New York State legislative history documents may be found in the New York State Archives Digital Collections at www.archives.nysed.gov/a/digital/images/browse.shtml. Click on "Legal" and browse the list for "Legislative Bill & Veto Jackets."

Legislative Documents (Contact Information)

<u>Commercial Services</u>

Legislative Retrieval System
1450 Western Avenue
Albany, NY 12203
(800) 356-6566
http://nyslrs.state.ny.us

New York Legislative Service, Inc.
15 Maiden Lane, Suite 1000
New York, NY 10038
(212) 962-2826
www.nyls.org

<u>Services at the NY Legislature</u>

Assembly Information Office
202 Legislative Office Building
Albany, NY 12247
(518) 455-4218

Secretary of the Senate
321 Legislative Office Building
Albany, NY 12247
(Requests only accepted in writing.)

<u>State Services</u>

Secretary of State's
Miscellaneous Records Office
(518) 474-4771

Tutorials

The Legislative History of a New York State Law: A Tutorial and Guide to Library Sources, New York State Library, available at www.nysl.nysed.gov/leghist.

Chapter 7

Administrative Law

I. Introduction to Administrative Law and Governmental Agencies

Governmental agencies are created by enabling statutes to carry out functions of government not typically administered by the legislature. For example, the legislature may enact laws that assign the length of incarceration for different classes of convicted criminals, but the legislature does not enact laws that govern what kind of clothing or hygiene habits are expected of inmates. The rules governing inmate behavior are created by governmental agencies.

Each enabling statute carefully defines the scope of the agency's power. Typically, that power includes rulemaking (legislative), administrative adjudication (judicial), and the collection and maintenance of information (executive). New York governmental agencies function within the bounds of the State Administrative Procedure Act (SAPA)[1] and mirror the three branches of the federal government in both form and function. Administrative law is the law created by administrative agencies and is considered primary source material.

As you read this chapter, consider the hypothetical introduced in Chapter 1. Your client is a male inmate in a New York state prison who has been told to cut his long hair and shave his beard. The warden offers no health or safety reasons for the request. Further, your client's hair and beard are not long enough to pose any identification

1. State Administrative Procedure Act § 100 (McKinney 2003). State agencies are bound by the SAPA unless specifically exempted by State Administrative Procedure Act §§ 102(1)–501 (McKinney 2003 & Supp. 2011).

Table 7-1. Outline for New York Administrative Law Research

1. Find and read the statutory or constitutional provision granting the agency power to act. For assistance with statutory or constitutional research, refer to Chapter 5.
2. Research case law to determine whether the agency acted within that power. For assistance with case law research, refer to Chapter 4.
3. Find the text of the relevant administrative rule(s) in *Official Compilation of Codes, Rules and Regulations of the State of New York* (NYCRR). Update the rule(s).
4. Find agency and judicial decisions applying the rule(s) in similar circumstances. Update the decisions.
5. Research other administrative law resources, if applicable.

problems. He objects to the warden's request, so he hires you. As his attorney, you will follow the steps for New York administrative law research in Table 7-1 to perform thorough research.

II. Administrative Rules

A. Overview

Administrative agencies promulgate *rules*,[2] similar to the legislature enacting statutes. Administrative rules are written in a format similar to statutes. While statutes are intentionally broad, agency rules are intentionally detailed. This detail delineated by agency experts reflects the legislatively enabled power given to the agency. Think of the legislature as the generalist in policymaking and think of the agency as a specialist in carrying out the details of the policy.

---

2. The State Administrative Procedure Act § 102(2) (McKinney 2003 & Supp. 2011) (SAPA) provides the definition of "rule" and exemptions from the definition.

Often, courts seek guidance and expertise from agencies.[3] Rules can provide guidance about an agency's understanding of a statute. Although rules and statutes are both primary authority, rules are subordinate to statutes. When there is conflict or inconsistency between a rule and a statute, the statute wins.[4] Moreover, a rule cannot "cure" a statute that a court has held unconstitutional.

Figure 7-1 provides an example of a New York rule that relates to the inmate hypothetical. Compare the outcome of this hypothetical case if the inmate were in a federal prison by examining a similar federal regulation in Figure 7-4. Consider the subtle difference in outcomes for hair and beards in state and federal prisons. In a case in which state and federal rules and regulations conflict, the Supremacy Clause of the United States Constitution[5] dictates that federal regulations preempt state regulations.

B. The Rulemaking Process

The SAPA sets the time frame, procedures, and other requirements for each step of the rulemaking process. Early in the process, the agency is required to file documents, including the proposed rule, with the Department of State. The *State Register*, a weekly SAPA-mandated publication, reports all Notices of Proposed Rulemaking reported by the agency. If the full text is fewer than 2,000 words, the proposed rule is reported in full. This date marks the beginning of a forty-five day comment period that provides the opportunity for regulated parties and other stakeholders to express their concerns, in

---

3. "[A]n administrative agency's construction and interpretation of its own regulations and of the statute under which it functions is entitled to the greatest weight." *Herzog v. Joy*, 74 A.D.2d 372, 375 (N.Y. Sup. Ct. 1980).

4. "[I]n situations where an agency's determination 'runs counter to the clear wording of a statutory provision,' its determination is given little weight." *Lincoln West Partners, L.P. v. Dep't of Hous. Pres. & Dev.*, 179 Misc. 2d 271, 275, 684 N.Y.S.2d 744, 748 (1998), *citing Kurcsics v. Merchants Mut. Ins. Co.*, 49 N.Y.2d 451, 459, 426 N.Y.S.2d 454, 458 (1980).

5. U.S. Const. art. VI, cl. 2.

Figure 7-1. Example of a New York Agency Rule and Historical Note

PRISONER PERSONAL HYGIENE, HAIR STYLES
N.Y. Comp. Codes R. & Regs. tit. 9, § 7005.5

(Statutory Authority Correction Law § 45[6], [15])

(a) Consistent with the requirements of Part 7024 of this Title, the chief administrative officer may establish rules for the permissible style and length of inmates' hair.

(b) Prisoners assigned to work in areas where food is stored, prepared, served or otherwise handled may be required to wear a hairnet or other head covering.

(c) The chief administrative officer may determine that certain work assignments constitute a safety hazard to those prisoners with long hair or beards. Prisoners unwilling or unable to conform to the safety requirements of such work assignments shall be assigned elsewhere.

(d) Should examination of a prisoner's hair reveal the presence of a health condition that may threaten the health of other persons, medical treatment shall be initiated immediately. Such medical treatment may include the cutting of a prisoner's hair upon the determination of the facility physician that such action is necessary. Such haircutting shall be performed under the direct supervision of a member of the facility health services staff.

(e) When in the opinion of the chief administrative officer, the growth or removal of a prisoner's hair, including facial hair, creates an identification problem, a new photograph may be taken of that prisoner.

Historical Note

Sec. filed July 27, 1977; amd. filed July 29, 1997 eff. Aug. 13, 1997.

Source: N.Y. Comp. Codes R. & Regs. tit 9, § 7005.5 (1997).

writing or at a hearing, about the proposed rule. If the full text is more than 2,000 words, a summary of the proposed rule is reported in the *State Register*. If a summary is published and the full text is not readily available on the agency's website, the comment period is extended to sixty days. For Notices of Revised Rulemaking, the comment period is limited to thirty days.

After the comment period, the agency may adopt, revise, or withdraw the rule. If the rule is adopted, notice of its adoption is published in the *State Register* and the full text of the rule is filed with the Department of State for publication in the *Official Compilation of Codes, Rules and Regulations of the State of New York* (NYCRR). The rule is formally adopted when a Notice of Adoption, along with the text of the final rule, is published in the *State Register*. The effective date is the date of publication in the *State Register* unless specified otherwise. The effective date is included in the Historical Notes immediately following the text of the rule in NYCRR. The Historical Note at the bottom of Figure 7-1, for example, shows the effective date "eff. Aug. 13, 1997."

Each rulemaking is assigned an identification number that represents the abbreviation of the adopting agency, the *State Register* issue number, the year, the Department of State number issued when notice is given, and an abbreviation representing the rulemaking activity. For example, the identification number ASA-52-07-00010-P represents:

ASA	Office of Alcoholism and Substance Abuse Services
52	The *State Register* issue number
07	The year of the rulemaking (i.e., 2007)
00010	The Department of State number
P	Proposed rulemaking.

Once the rulemaking process begins, the identification number remains the same throughout the rulemaking process. The only exception is the letter at the end. In the example above, the "P" represents a proposed rulemaking. Depending on the stage of the process or the kind of rule, that letter may change to any of the following letters:

A (adoption)

E (emergency rulemaking)

EA (emergency rulemaking that does not expire)

EP (combined emergency and proposed rulemaking)

RP (revised rulemaking).

The Secretary of State compiles and publishes rules issued by agencies and boards in New York in the multi-volume, loose-leaf set *Of-*

ficial Compilation of Codes, Rules and Regulations of the State of New York (NYCRR). It is cited as N.Y. Comp. Codes R. & Regs. tit. 9, § 7005.5 (1977) in Bluebook citation format and as 9 N.Y. Comp. Codes, R. & Reg. 7005.5 (1977) in ALWD citation format. Common practice in New York, however, is the citation format suggested in the "Explanatory Material" section at the front of each volume of the NYCRR. An example of this citation format is 9 NYCRR § 7005.5.

The NYCRR is arranged into twenty-two titles. Twenty of these titles are assigned to specific agencies, and each represents one of the twenty departments of New York state government. Labeled "Miscellaneous," Title 21 is the catch-all title that includes rules from any agency or department not assigned its own title. Title 22 is exclusively for the judiciary. Each title may include some or all of the following: a subtitle, chapters, subchapters, articles, subarticles, parts, subparts, sections, subdivisions, and paragraphs.

III. Administrative Law Research

A. Researching the Enabling Act

Analytically, the initial research question is whether the agency acted within its power. If that is in doubt, your first step in researching an administrative rule is to find the statute or the constitutional provision that gives the agency power to act. Chapter 5 explains the process of searching the codes to find statutes and constitutional provisions; the annotations in the annotated codes provide references to relevant cases.

A shortcut for locating the enabling statute or constitutional provision is to consult the beginning of the NYCRR part containing the relevant section. An example of the statutory authority is "(Statutory Authority: Correction Law § 45[6], [15])." Another possible source for the statutory authority is *The New York Red Book*'s "Twenty Departments of State Government" section. Most departments include a brief history of their origins and enabling legislation.

The next step is to find cases that interpret those provisions. This research will help determine whether the agency acted within the limits of its power in the situation that affects your client. Chapter 4 explains how to find judicial cases. If the agency's power is clear, skip this inquiry and move directly to finding relevant rules, as explained next.

B. Locating Rules

The NYCRR does not include all agency rules because the State Administrative Procedure Act § 102(1) outlines express exemptions from the statutory definition of "agency." Some examples of exempted agencies are the Office of the Governor and the Division of State Police. Consequently, exempted agencies may be the only sources of some rules. Note that when an inconsistency arises between the NYCRR and the version of a rule filed in the office of the Secretary of State, the NYCRR version is subordinate.[6]

The content of the print NYCRR is accessible by searching a two-volume index accompanying the set. The index allows access to the rule by keyword or subject. Full-text searches on Lexis, Westlaw, Legislative Retrieval System (LRS), and the Secretary of State's website also make the unofficial NYCRR accessible. Addresses are provided in Table 7-2.

The loose-leaf format of NYCRR allows for continuous updating. "The goal is to maintain the currentness of the NYCRR within one month of an amendment and to provide semi-monthly supplements to subscribers."[7] Although subscribers receive updates to the NYCRR semi-monthly, the time lag between the effective date of a new rule and the distribution of the update reflecting the new rule is at least a few months.

Each NYCRR volume contains a Table of Current Pages. Once you locate relevant sections, use this table to verify that the most current page has been filed. The time lag for updating the Lexis and Westlaw versions of the NYCRR can be as lengthy as the print NYCRR. LRS, conversely, updates the NYCRR whenever changes are made.

---

6. N.Y. Exec. Law § 102(5) (McKinney 2010).
7. NYCRR *User's Guide* at 3–4.

Table 7-2. Online Sources of Agency Rules—NYCRR and *State Register*

Source	Content	Web Address	Free or Commercial
HeinOnline	*State Register*	http://home.heinonline.org	Commercial
Legislative Retrieval System (LRS)	NYCRR	http://nyslrs.state.ny.us (Note: LRS works best with Internet Explorer)	Commercial*
New York Department of State	NYCRR *State Register*	www.dos.state.ny.us/info/nycrr.html www.dos.state.ny.us/info/register.htm	Free
Lexis	NYCRR and *State Register*	www.lexis.com	Commercial
Westlaw	NYCRR	www.westlaw.com	Commercial

* The fee is comparatively nominal.

After all relevant rules have been identified and obtained, read them carefully. Like statutes, a complex rule may need to be read more than once to fully understand the language. Outlining complex rules enables the identification of key issues and provides a summary of the rule for future reference throughout the research project.

C. Exploring Regulatory Intent

Sometimes, you will need to research a rule as it existed prior to an amendment. Typically, this research also triggers an inquiry into why the rule changed. To accomplish this inquiry, first locate the superseded rule. Next, review the rulemaking activity as reported in the *State Register*. Always begin your exploration of regulatory intent by locating the effective date of the new rule. Consult Table 7-3 to locate the effective date of 9 NYCRR § 7005.5 in the historical note. The effective date is August 1997.

Table 7-3. History Line from New York Rule 9 NYCRR § 7005.5

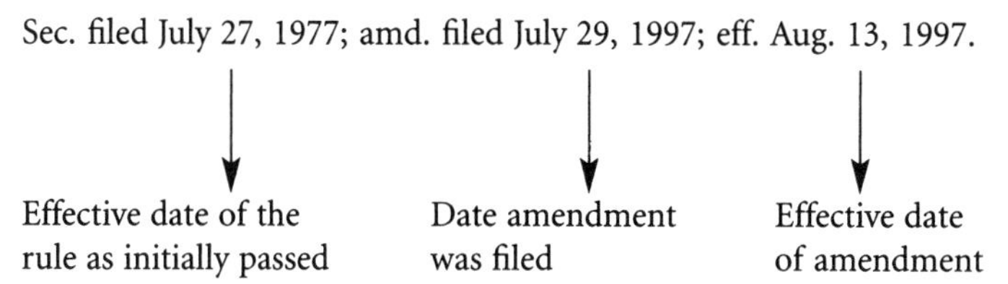

Consult the "takeouts," or NYCRR pages that were replaced because of new rules and amendments to rules. Because the NYCRR is supplemented semi-monthly, the superseded pages for a portion of the month are removed and new pages are inserted. The pages that are removed are the takeouts.

Libraries shelve takeouts in monthly or semi-monthly segments arranged by NYCRR section number. Begin by consulting the takeouts dated August 1997 for the superseded text of 9 NYCRR § 7005.5. The superseded rule may not be reported in that takeout. Considering the potential time lag associated with government entities printing enacted laws, the inclination to check for the superseded text of the rule in other takeouts should be in ascending order. In practice, takeouts for a rule amendment dated August 1997 may be found before or after the effective date. In the prison inmate example, the text of the rule prior to the August 13, 1997, amendment can be found in the July 31, 1997, takeouts.

Next, consult the *State Register* (1979–present) or one of its predecessors, such as the *State Bulletin* (1944–1979). The weekly *State Register* publishes notices concerning rulemaking activity. It includes *State Register Quarterly Index* issues that report the status of rulemaking to date during the current twelve-month period. The *State Register* is available as a print or online publication. Table 7-2 includes online sources of the *State Register*. The print *State Bulletin* is available in many libraries in New York State.

Referring to the Historical Note in Table 7-3, the effective date of the rule as initially passed was July 1977. Therefore, the *State Bulletin* for the year 1977 must be consulted. Browse the *State Bulletin*'s no-

Figure 7-2. Reproduction of Notice of Agency Action from the *State Bulletin*

STATE OF NEW YORK
STATE COMMISSION
OF CORRECTION

NOTICE OF
AGENCY ACTION

Relating to Prisoner Personal Hygiene

Pursuant to the provisions of the State Administrative Procedure Act (Chapter 82 of the Consolidated Laws), NOTICE is hereby given of the following agency action:

Action: Amendment of Subtitle aa, 9 NYCRR, to repeal the existing Part 7005 and adopt a new Part 7005.

Statutory Authority under which action was taken: Correction Law, 45(6).

Substance of Action: To repeal an existing rule and regulation addressing prisoner personal hygiene in county jails and penitentiaries and to adopt a new rule and regulation controlling that issue.

Express terms of terms of action may be obtained: By writing to James McSparron, Counsel N.Y.S. Commission of Correction, Empire State Plaza, Tower Bldg., 23rd Fl., Albany, N.Y. 12223.

Source: *New York State Bulletin*, August 2, 1977, at 3.

tices sections for the time period closest to the effective date of the rule, and locate the entry on the topic of "State of New York, State Commission of Correction—Notice of Agency Action Relating to Prisoner Personal Hygiene." This action, found in the August 2, 1977, *State Bulletin*, is reproduced in Figure 7-2. Useful information for determining regulatory intent can be gleaned from the notice posted in the *State Bulletin*:

- The proposed amendment is to repeal the existing 9 NYCRR Part 7005 and replace it with a new one.
- The full text of the proposed amendment can be obtained by writing to the person listed in the notice.

When researching notices in the *State Register*, consult the *State Register Quarterly Cumulative Index* covering the relevant time frame. The entry will provide the following information:

- The State Department number;
- A very brief description of the topic;
- The dates of publication in the *State Register* for the proposed, revised, and final rule.

Using the dates of the rulemaking from the index entries, locate the notices in the *State Register*. The notices will provide the text of the rule or the contact person for obtaining a copy of the rule in addition to:

- The statutory authority for the rulemaking;
- Brief statements of the subject and purpose of the rulemaking;
- A longer, more descriptive statement of the substance of the proposed rule;
- Any regulatory impact statement and/or other impact statements.

D. Judicial Interpretation of Rules

The next research step—finding judicial opinions—is done with annotations. In the context of researching administrative rules, an annotation is a short summary of an issue of law from a case that interpreted the rule. Annotations are available in the "Annotations" section of each print NYCRR volume and can be searched in full text on Westlaw's "New York Administrative Code" database (NY-CRR). An example of an annotation possibly relevant to the inmate hypothetical is reprinted in Figure 7-3.

Figure 7-3. Text of an NYCRR Annotation

C

◀ Previous Section **7 NY ADC 270.2** Next Section ▶

Approx. 34 pages

CASE NOTES:

State inmate's claim that prison regulation limiting length of his beard conflicted with his Rastafarian beliefs, in violation of his First Amendment rights, was to be evaluated under Religious Land Use and Institutionalized Persons Act (RLUIPA) pursuant to compelling governmental interest standard, rather than rational basis standard. Young v. Goord, C.A.2 (N.Y.)2003, 67 Fed.Appx. 638, 2003 WL 21243302, Unreported, on remand 2005 WL 562756

Source: Westlaw's New York Administrative Code Database (NY-CRR). Reprinted with permission of West, a Thomson Reuters business.

E. Updating and Tracking Tools

To update a New York rule in print, use *Shepard's New York Statute Citations* or consult the "Annotations" section of the NYCRR for judicial interpretations of a rule. In addition, consult the *NYCRR Sections Affected*, compiled by James R. Sahlem. For print researchers, the *NYCRR Sections Affected* provides notice of NYCRR sections affected by current rulemaking during the previous ten months. Unfortunately, as of the August 2009 release, this resource is no longer being updated. To update a New York rule online, use Shepard's or KeyCite. (See Chapter 8 for more information about updating with citators.) The *State Register* could also be used as a regulation tracking tool by researchers who monitor each weekly issue for relevant rulemaking.

Online resources are available to monitor current changes in agency rules. Westlaw's "New York Regulation Tracking" database also provides tracking information and the full text of proposed and recently adopted New York rules. It includes the text of the rule or proposed rule; the status, filing number, and date; the sponsoring agency; and the effective date. Lexis has a similar database, called "NY State Regulation Tracking." It includes the same information as Westlaw's database, but the Westlaw coverage extends beyond the Lexis coverage of recent proposals and adoptions to the most recent two years. Both Lexis and Westlaw have notification services—"Alerts" and "Westclip,"[8] respectively—that run custom searches in databases and deliver results via e-mail or printer at regular intervals. These services can be useful for tracking subject-specific rulemaking.

IV. Researching Agency Decisions

In addition to their rulemaking function, agencies also act in a quasi-judicial role, adjudicating cases pertaining to agency rules or actions and issuing opinions. For the inmate hypothetical, you should search for any relevant opinions by the New York Department of Cor-

8. Lexis Alerts were formerly known as Eclipse.

rectional Services, which is charged with establishing rules for and overseeing the operations of New York's correctional facilities.[9]

An appeal of an administrative decision loosely mirrors the elements and procedures of an appeals court in the judicial system. A hearing may be held before an Administrative Law Judge (ALJ). These proceedings may resemble short, informal trials. The ALJ will consider the initial determination and any additional evidence prior to making a determination. Check with the particular agency or its website to learn the specific procedure it follows. All of New York's agencies are accessible from New York's official website.[10]

In compliance with the SAPA, agencies must publish written decisions or determinations and maintain a publicly available name and subject index to the decisions.[11] Selected agencies make their decisions available on their websites, but many agencies do not. Some vendors make the full text of selected agency opinions available online.

A useful finding aid for locating compiled administrative decisions is *Sources of Published and Unpublished Administrative Opinions in New York State* by Robert Allan Carter.[12] This publication was available as a print publication initially and later added to the New York State Library Digital Image Project.[13] Within this finding aid, agencies are listed alphabetically with the name of the compilations listed below the entry. For the inmate hypothetical, browse the "C" entries for "Correction, Commission of," but none will be found there.

Absent availability through compiled print sources or commercial sources, the issuing agency is often the best, and possibly the only, source for obtaining a copy of a decision. Using the few full-text, fee-

9. N.Y. Comp. Codes R. & Regs. tit. 7, § 301(3) (1999).

10. The address is www.ny.gov (click on "Government" and then "Agency Listings (State Agencies)").

11. SAPA §§ 307(1), 307(3) (2003).

12. Originally published in 1985, a revised edition was published in 1994. Both editions are authored by Robert Allan Carter, formerly Senior Librarian at the New York State Library.

13. The address is www.nysl.nysed.gov/scandocs/nysdocsguides.htm (scroll down and click on "*Sources of Published and Unpublished Administrative Opinions in New York State*").

based databases made available by vendors benefits researchers who seek administrative opinions. The Commission of Correction, for example, does not provide agency decisions on its website, nor are the decisions available in commercial sources. The best source of this agency's decisions is the agency. A list of online sources of New York agency decisions is provided in Table 7-4.

V. Researching Attorney General Opinions

Under the New York Constitution, the New York Attorney General acts as the head of the Department of Law.[14] Under New York Executive Law §63, the Attorney General is charged with "prosecut[ing] and defend[ing] all actions and proceedings in which the state is interested, and ha[s] charge and control of all the legal business of the departments and bureaus of the state, or of any office thereof which requires the services of attorney or counsel, in order to protect the interest of the state...."

Formal opinions are issued by the state Attorney General upon the request of state agency officials. These opinions are considered formal, and therefore binding, because they are signed by the Attorney General, who is acting as the chief legal officer of New York. Informal opinions are requested by local governments. The opinions are informal because the state Attorney General does not have standing to impose the opinion on a local municipality. New York courts take the position that Attorney General opinions are subordinate to sources of judicial authority[15] and are persuasive authority.[16]

---

14. N.Y. Const. art. V, §4.

15. "The opinion of the Attorney-General ... [is] entitled to great weight in determining the construction and effect of the statute, but [is] not necessarily binding on this court." *Thruway Motel of Ardsley, Inc. v. Hellman Motel Corp.*, 11 Misc. 2d 418, 422, 170 N.Y.S.2d 552, 556 (1958).

16. "[A] court should not hide behind the ruling of an administrative officer or agency and thus escape the duty to interpret the statute.... Even though practical construction by an officer or agency charged with administration of a statute ... is entitled to great weight and may not be ignored,

Table 7-4. Online Sources of New York Agency Decisions

Source Name	Web Address	Free or Commercial
HeinOnline	www.heinonline.org This resource includes Attorney General Opinions and reports from 1890–present.*	Commercial
LLMC Digital	www.llmcdigital.org This resource includes Attorney General Opinions from 1888–present.*	Commercial
Lexis	www.lexis.com Lexis provides the full text of almost twenty agencies' decisions including: • New York Insurance General Counsel Opinions • New York Office of Administrative Trials & Hearings • New York State Workers' Compensation Board • New York Attorney General Opinions • New York Department of Environmental Conservation Decisions	Commercial
New York State Agencies	www.ny.gov click on "Government" and "Agency Listing (State Agencies)" Selected New York agencies make the full text of decisions available on their websites, such as the Department of Environmental Conservation located at www.dec.ny.gov/65.html. Information unavailable on agency websites might also be obtained by contacting the agency.	Free
Westlaw	www.westlaw.com Westlaw provides the full text of at least six agencies' decisions including: • City of New York Commission on Human Rights Decisions • New York Attorney General Opinions • New York Comptroller Decisions (selected) • New York Public Relations Board Decisions • New York Tax Administrative Decisions • New York Workers Compensation Administrative Decisions	Commercial

* The most current years may not be available due to a time lag.

---

such an interpretation is not necessarily binding on court." N.Y. Stat. Law § 129 (McKinney 1971).

The compilations of the earliest published formal and informal opinions of the New York Attorney General are available as far back as 1777. From their inception, compilations of Attorney General opinions were chronologically interfiled. However, it was not until 1923 that the distinction between formal and informal opinions became official. At the time, formal opinions were viewed as thoroughly researched interpretations of law tailored for state agencies and departments. On the other hand, informal opinions directed at towns, villages, counties, corporations, and individuals were mistakenly viewed as official opinions of the Department of Law.[17] Although the distinction between the two became official in 1923, formal and informal opinions continued to be compiled in an interfiled, and therefore less distinctive, fashion until 1932.

The varied publishing history of the opinions of the New York Attorney General is summarized in Table 7-5. The print resources in Table 7-5 publish the opinions in chronological order with a subject index available.

New York Attorney General opinions are available online from 1995 to the present through the Attorney General's website.[18] The opinions are accessible through numerical, subject, statutory, and keyword indexes available on the website. Attorney General opinions are also available with full-text search capabilities through commercial vendors. Table 7-6 lists online sources that include the full text of the New York Attorney General opinions.

VI. Researching Governor's Executive Orders and Proclamations

The Governor of New York has the power to issue executive orders, which are "merely voluntary arrangements or directions for imple-

---

17. Karl T.W. Swanson, *The Background and Development of the Office of the Attorney General in New York* 264, 269 (1958).

18. The address is www.ag.ny.gov/bureaus/appeals_opinions/search_intro.html.

Table 7-5. Print Sources of New York Attorney General Opinions

Title and Publisher	Formal or Informal Opinions	Dates of Microform Availability	Dates of Print Availability
New York Attorney General Reports and Opinions, W.S. Hein	Formal and informal interfiled until 1932	1777–present	
Opinions of the Attorneys-General of the State of New York, Banks & Brothers	Formal and informal interfiled		1777–1872
Report of the Attorney General of the State of New York, James B. Lyon	Formal and informal interfiled		1889–1892
Annual Report of the Attorney General of the State of New York, Attorney General's Office	Formal and informal interfiled		1893–1927
Annual Report of the Attorney General for the Year Ending..., New York State, Department of Law	Formal and informal interfiled		1928–1931
Annual Report of the Attorney General for the Year Ending..., New York State, Department of Law	Formal		1932–1958
Informal Opinions of the Attorney General, New York State, Department of Law	Informal		1932–1958
Opinions of the Attorney General for the Year Ending..., New York State, Department of Law	Formal and informal opinions in separate sections of the compilation		1959–1989
Opinions of the New York State Attorney General	Formal and informal opinions in separate sections of the compilation		1990–present

menting legislative enactments."[19] These orders are typically sought by, and therefore directed toward, state agencies.

Executive orders issued since 1960 are available in the *State Register*; prior to 1960, they were available in Governor's public papers compilations. Each volume of the public papers represents a year of a Governor's term, and each set of public papers includes a name and

19. *Citizens Util. Bd. v. State*, 267 A.D.2d 838, 839, 700 N.Y.S.2d 297, 298 (1999).

Table 7-6. Online Sources of Attorney General Opinions

Source Name	Web Address	Free or Commercial
Lexis	www.lexis.com	Commercial
Office of the Attorney General of New York	www.ag.ny.gov/bureaus/appeals_opinions/search_intro.html	Free
Westlaw	www.westlaw.com	Commercial

subject index. Executive orders are also compiled in Title 9 of the NYCRR. The Annotations section of the volume containing Title 9 includes summaries of judicial interpretation of executive orders.

Proclamations are an official way to recognize events or specific causes of local or regional interest. Proclamations can be initiated by an individual, a group, or the legislature.[20]

Table 7-7 lists sources of online access to executive orders and proclamations.

VII. Other Resources for Researching New York Administrative Law

A new resource available on Westlaw is the "Reg & Leg Center." It allows multiple federal and state jurisdiction searches for statutes and various agency publications including regulations and guidance documents. The output can be crafted into a custom report. In addition, researchers can set up Reg & Leg Center alerts.

The most valuable resource in administrative law research is the agency itself. While rules are relatively easy to find, additional policies, guidelines, and decisions exist that may be difficult to access. A large part of your research should be talking to the agency's repre-

20. For more information about proclamations, see www.governor.ny.gov/sl2/proclamationindex.

Table 7-7. Current Sources of Governor's Executive Orders and Proclamations Online

Source Name	Web Address	Coverage	Free or Commercial
Governor's Website	www.governor.ny.gov/sl2/ExecutiveOrderindex www.governor.ny.gov/sl2/proclamationindex	Executive Orders and Proclamations	Free
Lexis	www.lexis.com (NYADMN)	Executive Orders and Proclamations	Commercial
Westlaw	www.westlaw.com (NS-EO; NY-LEGIS; NY-LEGIS-OLD; NY-CRR)	Executive Orders and Proclamations	Commercial

sentatives to find out what material is available. In the inmate hypothetical, Attorney General opinions and Governor's executive orders will, most likely, not be relevant. The New York State Commission on Correction, however, is a potential resource for locating relevant administrative documents unique to that agency.

VIII. Federal Administrative Law

The federal government's agencies function much like New York's. Agencies such as the Department of Justice, the Internal Revenue Service, and the U.S. Fish and Wildlife Service are invaluable parts of the executive branch.

Like New York's Administrative Procedure Act, the goal of the federal Administrative Procedure Act[21] is to promote uniformity, public participation, and public confidence in the fairness of the procedures used by agencies of the federal government.

21. 5 U.S.C. §§ 551–59, 701–06, 1305, 3105, 3344, 4301, 5335, 5362, 7521 (2006).

A. *Code of Federal Regulations*

Federal administrative rules are called regulations. Federal regulations are published in the *Code of Federal Regulations* (CFR), which is published by the Government Printing Office (GPO). The CFR is a codification of regulations issued by federal agencies. Similar to New York rules in the NYCRR, federal regulations in CFR are organized by agency and subject. The fifty titles of the CFR do not necessarily correspond to the fifty-one titles of the *United States Code* (USC), although some topics do fall under the same title number. For instance, Title 7 in both the CFR and the USC pertains to agriculture, but Title 11 of the USC addresses bankruptcy, while the same title in the CFR deals with federal elections.

The CFR volumes are updated annually, with specific titles updated each quarter. Titles 1 through 16 are updated as of January 1; Titles 17 through 27 are updated as of April 1; Titles 28 through 41 are updated as of July 1; and Titles 42 through 50 are updated as of October 1. Title 3, "The President" is the exception. Published annually since 1976, each volume of Title 3 contains unique information and is retained by libraries as a compiled source of presidential documents.

Realize, though, that the updates to each title may only become available months after the schedule indicates. Each year, the covers of the CFR volumes are a different color, which makes it easy to tell whether a print volume has been updated. If no changes were made in a particular volume for the new year, a cover with the new color is pasted on the old volume.

To research a topic in the CFR, you may use the general index published with the set or *West's Code of Federal Regulations General Index*. Look up your research terms or the relevant agency's name, and then read the regulations referenced. It may be more efficient to begin your research in an annotated statutory code that contains references to related regulations for each statute. After finding a statute on point, review the annotations following the statutory language for cross-references to relevant regulations. You may notice that *United States Code Service* (USCS) tends to provide more references to regulations than does *United States Code Annotated* (USCA). Look up the citations given and review the regulations.

Another print product available for selected areas of law is *West's Code of Federal Regulations Annotated.* Examples include Title 8 (Aliens & Nationality), Title 29 (Labor), Title 42 (Medicare/Medicaid), and Title 49 (Transportation). Each set provides the full text of regulations along with related case summaries, law review and journal commentary references, and references to corollary provisions of USCA. Its online counterpart, "Regulations Plus," is available on Westlaw.

Federal regulations are available online via Federal Digital System (FDsys) from 1996 to the present in PDF, text, and xml formats.[22] Figure 7-4 provides examples of federal regulations from the GPO's FDsys website.

B. *Federal Register*

New regulations and proposed changes to existing regulations are published first in the *Federal Register*, the federal equivalent of the *State Register.* The *Federal Register* is the official daily publication for rules, proposed rules, and notices of federal agencies and organizations, as well as executive orders and other presidential documents. It is published almost every weekday, with continuous pagination throughout the year. This means that page numbers in the thousands are common. The online version of the *Federal Register* is available on FDsys[23] in addition to HeinOnline, Lexis, and Westlaw.

C. Updating Federal Regulations

Updating regulations refers to the process of determining if the text of a regulation has changed or if the regulation has been repealed.

---

22. The address is www.gpo.gov/fdsys/browse/collectionCfr.action?collection Code=CFR.

23. The address is www.gpo.gov/fdsys/browse/collection.action?collection Code=FR.

Figure 7-4. Examples of Federal Regulations

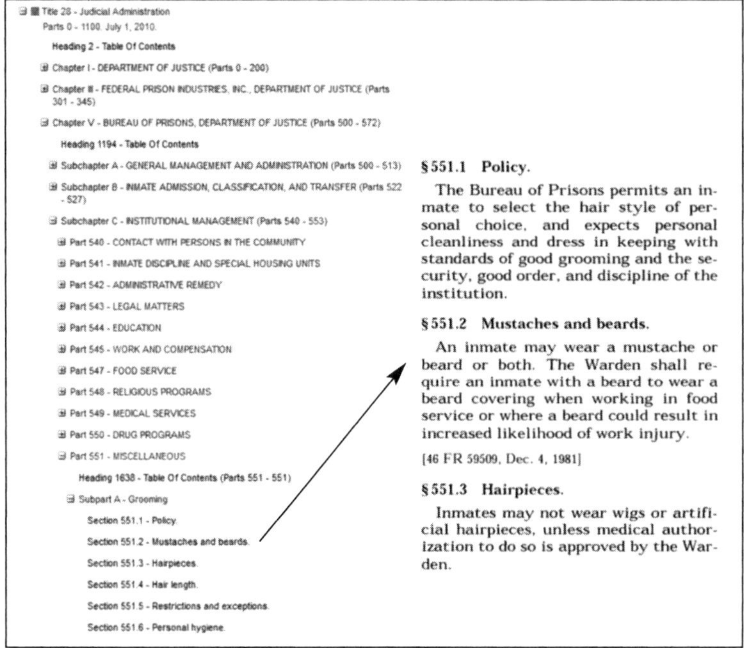

Title 28 - Judicial Administration
Parts 0 - 1100. July 1, 2010.
Heading 2 - Table Of Contents
Chapter I - DEPARTMENT OF JUSTICE (Parts 0 - 200)
Chapter III - FEDERAL PRISON INDUSTRIES, INC., DEPARTMENT OF JUSTICE (Parts 301 - 345)
Chapter V - BUREAU OF PRISONS, DEPARTMENT OF JUSTICE (Parts 500 - 572)
Heading 1194 - Table Of Contents
Subchapter A - GENERAL MANAGEMENT AND ADMINISTRATION (Parts 500 - 513)
Subchapter B - INMATE ADMISSION, CLASSIFICATION, AND TRANSFER (Parts 522 - 527)
Subchapter C - INSTITUTIONAL MANAGEMENT (Parts 540 - 553)
Part 540 - CONTACT WITH PERSONS IN THE COMMUNITY
Part 541 - INMATE DISCIPLINE AND SPECIAL HOUSING UNITS
Part 542 - ADMINISTRATIVE REMEDY
Part 543 - LEGAL MATTERS
Part 544 - EDUCATION
Part 545 - WORK AND COMPENSATION
Part 547 - FOOD SERVICE
Part 548 - RELIGIOUS PROGRAMS
Part 549 - MEDICAL SERVICES
Part 550 - DRUG PROGRAMS
Part 551 - MISCELLANEOUS
Heading 1638 - Table Of Contents (Parts 551 - 551)
Subpart A - Grooming
Section 551.1 - Policy.
Section 551.2 - Mustaches and beards.
Section 551.3 - Hairpieces.
Section 551.4 - Hair length.
Section 551.5 - Restrictions and exceptions.
Section 551.6 - Personal hygiene.

§ 551.1 Policy.

The Bureau of Prisons permits an inmate to select the hair style of personal choice, and expects personal cleanliness and dress in keeping with standards of good grooming and the security, good order, and discipline of the institution.

§ 551.2 Mustaches and beards.

An inmate may wear a mustache or beard or both. The Warden shall require an inmate with a beard to wear a beard covering when working in food service or where a beard could result in increased likelihood of work injury.

[46 FR 59509, Dec. 4, 1981]

§ 551.3 Hairpieces.

Inmates may not wear wigs or artificial hairpieces, unless medical authorization to do so is approved by the Warden.

Source: *Code of Federal Regulations* via FDsys is available at http://www.gpo.gov/fdsys/search/home.action.

To update a federal regulation in print or on the government's website, begin with the small booklet or the database called *List of CFR Sections Affected* (LSA). As its name suggests, the LSA lists all sections of the CFR that have been affected by recent agency action. The LSA provides page references to *Federal Register* issues when action affecting a section of the CFR is included. If the section you are researching is not listed in the LSA, then it has not been changed since its annual revision. The LSA is issued monthly. On FDsys,[24] the LSA also contains three supplemental services: *Last Month's List of CFR Sections Affected*, *Current List of CFR Parts Affected*, and the *List of CFR*

24. The LSA on FDsys is available at www.gpo.gov/fdsys/browse/collection.action?collectionCode=LSA.

Table 7-8. Updating Federal Regulations Using the Print LSA

1. Note the date of the CFR volume containing the section you want to update.
2. Locate the most current LSA that updates your CFR title. The tables inside list the CFR sections that have been amended or repealed. If a section is affected, a page number where the text of this change appears in the *Federal Register* will be provided. At the end of this step, you have updated your CFR section through the time period noted on the cover of the LSA pamphlet used.
3. Final updating in print requires reference to a table at the back of the *Federal Register* called "CFR Parts Affected During [the current month]." (Do not confuse this table with the "CFR Parts Affected in this [Current] Issue" located in the Contents at the beginning of each issue.) Refer to this table in each *Federal Register* for the last day of each month for all the months between the most recent monthly LSA issue and the current date. Also check the most recent issue of *Federal Register* for the present month. The table contains more general information (whether a "part" has been affected, not a "section"), but it will note changes made since the most recent LSA.

Parts Affected Today. A complete list of steps for updating federal regulations using the print and online LSA are provided in Tables 7-8 and 7-9.

In addition to updating federal regulations with the LSA, you can also update them by using Shepard's or KeyCite. Note that when you retrieve a regulation online using fee-based databases you are viewing the most current form of the regulation unless otherwise noted. Therefore, the value of using Shepard's or KeyCite for federal regulations is in the treatment of codes and other editorial analysis, not finding updated language.

D. Agency Decisions

Like New York agencies, federal agencies hold quasi-judicial hearings to decide cases that arise under the agencies' regulations. Some of

Table 7-9. Updating Federal Regulations Online via GPO Access

Each of the following steps can be completed on the FDsys website.* Check each of the following four lists for your regulation's section or part, as applicable.**

In each list, if your regulation's section or part is affected, a *Federal Register* page number will be provided so that you can locate the text of the change. If your section or part is not affected, it will not be listed.

List	Coverage
List of CFR Sections Affected	Sections affected by changes during the current month
Last Month's List of CFR Sections Affected	Sections affected by changes during the past month
Current List of CFR Parts Affected	Parts changed since the most recent monthly issue of LSA
List of CFR Parts Affected Today	Parts affected by changes in the most recent issue of *Federal Register*

* The address is www.gpo.gov/fdsys/browse/collection.action?collection Code=LSA.

** Remember that a "section" is a narrower citation than a "part." The most current information reports on parts, so it's possible that the change listed does not affect your particular section. You must read the *Federal Register* page to determine whether the change is important for your work.

these decisions are published in reporters specific to each agency, for example, *Decisions and Orders of the National Labor Relations Board.*

E. Judicial Opinions

The method of case research explained in Chapter 4 will lead to opinions in which the judiciary reviewed decisions of federal agencies. Additionally, *Shepard's Code of Federal Regulations Citations* in print and online are useful research tools both for updating federal regulations and for finding cases relevant to regulatory research. Federal regulations and judicial opinions can also be updated in KeyCite. The process of updating is described in Chapter 8.

Chapter 8

Updating Research with Citators

I. The Role of Citators in Legal Research

Before using any legal authority to analyze a problem, a lawyer must know how that authority has been treated by later actions of a court, legislature, or agency. A case may have been reversed or overruled; a statute or regulation may have been amended, repealed, or superseded. Ensuring that cases, statutes, and other authorities represent the current law or "good law" requires an additional step; the generic term for this step is *updating*, though it is often called "Shepardizing" because the first major updating tool was *Shepard's Citations*.

In addition to determining that a case is still good law, there are two other reasons to update. First, the significance of a case may have been undercut because either (a) a later decision criticized the case without explicitly overruling the prior case or (b) a subsequent decision's holding distinguished itself from the case by asserting that the case's holding does not apply to the facts of the later case. Second, updating can be an effective finding tool; updating a single case or statute can provide links to many other cases on the same topic.

To update an authority, you must find every subsequent legal source that has cited that authority and determine how the subsequent source treated the authority on a particular issue. A *citator* provides a comprehensive list of citations to sources that refer to your authority. Analyzing this list of citations will help determine whether the case is good law.

This chapter's primary focus is updating cases with online sources; this focus reflects the frequency with which cases are updated in comparison to other sources of law. Other authorities—including statutes, constitutional provisions, regulations, and some secondary sources—can also be updated and will be addressed briefly.

The chapter concentrates on updating with online sources for one reason: print citators tend to lag behind their online counterparts by at least a few months, impacting the currentness and, potentially, the validity of your research. Moreover, fewer libraries are maintaining their print citator collections. Whether you choose an online or print citator, you must take the time to interpret the information presented and read the later authorities to determine how they affect your analysis.

II. When to Update

Updating can be a valuable tool at several points in the research process. You should do a cursory update as soon as you find a potentially relevant case to learn immediately whether the case is still respected authority. At the same time, you will find other cases and secondary sources that discuss the same points of law as the first case, which will expand your research.

Later in the research process, you should carefully update the cases that will likely appear in your document. This time, updating should ensure that the case has not been undercut, implicitly or explicitly. For example, a case might not have been overruled, but if many cases distinguish its facts or criticize its reasoning, you might be reluctant to rely heavily on the case in your analysis. In this more careful updating, you will need to review each relevant source that has cited your case.

You should continue updating your authorities until the moment your final document is submitted, and again prior to any hearings, trials, or other actions associated with your case. The end result should be that you find all current and relevant authorities for your legal issues and base your analysis on them. Simply stated, failure to update thoroughly is a disservice to your client and could be grounds for malpractice.

III. Shepard's and KeyCite

Use of online citators is recommended over print citators because they are easier to use and provide the most comprehensive, up-to-date information about the status of an authority. Researchers consider Shepard's (Lexis) and KeyCite (Westlaw) the most comprehensive online case citators available.[1] Shepard's has been available in print for over one hundred years and online since 1980.[2] KeyCite has been an online product in the legal marketplace since 1997.

Researchers without free access to an online citator have a few options. They can seek institutions in the community such as public and academic libraries that provide public access to these online citator services. Researchers may also purchase a subscription or use a credit card on the Westlaw website to KeyCite for a single use or a la carte service.[3]

Once Lexis or Westlaw is accessible, there are at least two ways to find to Shepard's or KeyCite information. When retrieving a case or searching for a list of cases, both Shepard's and KeyCite automatically provide citator symbols within or next to the documents. Clicking on that symbol from within the full text of a document or, in the case of a list of citations, next to a document, will open the full citator report.

Another way to access the citator services after logging into Lexis or Westlaw is to click on the Shepard's tab or the KeyCite button. The location of the tab or button is ever changing as vendors try to improve their online interfaces. However, the Shepard's tab and the KeyCite button are typically found near the top of the screen.

---

1. Both Shepard's and KeyCite include cases beginning in the following volumes: 40 N.Y. 1 (1869–present), 1 A.D. 1 (1895–present), and 1 Misc. 1 (1892–present).

2. Shepard's was available on Westlaw from 1980 through 1999.

3. Lexis offered a pay-as-you-go service in the past, but it is no longer offered.

A. Updating a Case

When updating a case, your main goal is to determine whether the case has been overruled or reversed. If it has been, you must determine whether it was overruled or reversed for the same issue or point of law that you are relying on. Note, for example, that if you are relying on a case for its support of a substantive issue and the case was reversed because of a procedural issue, you can still rely on this case substantively (with an explanation of this distinction).

If the case has not been overruled or reversed, you must still explore the subsequent treatment of this case by other courts to assess the impact on its precedential value. A case that has frequently been criticized and never followed is weaker precedent than a case that has been followed often by other courts. Shepard's and KeyCite provide different tools to make this assessment, but the research process is similar in each.

Although novice researchers are tempted to rely strictly on the colored symbols provided by Shepard's and KeyCite, doing so can be perilous. You know your research project better than an anonymous attorney-editor employed by one of the vendors to make generic determinations about the value of cases. Thus, you need to analyze the history and read the citing references to form your own judgment about whether a particular authority is valuable for your analysis.

B. Updating with Shepard's and KeyCite

Both Shepard's and KeyCite produce comprehensive reports with information about the case being updated. Both include colored symbols that quickly tell you that service's opinion about the value of the case. Both services use a similar spectrum of color codes ranging from red (connoting negative treatment by later cases) to green (connoting positive treatment). Table 8-1 includes information about each Shepard's signal and KeyCite symbol.

Table 8-1. Case Treatment Symbols

Treatment Category	Shepard's	KeyCite
Negative Treatment	Red Stop Sign *Warning: Negative treatment is indicated*	Red Flag *No longer good for at least one point of law*
Possible Negative Treatment	Orange Q *Questioned: Validity questioned by citing references* Yellow Triangle *Caution: Possible negative treatment*	(no similar symbol) Yellow Flag *Some negative history but not overruled*
Neutral or Positive Treatment	Blue A *Citing references with analysis available* Blue I *Citation information available* Green Diamond *Positive treatment indicated*	Blue H *Case has some history* (no similar symbol) Green C *Citing references available*

1. Updating Basics

Both Shepard's (shown in Figures 8-1 and 8-3) and KeyCite (shown in Figures 8-2 and 8-4) produce lists of other authorities that cite your case; these authorities are referred to as *citing references.* These references include later cases, secondary sources, and other material available on that service that cites your case.

Both Shepard's and KeyCite offer two levels of updating—one simply to determine whether the case has been reversed, overruled, or otherwise treated negatively, and another to find an exhaustive list of all citing references. The more limited list provides the "history" of the case you are updating as seen in Figure 8-1 and Figure 8-2. The more expansive list is useful when using one case as a launching point in research to find additional cases, which is shown in Figure 8-3 and Figure 8-4.

Figure 8-1. Shepard's for Validation

The green diamond at the top of the summary represents positive treatment of the Shepardized case.

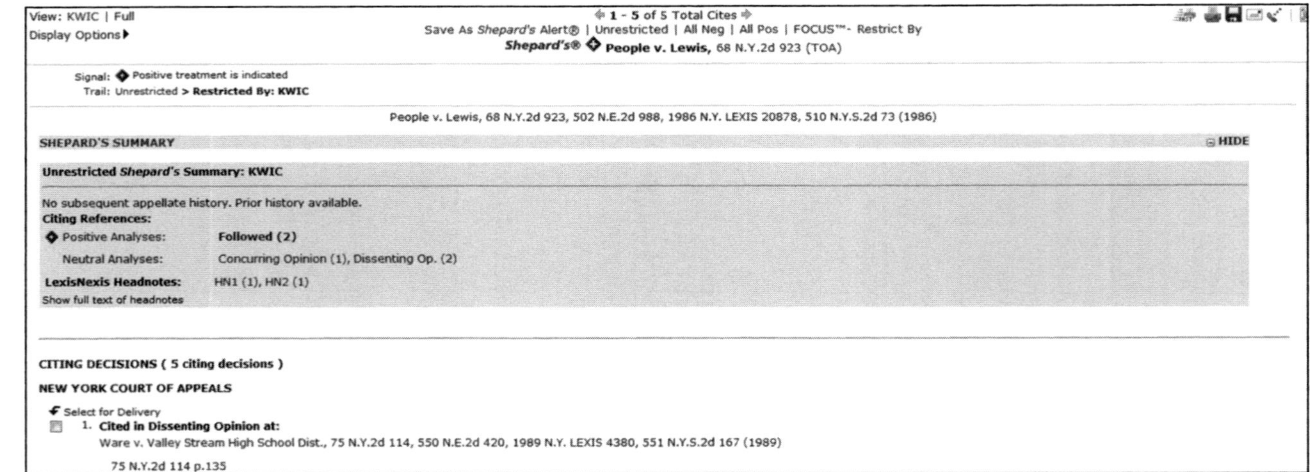

Figure 8-2. KeyCite Direct History

The blue H at the top left of this image indicates that the KeyCited case is still good law. Under a lower heading, the flag next to the ninth case is yellow. The yellow flag indicates that the case on that line has some negative history, but it has not been overruled.

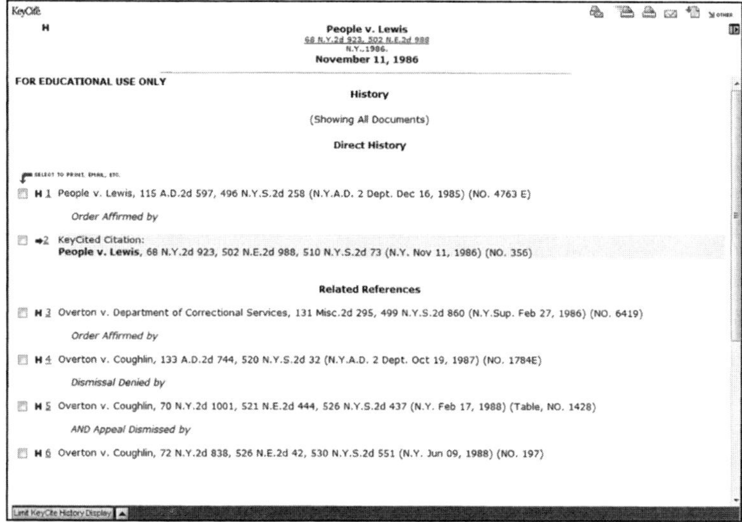

Source: Westlaw. 2011. Reprinted with permission of West, a Thomson Reuters business.

When Shepardizing a New York case, clicking the radio button "Shepard's for Validation" produces a list of citing sources limited to New York decisions, a Shepard's summary limited to New York decisions and headnotes, and the subsequent appellate history of the case. An example of Shepard's for Validation is shown in Figure 8-1. By contrast, clicking the radio button "Shepard's for Research" produces a list of all sources in the Lexis system that have cited that case. An example of Shepard's for Research is shown in Figure 8-3.

With KeyCite, the default setting is usually "Full History." While that name implies a full listing of citing references, Full History gives just the history of the case you are updating and any negative treatment. Thus, Full History is similar to Shepard's for Validation. To find a complete list of citing references on KeyCite, click on the link "Citing References" in the left frame.

Although both services contain a lot of similar information, they are organized differently and do not contain the same features. For instance, Shepard's provides a summary of the Shepard's report first. This summary information is designed to give a first impression about the status of a case. It includes a Shepard's symbol for the cited case and hyperlinks to citing cases by categories such as "Concurring Opinion" or "Dissenting Opinion." Next, Shepard's lists the history of the case you are updating; this is the litigation trail of the case, showing the results of various appeals. Finally, Shepard's provides citing references. Cases are arranged by jurisdiction and date, followed by secondary sources.

KeyCite begins with "Direct History," which is the procedural history of the case. Direct History is available in text form (see Figure 8-2) or in chart form known as "Direct History (Graphical View)" After reviewing the Direct History, click on the "Citing References" link in the left frame. "Negative Cases" and "Positive Cases" are listed respectively as shown in Figure 8-4.

Shepard's and KeyCite both include headnote references. As explained in Chapter 4, headnotes summarize each issue of law in a case. The concepts covered in the headnotes in Shepard's and KeyCite should be quite similar because they represent the same issues of law in each case. However, each vendor creates its own headnotes under the direction of staff editors. An important concept for any researcher using a citator is that the Shepard's headnotes are different from KeyCite headnotes.

2. *Limiting Shepard's and KeyCite Results*

Updating a case will often retrieve a very large number of citing decisions. Both Shepard's and KeyCite enable you to limit your results by jurisdiction, holding (or headnote), and specific terms or phrases. Shepard's uses descriptive phrases such as "Distinguished by," "Cited by," or "Mentioned" to express how a case has been treated. Citing decisions in the Shepard's report can be organized according to these categories. KeyCite has a depth-of-treatment feature that

Figure 8-3. Shepard's for Research

The green diamond indicates positive treatment.

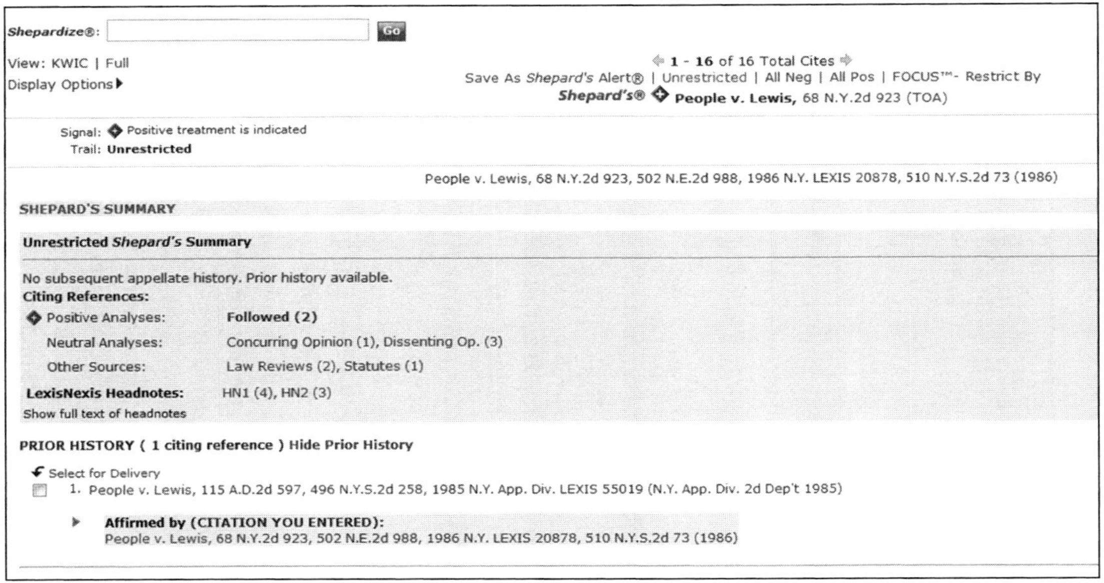

Shepardize®: Go

View: KWIC | Full
Display Options ▸

1 - 16 of 16 Total Cites
Save As *Shepard's* Alert® | Unrestricted | All Neg | All Pos | FOCUS™- Restrict By
Shepard's® ◆ **People v. Lewis,** 68 N.Y.2d 923 (TOA)

Signal: ◆ Positive treatment is indicated
Trail: **Unrestricted**

People v. Lewis, 68 N.Y.2d 923, 502 N.E.2d 988, 1986 N.Y. LEXIS 20878, 510 N.Y.S.2d 73 (1986)

SHEPARD'S SUMMARY

Unrestricted *Shepard's* Summary

No subsequent appellate history. Prior history available.
Citing References:

◆ Positive Analyses:	**Followed (2)**
Neutral Analyses:	Concurring Opinion (1), Dissenting Op. (3)
Other Sources:	Law Reviews (2), Statutes (1)
LexisNexis Headnotes:	HN1 (4), HN2 (3)

Show full text of headnotes

PRIOR HISTORY (1 citing reference) Hide Prior History

Select for Delivery
1. People v. Lewis, 115 A.D.2d 597, 496 N.Y.S.2d 258, 1985 N.Y. App. Div. LEXIS 55019 (N.Y. App. Div. 2d Dep't 1985)

▸ **Affirmed by (CITATION YOU ENTERED):**
People v. Lewis, 68 N.Y.2d 923, 502 N.E.2d 988, 1986 N.Y. LEXIS 20878, 510 N.Y.S.2d 73 (1986)

Figure 8-4. KeyCite Citing References

The H at the top left is blue, which indicates the case has some history, but is still good law.

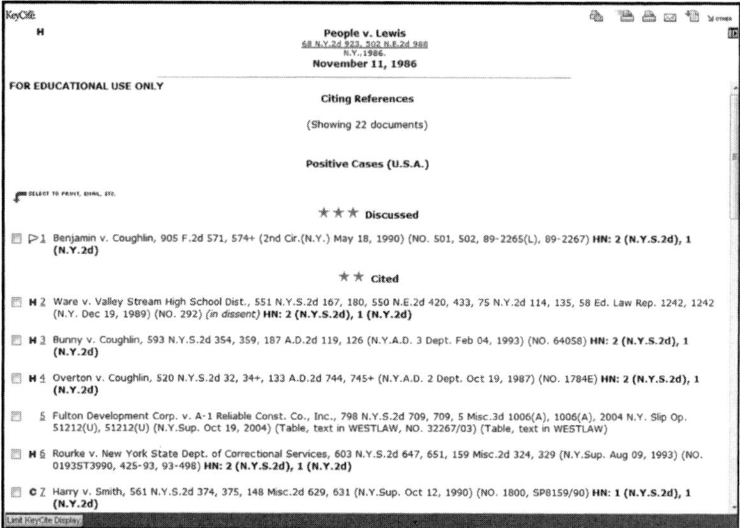

Source: Westlaw. 2011. Reprinted with permission of West, a Thomson Reuters business.

measures how much the KeyCited case is discussed. Depth of treatment is represented by the number of stars next to the citation. Four stars indicates a lengthy discussion about the KeyCited case, three stars typically indicates that there is more than a paragraph of discussion, and two stars or one star typically indicate a mere mention of the KeyCited case. In addition to the depth-of-treatment stars, KeyCite provides purple quotation marks to convey that the citing reference includes a quote in its discussion of the case you are updating. A visual example of depth-of-treatment stars is in Figure 8-4.

3. *Comparison of Shepard's and KeyCite*

Based on this understanding of the technical differences between these services, Table 8-2 demonstrates the differences in the process of updating a case in KeyCite and Shepard's using the New York case *People v. Lewis*, 68 N.Y.2d 923, 510 N.Y.S.2d 73 (1986). Each step of the process is emphasized in **bold** font in Table 8-2.

These two citator services have philosophical differences, as exemplified by the different treatment codes assigned to *Lewis*. On one hand, this case was assigned a relatively definitive symbol (a green diamond) to *Lewis* by the Shepard's attorney-editors that indicates positive treatment. On the other hand, the KeyCite attorney-editors assigned a more neutral symbol (a blue H). Both approaches are acceptable. However, an astute researcher must be aware of these different approaches and factor them into the use of these services. Most of all, the astute researcher will read all citing references and analyze them independent of the services' symbols.

4. *Westlaw's Direct History (Graphical View)*

Many cases have a complex history. You can view the history of a case in a color-coded diagram format in Westlaw's Direct History (Graphical View) service. Indirect history and citing references are not available in Direct History (Graphical View). You will have to use the traditional KeyCite service for this information.

5. *Shepard's Alert and KeyCite Alert*

You can monitor the status of cases by using alert services available in Shepard's and KeyCite. To monitor the status of a case in Shepard's, click on the "Save As Shepard's Alert" link at the top of the page. The next screen will allow you to customize your Shepard's Alert. To set up KeyCite Alert from within a KeyCite report, click on the "Monitor With KeyCite Alert" link. The setup wizard will guide you through the rest of the process.

Table 8-2. Steps for Updating with KeyCite and Shepard's Online Using *People v. Lewis*, 68 N.Y.2d 923, 510 N.Y.S.2d 73 (1986)

Step	*Shepard's*	*KeyCite*
1	**Login** at www.lexis.com.	**Login** at www.westlaw.com.
2	**Click on the "Shepard's" tab** at the top of the page.	**Click on the "KeyCite" link** at the top of the page *or* use the "KeyCite this Citation" box on the left frame of the page.
3	**Enter the full citation:*** 68 N.Y.2d 923 **Click the radio button "Shepard's for Research."**	**Enter the full citation:** 68 N.Y.2d 923 **Select "Citing References" in the left frame.**
4	**Look for the Shepard's signal to begin your assessment of this case.** There is a green diamond with a plus sign, which means *Positive treatment is indicated.*	**Look for the KeyCite symbol to begin your assessment of this case.** There is a blue H symbol, which means *Case has some history.*
5	**How has this case been treated by New York courts?** Explore the positive treatment of *Lewis* by evaluating the *citing decisions* in New York first. • Scroll down to the section marked *Citing Decisions.* To limit the number of citing references, use the "FOCUS —Restrict By" link to limit your citing references by date, jurisdiction, Lexis headnote number, type of analysis, or *Focus* keyword. Next, evaluate the relevance of citing opinions. • Click on the hyperlink in the pinpoint cite below the citing case. This will open the full text of the citing opinion and take you to the area that mentions *Lewis.* Evaluating this area of the citing opinion should help you decide whether the citing opinion has any impact on the standing of your case for your legal issue.	**How has this case been treated by New York courts?** Browse the *citing references* in New York first. • To limit the number of citing references, click on the "Limit KeyCite Display" button at the bottom of the page to limit the citing references by jurisdiction, document type, date, depth of treatment, or headnote. Next, evaluate the relevance of citing opinions. • Use the depth-of-treatment codes and other editorial analysis for this evaluation. Click on the hyperlinked number next to the citing decision. This will open the full text of the citing opinion and take you to the area that mentions *Lewis.* Evaluating this area of the citing opinion should help you decide whether the citing opinion has any impact on the standing of your case for your legal issue.

* The parallel citation for any case can be used to update in Shepard's and KeyCite. The use of vendor-specific citations is an exception to this rule. A Westlaw citation will not work in Shepard's. Likewise, a Lexis citation will

Table 8-2. Steps for Updating with KeyCite and Shepard's Online, *continued*

Step	*Shepard's*	*KeyCite*
6	Citing references are categorized by jurisdiction. After evaluating the New York cases, **evaluate the citing references in the Second Circuit and then other federal courts.**	Citing references are categorized first by depth-of-treatment. Under each depth-of-treatment category, the citing references are then organized by jurisdiction with cases from the highest court listed first. After evaluating the New York cases, **evaluate the citing references in the Second Circuit or other federal courts. Take a careful look at the citing references that have a four-star or a three-star depth-of-treatment code.**
7	**Use related documents and secondary sources.** Evaluate whether the related documents listed at the end of the Shepard's report add anything to your research generally or to your assessment of whether *Lewis* is still good law for your legal issue. Related documents include statutes, law review articles, encyclopedias, treatises, and other related resources available on Lexis.	**Use related documents and secondary sources.** Evaluate whether the related documents listed at the end of the KeyCite report add anything to your research generally or to your assessment of whether *Lewis* is still good law for your legal issue. Related documents include statutes, law review articles, encyclopedias, treatises, and other related resources available on Westlaw.

not work in KeyCite. Each vendor assigns its own citation to unreported cases and to cases that have not yet been assigned a reporter citation. A typical Westlaw citation may look like this: 2008 WL 1944571. The same case in Lexis citation format looks like this: 2008 N.Y. Lexis 1181.

6. *Using Online Citators to Find Cases*

Citators are excellent case-finding tools. When you have one relevant case, use a citator to find other relevant cases from the history or direct history of the case or from the citing references list. Often, citing references lists are long. Both Shepard's and KeyCite provide the ability to restrict or limit your citing references by jurisdiction, case treatment, or headnote number, as pointed out earlier. Restricting by a headnote number is especially advantageous because the headnote number represents an issue of law from the case you started with.

7. Table of Authorities Feature

Another effective case-finding feature of Shepard's and KeyCite is the Table of Authorities (TOA). On Lexis, look for the "TOA" link at the top of the page. On Westlaw, look for the "Table of Authorities" link toward the bottom of the left frame.

After locating a relevant case, the Table of Authorities feature allows you to compile a list of cases cited by that relevant case. The list includes treatment codes so that you are able to easily select the cases worth pursuing and identify hidden weaknesses of the relevant case. Note that the treatment codes in the TOA indicate the way other cases have treated the cases in the TOA list. Images of the Table of Authorities for Shepard's and KeyCite are available in Figures 8-5 and 8-6, respectively, showing the cases cited in *People v. Lewis*.

IV. Online Statutory Citators

Researchers can explore whether a statute has been repealed or amended by using Shepard's or KeyCite. In addition, researchers can consult these citators to identify citing decisions that have interpreted the statute or clarified ambiguous language. A unique feature of KeyCite is the availability of pending legislation that would affect the statute in question.

While online citators have their benefits, they also have their drawbacks, including the extent of their coverage. For example, the New York session laws and local laws can be updated using the print *Shepard's New York Statute Citations*, but they cannot be updated online. More discussion of print citators is in Part VII of this chapter.

V. Online Citators for Other Legal Materials

Online citators are available to update legal materials other than cases and statutes. For example, you can update state and federal regulations in Shepard's and KeyCite. In addition, you can run New York

Figure 8-5. Table of Authorities for *People v. Lewis* in Shepard's

The yellow Q next to some of the citing references indicates that the validity of those cases has been questioned. The yellow triangle next to the second case means that the case has some negative history but has not been overruled.

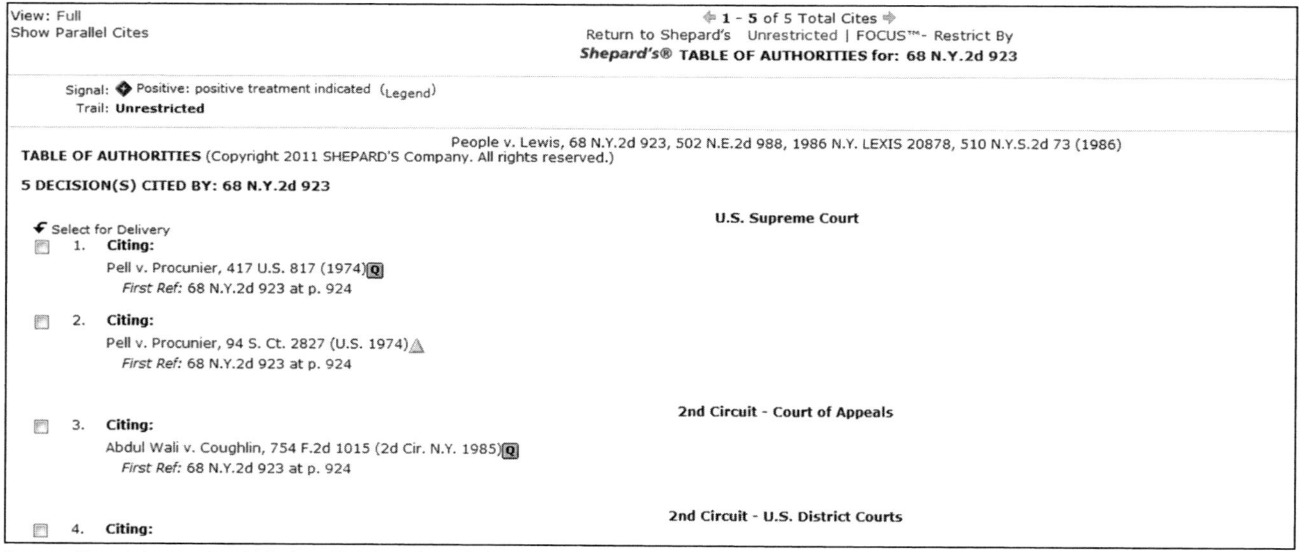
View: Full
Show Parallel Cites

1 - 5 of 5 Total Cites
Return to Shepard's Unrestricted | FOCUS™- Restrict By
Shepard's® TABLE OF AUTHORITIES for: 68 N.Y.2d 923

Signal: Positive: positive treatment indicated (Legend)
Trail: **Unrestricted**

People v. Lewis, 68 N.Y.2d 923, 502 N.E.2d 988, 1986 N.Y. LEXIS 20878, 510 N.Y.S.2d 73 (1986)
TABLE OF AUTHORITIES (Copyright 2011 SHEPARD'S Company. All rights reserved.)

5 DECISION(S) CITED BY: 68 N.Y.2d 923

U.S. Supreme Court

Select for Delivery

1. **Citing:**
Pell v. Procunier, 417 U.S. 817 (1974) Q
First Ref: 68 N.Y.2d 923 at p. 924

2. **Citing:**
Pell v. Procunier, 94 S. Ct. 2827 (U.S. 1974)
First Ref: 68 N.Y.2d 923 at p. 924

2nd Circuit - Court of Appeals

3. **Citing:**
Abdul Wali v. Coughlin, 754 F.2d 1015 (2d Cir. N.Y. 1985) Q
First Ref: 68 N.Y.2d 923 at p. 924

2nd Circuit - U.S. District Courts

4. **Citing:**

Source: Copyright 2011 LexisNexis, a division of Reed Elsevier Inc. All Rights Reserved. LexisNexis and the Knowledge Burst logo are registered trademarks of Reed Elsevier Properties Inc. and are used with the permission of LexisNexis.

Figure 8-6. Table of Authorities for *People v. Lewis* in KeyCite

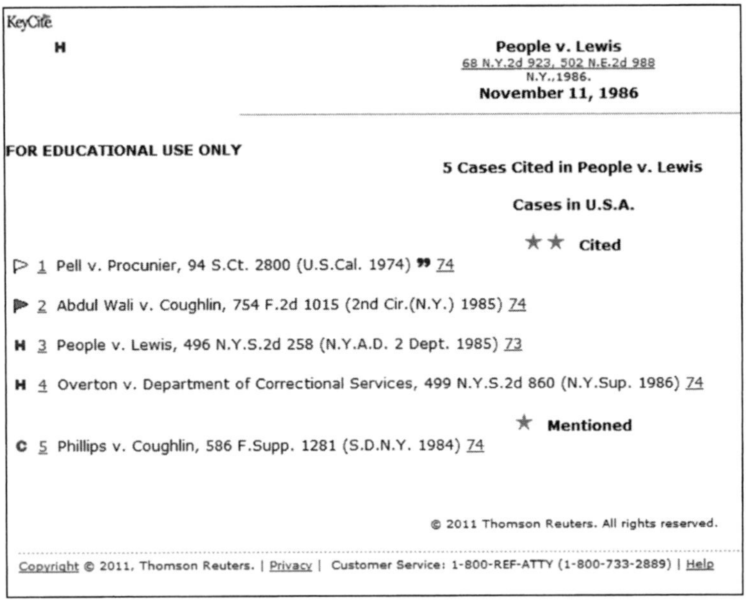
KeyCite
H
People v. Lewis
68 N.Y.2d 923, 502 N.E.2d 988
N.Y.,1986.
November 11, 1986

FOR EDUCATIONAL USE ONLY

5 Cases Cited in People v. Lewis

Cases in U.S.A.

★★ Cited

1 Pell v. Procunier, 94 S.Ct. 2800 (U.S.Cal. 1974) " 74

2 Abdul Wali v. Coughlin, 754 F.2d 1015 (2nd Cir.(N.Y.) 1985) 74

H 3 People v. Lewis, 496 N.Y.S.2d 258 (N.Y.A.D. 2 Dept. 1985) 73

H 4 Overton v. Department of Correctional Services, 499 N.Y.S.2d 860 (N.Y.Sup. 1986) 74

★ Mentioned

C 5 Phillips v. Coughlin, 586 F.Supp. 1281 (S.D.N.Y. 1984) 74

© 2011 Thomson Reuters. All rights reserved.

Copyright © 2011, Thomson Reuters. | Privacy | Customer Service: 1-800-REF-ATTY (1-800-733-2889) | Help

Source: Westlaw. 2011. Reprinted with permission of West, a Thomson Reuters business.

law review articles through Shepard's and KeyCite for citing references.

VI. Online Tutorials

Both Lexis and Westlaw provide online tutorials. If your updating needs are beyond the scope of this chapter, consult one of the vendor-sponsored tutorials available online.[4]

4. The *Shepard's* tutorial is available at http://web.lexis.com/help/multimedia/detect.asp?sPage=mom2010. The KeyCite tutorial is available at http://lawschool.westlaw.com/shared/marketinfodisplay.asp?code=re&id=2&subpage=1 (click on "KeyCite" under the "Interactive Tours and Tutorials" heading).

VII. Print Citators

The following print citators are available when updating New York law:

- *Shepard's New York Court of Appeals Citations*
- *Shepard's New York Miscellaneous Citations*
- *Shepard's New York Statute Citations*
- *Shepard's New York Supplement Citations*
- *Shepard's New York Supreme Court Citations* and
- *Shepard's North Eastern Reporter Citations.*

Updating in print entails the use of multiple volumes and steps. Each citator title uses a combination of bound volumes and supplementary pamphlets to list the citing references that are summarized in one place on an online citator. To know which volumes and pamphlets you need to update a particular authority, refer to the most recent pamphlet. Usually, this will be a red-cover pamphlet that is no more than one month old. On the cover, you will see a box entitled "What Your Library Should Contain." Gather the volumes and pamphlets listed there, and look up your authority in each.

Listed under your authority will be its citing references. Note that each volume or pamphlet contains citing references from a specific period. The volumes are not cumulative, so you must check each one for a complete list of citing references. Introductory pages at the front of each volume or supplement show how to interpret the citing references and the symbols that show how they treated your authority.

There is a considerable lag from the time new information becomes available and when it is printed in *Shepard's* and subsequently made available on library shelves. Relying on a citator that is not timely can pose both practical and ethical concerns. Caution must be exercised about complete reliance on a print citator for updating.

Chapter 9

New York City Legal Research

I. Introduction

New York City's rich colonial history can be felt today in its legal structures. In 1653, New Amsterdam was incorporated by the Dutch West India Company, and a court structure was defined. As New Amsterdam changed hands through the colonial period, its charter and court and administrative structures shifted, leaving a meandering trail for the legal historian.

For clarity, this chapter will focus on the current sources of law in New York City, including the New York City Charter, city legislation and administrative law, and the city's courts.

II. New York City's Charter

New York City's charter is an outgrowth of hundreds of years of governance. From the Dutch to the English to the United States, the charter has seen both minor revisions and complete overhauls in which city departments and courts were added or purged. The current charter is a blueprint for the overall legislative and administrative structure of New York City, and is a critical starting point for any legal question involving New York City.

A. The Current Charter

New York City's current charter reflects revisions through 2009. It is organized by chapter and section range, and each chapter defines the role of office or officer. As an example, Table 9-1 is an excerpt of Chapter 1 of the 2009 Charter, defining the role of mayor.

Table 9-1. New York City Charter Excerpt

CHAPTER 1
MAYOR

§ 3. Office powers. The mayor shall be the chief executive officer of the city.

§ 4. Election; term; salary. The mayor shall be elected at the general election in the year nineteen hundred sixty-five and every fourth year thereafter. The mayor shall hold office for a term of four years commencing on the first day of January after each such election. A mayor who resigns or is removed from office prior to the completion of a full term shall be deemed to have held that office for a full term for purposes of section 1138 of the charter. The salary of the mayor shall be two hundred twenty-five thousand dollars a year.

§ 5. Annual statement to council. The mayor shall communicate to the council at least once in each year a statement of the finances, government and affairs of the city with a summary statement of the activities of the agencies of the city. Such statement shall include a summary of the city's progress in implementing the goals and strategies contained in the most recent final strategic policy statement submitted by that mayor pursuant to section seventeen.

Note that the chapter begins at section three; sections one and two are included as an introduction to the charter. Also, note that, in this example, the charter defines the role of the mayor, including salary, term length, and job description and duties. Throughout the charter, a role, office, or department is defined at length within its respective chapter. If you are researching a legal question in New York City, the most recent charter is a good place from which to cull definitions, explanations, job descriptions, and procedures.

The Charter of 2009 is arranged as indicated in Appendix 9-A.

B. Revisions to the Charter

Before 1924, revisions to New York City's charter were written by the state legislature. The Home Rule Amendment was passed in 1914 for most cities in New York and in 1924 for New York City. New York State's Municipal Home Rule Law §§ 36 and 37 outlines a municipality's power to establish charter revisions via commission. This general rule established by the state legislature is delineated in the New York City charter in Chapter 2—Council, §§ 32 through 39, generally, and in § 40, specifically ("Amendment of the charter").

Currently, the Charter Revision Commission (CRC) has been granted the power to propose revisions to the City's charter. Appointed by the mayor, the most recent commission consists of fourteen community members and a chair. Typically, the CRC proposes changes to the charter and organizes public forums in the five boroughs of New York City to solicit public input on the proposed changes.

Occasionally, the mayor will charge the commission with a particular focus. For example, in 2010, Mayor Bloomberg charged the group

> with reviewing the entire Charter in order to propose amendments that would increase the efficiency and effectiveness of government. In addition, he requested that the Commission consider presenting the issue of term limits to the voters. The Mayor has also charged the Commission with conducting an extensive outreach program that encourages broad and diverse public participation and seeks ideas and opinions from a wide variety of civic and community leaders.[1]

After investigation, the commission will publish its preliminary findings and recommendations. Such documents highlight current

1. *See* www.nyc.gov/html/charter/downloads/pdf/preliminary_report_final.pdf, under "About the Commission," page 4.

issues in city governance and may be useful in an investigation of an area of the established charter. The proposed revisions are meant to reflect the collective wisdom of the commission members and the public input gathered from forums throughout the boroughs.

According to § 40 of the current charter, proposed amendments to the charter may be made final amendments by local law,[2] by a sufficient number of electors filing petition to have an amendment placed on a ballot, or "in any other such manner as provided by law."

C. Finding the Charter and Related Documents

1. *In Print*

You may purchase an unannotated copy of the charter, updated through December 18, 2009, on the New York City CityStore website. New York Legal Publishing Corporation offers a print version of *New York City Charter and Administrative Code Annotated*, available for purchase via its website.[3] Also, many New York law libraries have various print copies of the charter.

2. *Online*

Westlaw has two databases containing the charter. NYC-C searches the current charter only, including local laws up to 2009. NYC-AMEND has the current charter and recent amendments, including up to Local Laws 1–9 of 2011. Both databases provide historical and case notes at the bottom of the entries, and are managed by New York Legal Publishing Corporation.

Lexis also has two databases with the charter. NYCCH is updated annually and annotated with information dating back to 1937. NY-CMUN is updated within one week of publication. It is also anno-

---

2. Local law is discussed in Part III of this chapter.

3. The address of New York Legal Publishing Corporation is www.nylp.com.

tated and includes the charter, code, and rules of NYC. The database materials are also from New York Legal Publishing Corporation.

The New York City website provides access to versions of the charter from recent years. The most recent version available is from 2009.[4] The 2004 version is also available.[5] The Law Department of New York City has also contracted with New York Legal Publishing Corporation to provide a publicly accessible website for the charter, administrative code, and rules of New York City.[6]

The charter is also available on the state's legislature website, under the Laws of New York link.[7] Scroll down to the "Miscellaneous" section, to the Charter, labeled as "NYC."

3. *Charter Revision Commission Documents*

The Charter Revision Commission website has many of its reports available in its archives.[8] As of late 2011, the site has the 1988, 1989, 1998, 2001, 2002, 2003, and 2004 Full Staff Report of recommendations.

In print, some of the commission's proposed revisions are available. Search your local law library catalog for "charter revision commission" or "proposed charter amendments." Also, if you want to search a little further afield, search through New York City Hall's library catalog, available online.[9]

Alternatively, in your local library, scan the stacks in which the versions of the charter are shelved; the amendments and proposed amendments will be shelved nearby.

---

4. The address is www.nyc.gov/html/charter/downloads/pdf/citycharter 2009.pdf.
5. The address is www.nyc.gov/html/charter/downloads/pdf/citycharter 2004.pdf.
6. The address is http://home2.nyc.gov/html/law/html/about/laws.shtml.
7. The address is http://public.leginfo.state.ny.us.
8. The address is www.nyc.gov/html/charter/html/archives/reports.shtml.
9. The address is www.nyc.gov/html/records/html/about/chlibrary.shtml.

D. Historical Background of Charter Sections

While using an annotated version of the charter, you may notice the historical and revision notes included in many of the sections. If you are beginning with the 2009 version, follow the historical notes back through the different versions of the charter to monitor revisions.

Also, you can use Lexis to locate a section of the charter and use Shepard's to confirm its validity and relevance in case law. Click on the "Shepard's" tab, and enter in the name of the publication as "N.Y. City Charter." Then, enter in the section number you are interested in.

III. New York City's Legislative Structure

The Council of New York City is defined by New York City's 2009 Charter, under Chapter 2—Council, and it is "vested with the legislative power of the city."[10] The City Council is made up of fifty-one members and a public advocate.[11] No qualifications for the members are defined, except that no member may be employed in any capacity by an agency of New York City.[12]

A. Legislation

The legislative process of the Council is similar to that of the state legislature. A bill, named an "intro," is introduced in the Council's regularly stated meeting that occurs bimonthly at City Hall and follows the path illustrated in Figure 9-1.

10. *Charter of the City of New York*, ch. 2, § 21 (2009).
11. *Id.* at § 22.
12. *Id.* at § 23.

Figure 9-1. New York City Council Process Flowchart

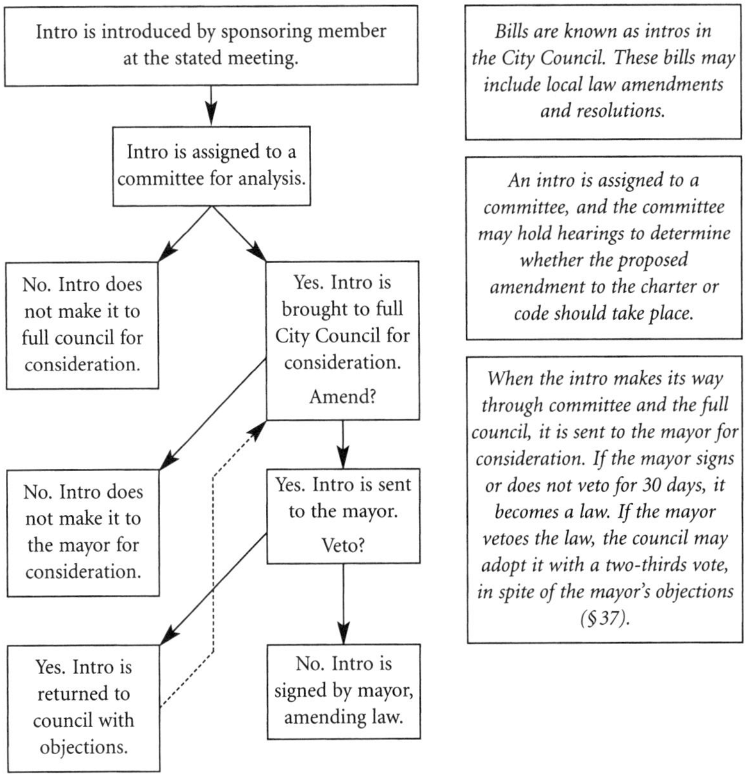

Intro is introduced by sponsoring member at the stated meeting.

Intro is assigned to a committee for analysis.

No. Intro does not make it to full council for consideration.

Yes. Intro is brought to full City Council for consideration. Amend?

No. Intro does not make it to the mayor for consideration.

Yes. Intro is sent to the mayor. Veto?

Yes. Intro is returned to council with objections.

No. Intro is signed by mayor, amending law.

Bills are known as intros in the City Council. These bills may include local law amendments and resolutions.

An intro is assigned to a committee, and the committee may hold hearings to determine whether the proposed amendment to the charter or code should take place.

When the intro makes its way through committee and the full council, it is sent to the mayor for consideration. If the mayor signs or does not veto for 30 days, it becomes a law. If the mayor vetoes the law, the council may adopt it with a two-thirds vote, in spite of the mayor's objections (§ 37).

The committees, subcommittees, and task forces under the Council are included in Appendix 9-B.

The citation format for Council legislation is straightforward. Each intro is assigned a number, reflecting its consecutive placement within the year. For example, Intro 70 of 2002 (also written as Int. 70-2002) was the seventieth intro proposed in 2002; it was a proposed local law to amend the administrative code of the city in relation to civil penalties for violations of the littering law. If the intro is accepted by the mayor and passed into law, it is relabeled as a local law. Using that same example, Int. 70-2002 was accepted and became Local Law 2003/001, the first local law of 2003, enacted on the seventh of January. Each intro and local law must deal with only one subject, and the title "shall briefly refer to the subject matter."[13]

Frequently, the Council passes resolutions that may rename streets or local landmarks, or make a general statement of policy on global issues affecting New York City. The citation format for resolutions is as follows: Reso. 01-2009, where 01 indicates the consecutive order in which the resolution was proposed and 2009 indicates the year.

B. Finding Council Bills and Meeting Minutes

1. *Bills*

For more recent intros, local laws, and resolutions, the City Council website allows the public to narrow by date and search through committee reports.

For older intros and bills, much of the material was duplicated in the *Proceedings of the Council of the City of New York* and the *City Record* via the keeping of minutes during Council sessions. See Table 9-2 for more information on where to locate bills.

Westlaw has local laws dating back to 1985 and Council Reports dating back to 1999 (NYC-MUN).

Your local law library may have one or many of the sources listed in Table 9-2. Search the catalog by publisher or by title to locate results. For publisher searches, try searching for "New York Legislative Service" or "New York City Council."

2. *Meeting Minutes*

Meeting minutes are available in a printed format in the *Proceedings of the Council of the City of New York* and the *City Record*. In ad-

13. *Charter of the City of New York*, § 32 (2009).

Table 9-2. Locations of Current and Past Intros and Local Laws

Title	Date Range	Location	Commercial or Free
City Record	1873–present	New York State Library	Free
Proceedings of the Council of the City of New York	1898–1901, 1938–present	New York State Library (1938–present) New York Public Library (1898–1901, 1938–present)	Free
New York City Report	1977–present	New York Legislative Service, www.nyls.org	Commercial
*New York City Legislative Annual**	1980–present	New York Legislative Service, www.nyls.org	Commercial
City of New York Council Digest (aka "The Pink Book")	1990–present	New York Legal Publishing Corporation, www.nylp.com	Commercial
New York Legal Advance Service: Local Laws of the City of New York	1991–present	New York Legal Publishing Corporation, www.nylp.com	Commercial
NYC Council Website	1998–present	http://legistar.council.nyc.gov/Legislation.aspx	Free

* From 1991 on; includes full text of intros and local laws, and includes full text committee reports.

dition to being available in print, recent editions of the *City Record* are available on the City's government website.[14]

With coverage back to 1998, the proceedings are also available on the Council's website. In addition to the meeting minutes, an agenda is available for most committee meetings. The bimonthly stated meetings include an agenda, minutes, and a video recording of the meeting.

14. The address is www.nyc.gov/html/dcas/html/vendors/cityrecord_editions.shtml.

IV. New York City's Administrative System

A. Origin of the Administrative Code

New York City's administrative code is much like the *United States Code* and New York's state statutes in function. It reflects the City Council's legislative process and organizes local laws and ordinances by topic.

However, New York City's administrative code has a complicated history. Throughout the years, the City's legislative body made attempts to organize its local laws and ordinances into a coherent structure. These attempts were convoluted and difficult to understand.

The state legislature addressed the confusion caused by poor organization by recodifying New York City's local laws into an administrative code, first in 1937 and then in 1985.[15] Now, the administrative code may be amended by state or local law, and there have been many revisions since the recodification in 1985.

B. The Administrative Code

New York City's administrative code is divided into titles, chapters, subchapters, sections, and subsections. Table 9-3 is an excerpt from the administrative code.

The current code has thirty titles, as outlined in Appendix 9-C.

C. Finding the Administrative Code

1. *In Print*

The *New York City Charter and Administrative Code* is published by New York Legal Publishing Corporation. It is annotated with materials dating back to 1937, including case notes, historical notes, and

15. William H. Manz, *Gibson's New York Legal Research Guide* 458 (3d ed. 2004). The recodification of 1937 is called the New York City Administrative Code of 1938.

Table 9-3. Administrative Code Excerpt

Title 3—Elected Officials
Chapter 2—City Council and County Clerk
Subchapter 3—Prohibition of Gifts by Lobbyists
Section 3-226—Enforcement
Complaints alleging violations of this subchapter shall be made, received, investigated and adjudicated in a manner consistent with investigations and adjudications of conflicts of interest pursuant to chapters sixty-eight and thirty-four of the charter.

old code derivations.[16] In print, it is updated semi-annually with pocket parts. The resource also includes a complementary set of all New York State Session Laws that impact the administrative code in New York City.

The city of New York does not sell the complete administrative code, but you can purchase individual portions of the code at the CityStore.[17] For example, the plumbing, building, construction, mechanical, and fire codes from various years are for sale.

2. *Online*

Lexis provides an annotated version of the code and charter, including historical notes (NYCCDE). The materials are from New York Legal Publishing Corporation. Westlaw also provides the administrative code from New York Legal Publishing Corporation and is listed as being current through 2010 (NYC-CODE).

New York Legal Publishing Corporation also offers online, paid access to the administrative code at its website.[18] The Law Department

16. As mentioned in the introduction to this section, there were many embodiments of the code before the 1985 version. *Old code derivations* are editorial notes that link the current code section to its origins in older versions of the administrative code.

17. The address is www.nyc.gov/citystore.

18. The address of New York Legal Publishing Corporation is www.nylp.com.

of New York City has contracted with New York Legal Publishing Corporation to provide a publicly accessible website for the charter, administrative code, and rules of New York City.[19]

The online Laws of New York have a section that includes New York City's unannotated administrative code. On the state legislature's website, click on the link to the "Laws of New York."[20] Scroll down through the listings of laws to find the "Miscellaneous" category, under which the administrative code is listed as "ADC."

V. New York City's Rules

A. Origin of Rules and Authority to Promulgate

The *Rules of the City of New York* are much like the *Code of Federal Regulations* and the *New York Code of Rules and Regulations* in function. The rules are promulgated by agencies of New York City government and outline the activities and procedures of agencies. The City Administrative Procedure Act, chapter 45 of the current charter, defines a rule as follows:

> 5. "Rule" means the whole or part of any statement or communication of general applicability that (i) implements or applies law or policy, or (ii) prescribes the procedural requirements of an agency including an amendment, suspension, or repeal of any such statement or communication.
>
> a. "Rule" shall include, but not be limited to, any statement or communication which prescribes (i) standards which, if violated, may result in a sanction or penalty; (ii) a fee to be charged by or required to be paid to an agency; (iii) standards for the issuance, suspension or revocation of a license or permit; (iv) standards for any product, material, or service which must be met before manufacture, distribution,

19. The address is http://home2.nyc.gov/html/law/html/about/laws.shtml.
20. The address is http://public.leginfo.state.ny.us/menuf.cgi.

sale or use; (v) standards for the procurement of goods and services; (vi) standards for the disposition of public property or property under agency control; or (vii) standards for the granting of loans or other benefits.[21]

Section 1043 (a) of the charter "empower[s] [agencies] to adopt rules necessary to carry out the powers and duties delegated to it by or pursuant to federal, state or local law."[22] An agency is required to publish any proposed amendment or change to its rules in the *City Record* at least thirty days prior to a public hearing or the final date of receipt for written comments.[23]

Appointed by the mayor, the Corporation Counsel serves as the head of the New York City Law Department. The Corporation Counsel and New York City Law Department review any proposed amendment or change to an agency's rules,[24] and no rule is effective until filed with the Corporation Counsel so that it may be published in the *Rules of the City of New York*.[25]

B. Organization of Rules

The rules are organized by agency, with titles reserved for future growth. The organization is reflected in Appendix 9-D.

C. Sources of Rules

1. In Print

The official compilation of agency rules is in the *Rules of the City of New York*, published by New York Legal Publishing Corporation.

---

21. *See* www.nyc.gov/html/charter/downloads/pdf/citycharter2009.pdf.

22. The address of the City's charter is www.nyc.gov/html/charter/downloads/pdf/citycharter2009.pdf.

23. *Charter of the City of New York* § 1043(b) (2009).

24. *Id.* § 1043(c).

25. *Id.* § 1043(e)(a).

This compilation includes historical and case notes, and is updated semi-annually.

2. *Online*

The Law Department of New York City has contracted with New York Legal Publishing Corporation to provide a publicly accessible website for the charter, administrative code, and rules of New York City.[26] New York Legal Publishing also offers online paid subscriptions to the annotated official compilation via its website.[27]

Both Lexis (NYCRUL) and Westlaw (NYC-RULES) have collections of New York City's annotated rules, as provided by New York Legal Publishing Corporation. Updated intermittently, the entries provide historical references and research notes.

In addition to the various formats of New York Legal Publishing Corporation's compilation, you may also search the agency website for its rules or contact the agency directly.

D. Opinions and Rulings

New York City administrative law includes agency rules and court opinions based on appeals of those rulings.

1. *Agency Rulings*

Much like agencies at the federal and state levels, New York City agencies hear and pass rulings on complaints. New York Law School publishes *CITYLAW*, a quarterly periodical, through its Center for New York City Law. Agency decisions of interest and court decisions that may impact agency rules are published, organized by topics such as education, environment, torts, contracts, and land use. The entries include a detailed summary of the case or complaint, and a citation reference. The coverage does not include all agency decisions.

---

26. The address is http://home2.nyc.gov/html/law/html/about/laws.shtml.

27. The address of New York Legal Publishing Corporation is www.nylp.com.

Table 9-4. Agency Decisions Included in New York Law School's CityAdmin

Business Integrity Commission	Commission on Human Rights
City Council Land Use	City Planning Commission
Conflicts of Interest Board	Dept. of Consumer Affairs
Dept. of Buildings	Landmarks Preservation Committee
Dept. of Investigation	Environmental Control Board
Loft Board	Office of Administrative Trials & Hearings
Mayor's Office of Contract Services	Tax Appeals Tribunal
Office of Collective Bargaining	Mayor's Executive Orders
Opinions of the Corporation Council	Board of Standards & Appeals
Taxi and Limo Commission	

Source: www.nyls.edu/centers/harlan_scholar_centers/center_for_new_york_city_law/city admin_library.

The Center for New York City Law at New York Law School houses a library of agency decisions in an Internet database, known as CityAdmin.[28] CityAdmin includes decisions from agencies listed in Table 9-4.

Each agency listing within CityAdmin includes a link that opens up a separate window. Clicking on an agency name in CityAdmin will lead to a definition of the agency, the scope and dates of coverage offered by the database, and an embedded link to the external official website of the agency.

2. *Actions Against Agencies, Opinions of the Corporation Counsel*

The Law Department of New York City is "attorney and counsel for the city and every agency thereof and shall have charge and con-

---

28. The address is www.nyls.edu/centers/harlan_scholar_centers/center_for_new_york_city_law/cityadmin_library.

duct of all the law business of the city and its agencies and in which the city is interested."[29] The Law Department defends agencies when they are sued and provides opinions on legal questions presented by agencies.

Lexis has opinions of the corporation counsel from November 7, 1980, through December 26, 2001 (NYCCC). Westlaw has coverage from 1980 to the present (NYC-CCO).

VI. New York City's Court System

A. Court Structure

Article 6, § 15 of the New York State Constitution established a "single court of city-wide civil jurisdiction and a single court of city-wide criminal jurisdiction in and for the city of New York." Hence, New York City has its own Civil Court and Criminal Court, from which appeals move to the Appellate Terms of the Supreme Court. There is a civil and criminal court in each county of New York City.

1. New York City Civil Court

New York City's civil court was defined by a 1962 state statute, the New York City Civil Court Act. Article 6, § 15(b) of the state constitution restricts New York City's civil court jurisdiction to

> actions and proceedings for the recovery of money, actions and proceedings for the recovery of chattels and actions and proceedings for the foreclosure of mechanics liens and liens on personal property where the amount sought to be recovered or the value of the property does not exceed twenty-five thousand dollars exclusive of interest and costs, or such smaller amount as may be fixed by law; over summary proceedings to recover possession of real property and to remove tenants therefrom and over such other actions and

29. *Charter of the City of New York* § 394(a) (2009).

> proceedings, not within the exclusive jurisdiction of the supreme court, as may be provided by law.

Under the New York City Civil Court Act § 1701, appeals move to the Appellate Terms of the Supreme Court.

2. New York City Criminal Court

In tandem with the Civil Court Act, the state legislature also passed the New York City Criminal Court Act in 1962. Section 31 of the Act defines the court's jurisdiction as covering crimes and offenses committed within New York City, including all charges of misdemeanor, except charges of libel and all offenses of a grade less than misdemeanor.

3. Other Courts in New York City

In addition to the civil and criminal courts in each county, New York City also has the following courts within its boundaries:

1) The Appellate Division, 1st Dept. (Bronx and New York Counties) and 2nd Dept. (Kings, Queens, Richmond Counties);
2) Surrogate's Court;
3) United States District Courts for the Southern and Eastern District;
4) Family Court;
5) Integrated Domestic Violence Court;
6) New York City Supreme Court;
7) Drug Treatment Court;
8) Mental Health Court;
9) Youthful Offender Domestic Violence Court; and
10) Community Court.

For more information about the state and city courts and the court system in general, consult the Unified Court System website.[30]

30. The website is www.nycourts.gov/courts/.

B. Court Rules

The rules of New York City's courts appear with the rules of the state's courts, published in the *New York Code of Rules and Regulations* (NYCRR). The New York City Civil Court rules are in 22 NYCRR part 208, titled "Uniform Civil Rules for the New York City Civil Court." The New York City Criminal Court rules are contained in 22 NYCRR part 200, titled "Uniform Rules for Courts Exercising Criminal Jurisdiction."

An unofficial version of the NYCRR is available online at www.dos.state.ny.us/info/nycrr.html. You may also consult Westlaw (NY-ADC) or Lexis (NYADMIN) for unofficial versions of NYCRR.

The court rules are also published in *Consolidated Laws Service* (CLS) and *McKinney's New York Rules of Court.* Lexis (NYRULE) and Westlaw (NY-RULES) offer searchable databases of all New York State court rules.

In addition, the Uniform Rules for the Civil Court of New York City[31] are available on the Unified Court System's website, and the Uniform Rules for Courts Exercising Criminal Jurisdiction[32] are available as well.

C. Case Law of New York City

1. In Print

Recent New York City cases are published in New York's *Miscellaneous Reports* (official) and West's *New York Supplement* (unofficial). The decisions are not organized by geographic location, however, so a citation is necessary to locate a case.

2. Online

Lexis provides decisions from New York City's civil court (CIVCT) and criminal court (CRIMCT). It also has New York City court opin-

---

31. The address for the civil rules is www.courts.state.ny.us/rules/trial courts/208.shtml.

32. The address for the criminal rules is www.courts.state.ny.us/rules/trialcourts/200.shtml.

ions (CITYCT) from 1888 to present. Westlaw has coverage of New York state court opinions since 1799 (NY-CS), but doesn't have a separate database for New York City decisions.

Appendix 9-A. Arrangement of the New York City Charter

Chapter/Title	Chapter/Title
1 Mayor	2 Council
2-A Districting Commission	4 Borough Presidents
5 Comptroller	6 Expense Budget
7 Tax Appeals	8 City Planning
9 Capital Projects and Budget	10 Budget Process
11 Independent Budget Office	12 Obligations of the City
13 Procurement	14 Franchises, Revocable Consents and Concessions
15 Property of the City	16 Heads of Mayoral Agencies
17 Law Department	18 Police Department
18-A Civilian Complaint Review Board	18-B Independent Police Investigation and Audit Board
18-C Public Safety	18-D Sale, Purchase and Possession of Weapons
19 Fire Department	19-A Emergency Management Department
20 Education	21 Department of Parks and Recreation
21-A New York City Sports Commission	22 Department of Health and Mental Hygiene
24 Department of Social Services	24-A Department of Homeless Services
24-B Administration for Children's Services	25 Department of Correction
26 Department of Buildings	27 Board of Standards and Appeals
28 Department of Juvenile Justice	30 Department of Youth and Community Development
31 Department of Sanitation	34 Department of Investigation

Appendix 9-A. Arrangement of the New York City Charter, *continued*

Chapter/Title	Chapter/Title
35 Department of Citywide Administrative Services	36 Equal Employment Practices Commission
37 Art Commission	38 Financial Information Services Agency
39 Office of Payroll Administration	40 New York City Human Rights Commission
45 City Administrative Procedure Act	45-A Office of Administrative Trials and Hearings
46 Elections and Voter Assistance	47 Public Access to Meetings and Information
48 Department of Information Technology and Telecommunications	49 Officers and Employees
50 Term Limits	51 Transitory Provisions
52 General Provisions	54 Collective Bargaining
55 Department of Design and Construction	56 Department of Small Business Services
57 Department of Environmental Protection	58 Department of Finance
61 Department of Housing Preservation and Development	63 Business Integrity Commission
64 Department of Consumer Affairs	65 New York City Taxi and Limousine Commission
66 Department for the Aging	67 Department of Cultural Affairs
68 Conflicts of Interest	69 Community Districts and Coterminality of Services
70 City Government in the Community	71 Department of Transportation
72 Department of Records and Information Services	73 Department of Employment
74 Landmarks Preservation Commission	

Appendix 9-B. Committees, Subcommittees, and Task Forces of the New York City Council

Aging	Civil Rights
Civil Service and Labor	Community Development
Consumer Affairs	Contracts
Cultural Affairs, Libraries and International Intergroup Relations	Economic Development
Education	Environmental Protection
Finance	Fire and Criminal Justice Services
General Welfare	Governmental Operations
Health	Higher Education
Housing and Buildings	Immigration
Juvenile Justice	Land Use
Lower Manhattan Redevelopment	Mental Health, Mental Retardation, Alcoholism, Drug Abuse and Disability Services
Oversight and Investigations	Parks and Recreation
Public Housing	Public Safety
Rules, Privileges and Elections	Sanitation and Solid Waste Management
Small Business	Standards and Ethics
State and Federal Legislation	Technology
Transportation	Veterans
Waterfronts	Women's Issues
Youth Services	Select Committee on Libraries
Subcommittee on Drug Abuse	Subcommittee on Landmarks, Public Siting and Maritime Uses
Subcommittee on Planning, Dispositions and Concessions	Subcommittee on Senior Centers
Subcommittee on Zoning and Franchises	Task Force on Hospital Closings
Task Force on Infrastructure	Task Force on the Operations & Improvements of the Department of Buildings

Source: http://legistar.council.nyc.gov/Departments.aspx.

Appendix 9-C. New York City's Current Administrative Code

TITLE 1. General Provisions	TITLE 2. City of New York
TITLE 3. Elected Officials	TITLE 4. Property of the City
TITLE 5. Budget; Capital Projects	TITLE 6. Contracts, Purchases and Franchises
TITLE 7. Legal Affairs	TITLE 8. Civil Rights
TITLE 9. Criminal Justice	TITLE 10. Public Safety
TITLE 11. Taxation and Finance	TITLE 12. Personnel and Labor
TITLE 13. Retirement and Pensions	TITLE 14. Police
TITLE 15. Fire Prevention and Control	TITLE 16. Sanitation
TITLE 16-A (Enacted without title. Subtitle: NYC Trade Waste Commission)	TITLE 17. Health
TITLE 18. Parks	TITLE 19. Transportation
TITLE 20. Consumer Affairs	TITLE 20-A. Shipboard Gambling
TITLE 21. Social Services	TITLE 22. Economic Affairs
TITLE 23. Communications	TITLE 24. Environmental Protection and Utilities
TITLE 25. Land Use	TITLE 26. Housing and Building
TITLE 27. Construction and Maintenance	TITLE 28. New York City Construction Codes
TITLE 29. New York City Fire Code	TITLE 30. Emergency Management (Effective date: 8/5/2011)

Source: http://public.leginfo.state.ny.us/menuf.cgi.

Appendix 9-D. Current Organization of Rules of the City of New York

TITLE 1. Department of Buildings	TITLE 2. Board of Standards and Appeals
TITLE 3. Fire Department	TITLE 4. [Reserved]
TITLE 5. [Reserved]	TITLE 6. Department of Consumer Affairs
TITLE 7. [Reserved]	TITLE 8. [Reserved]
TITLE 9. Procurement Policy Board Rules	TITLE 10. [Reserved]
TITLE 11. [Reserved]	TITLE 12. Franchise and Concession Review Committee
TITLE 13. [Reserved]	TITLE 14. [Reserved]
TITLE 15. Department of Environmental Protection	TITLE 16. Department of Sanitation
TITLE 17. Business Integrity Commission	TITLE 18. [Reserved]
TITLE 19. Department of Finance	TITLE 20. Tax Appeals Tribunal
TITLE 21. Tax Commission	TITLE 22. Banking Commission
TITLE 23. [Reserved]	TITLE 24. Department of Health and Mental Hygiene
TITLE 25. Department of Mental Health and Retardation	TITLE 26. [Reserved]
TITLE 27. [Reserved]	TITLE 28. Housing Preservation and Development
TITLE 29. Loft Board	TITLE 30. Rent Guidelines Board
TITLE 31. Mayor's Office of Homelessness and Single Room Occupancy	TITLE 32. [Reserved]
TITLE 33. [Reserved]	TITLE 34. Department of Transportation
TITLE 35. Taxi and Limousine Commission	TITLE 36. [Reserved]
TITLE 37. [Reserved]	TITLE 38. Police Department
TITLE 38-A. Civilian Complaint Review Board	TITLE 39. Department of Correction

Source: http://24.97.137.100/nyc/rcny/entered.htm.

Appendix 9-D. Current Organization of Rules of the City of New York, *continued*

TITLE 40. Board of Correction	TITLE 41. Department of Juvenile Justice
TITLE 42. Department of Probation	TITLE 43. Mayor
TITLE 44. Comptroller	TITLE 45. Borough Presidents
TITLE 46. Law Department	TITLE 47. Commission on Human Rights
TITLE 48. Office of Administrative Trials and Hearings (OATH)	TITLE 49. Department of Records and Information Services
TITLE 50. Community Assistance Unit	TITLE 51. City Clerk
TITLE 52. Campaign Finance Board	TITLE 53. Conflicts of Interest Board
TITLE 54. [Reserved]	TITLE 55. Department of Citywide Administrative Services
TITLE 56. Department of Parks and Recreation	TITLE 57. Art Commission
TITLE 58. Department of Cultural Affairs	TITLE 59. [Reserved]
TITLE 60. Civil Service Commission	TITLE 61. Office of Collective Bargaining
TITLE 62. City Planning	TITLE 63. Landmarks Preservation Commission
TITLE 64. [Reserved]	TITLE 65. [Reserved]
TITLE 66. Department of Small Business Services	TITLE 67. Department of Information Technology and Telecommunications
TITLE 68. Human Resources Administration	TITLE 69. Department of Aging
TITLE 70. In Rem Foreclosure Release	TITLE 71. Voter Assistance Commission

Chapter 10

Legal Ethics Research

I. Introduction to Legal Ethics Research

Having the skills necessary to research legal ethics issues will benefit anyone in the legal profession on more occasions than expected. For example, is a particular conversation covered by the attorney-client privilege? Are you asking your legal assistant to perform the duties of a lawyer? What duties do you owe to former clients?

Earlier chapters addressed locating cases, statutes, administrative regulations, and secondary sources. This chapter applies the skills from those chapters to locate relevant cases and statutes, and their counterparts such as model rules, ethics opinions, disciplinary proceedings, and commentary. Pieced together, these relevant sources provide answers to legal ethics issues.

Unlike other chapters in this book in which state and federal resources are considered separately, this chapter recognizes that the process of researching a New York ethics issue may naturally include resources from jurisdictions outside of New York. Typically, resources from other jurisdictions are considered when there is not enough New York precedent. American Bar Association (ABA) resources, for example, can be persuasive in New York courts when New York precedent is lacking. Consequently, the process of doing state-level ethics research may reach beyond the bounds of state resources and, therefore, this chapter considers sources from other jurisdictions at the same time.

II. The Model Code and Model Rules: A Brief History

The ABA has adopted many versions of rules governing conduct in the legal profession since its inception in 1878. Most notable for New York practitioners are the ABA's adoption of the *Model Code of Professional Responsibility* (Model Code) in 1969 and the ABA's subsequent adoption of the *Model Rules of Professional Conduct* (Model Rules) in 1983. To date, all fifty states have abandoned the Model Code and adopted the Model Rules in whole or in part.[1]

New York was the last state to transition from the Model Code format.[2] The New York State Bar Association (NYSBA) Committee on Standards of Attorney Conduct (COSAC) began reviewing the *New York Lawyer's Code of Professional Responsibility* (NYLCPR) in 2003. In 2007, COSAC presented the bar association with an overhauled version of the NYLCPR. The NYSBA House of Delegates adopted a resolution approving the *Proposed New York Rules of Professional Conduct* and forwarded them to the Appellate Division for consideration. The *New York Rules of Professional Conduct* were subsequently approved in 2008 and given an effective date of April 1, 2009.[3]

Table 10-1 provides a timeline of the development of rules regulating attorney conduct. The portions of the table in bold have or have had a direct impact on New York's code of ethics.

---

1. Model rules are not binding in a jurisdiction until adopted by the legislature, the highest court, or the bar association of the jurisdiction.

2. Roy Simon, *Comparing the New York Rules of Professional Conduct to The New York Code of Professional Responsibility* 2 (2009), *available at* www.nysba.org/Content/NavigationMenu/ForAttorneys/ProfessionalStandardsforAttorneys/CorrelationtableofnewNYrules.pdf.

3. *Id.*

Table 10-1. Timeline of Historical Development of Rules of Professional Ethics

1836	David Hoffman, founder of University of Maryland Law School, wrote fifty *Resolutions in Regard to Professional Development* for his students.
1854	Honorable George Sharswood, professor of law at University of Pennsylvania, published *A Compend[ium] of Lectures on the Aims and Duties of the Profession of Law.*
1887	David Goode Jones, an Alabama attorney, provided leadership that led to the adoption of the *Code of Ethics* by the Alabama Bar Association.
1908	The American Bar Association adopted the *Canons of Professional Ethics.*
1969	**The Special Committee on Evaluation of Ethical Standards produced, and the ABA adopted, the *Model Code of Professional Responsibility* (Model Code).**
1970	**New York adopted the Model Code, referred to as the *New York Lawyer's Code of Professional Responsibility* (NYLCPR).**
1977	The ABA Commission on Evaluation of Professional Standards (Kutak Commission) was formed to evaluate the Model Code. The Kutak Commission was instrumental in drafting the *Model Rules of Professional Conduct* (Model Rules).
1978	**The NYLCPR was extensively revised.**
1983	The ABA House of Delegates adopted the *Model Rules of Professional Conduct* (Model Rules), and most states subsequently adopted them.
1985	The New York State Bar Association House of Delegates rejected the proposal to adopt the Model Rules.
1990	**The NYLCPR was extensively revised.**
1997	The ABA Ethics 2000 Commission began writing new rules to address current issues. Subsequently, most remaining Model Code states adopted all or part of the Model Rules.
1999	**The NYLCPR was extensively revised under the Special Committee to Review the Code of Professional Responsibility (Krane Committee).**
2002	The ABA House of Delegates adopted significant revisions of the Model Rules based on the recommendations of the Kutak Commission.
2003	**The New York State Bar Association Committee on Standards of Attorney Conduct began evaluating the 2002 revisions to the Model Rules. The committee compared each Model Rules provision with the corresponding Model Code provision and selected the best characteristics of both.**
2007	**The New York State Bar Association House of Delegates adopted a resolution approving the Proposed New York Rules of Professional Conduct and forwarded them to the Appellate Division for consideration. The NYLCPR was extensively revised during the same year.**
2008	**The New York Rules of Professional Conduct were approved.**
2009	**New York Rules of Professional Conduct went into effect on April 1.**

III. Comparing the Style of the Old Rules to the New York Rules of Professional Conduct

A. New York Lawyer's Code of Professional Responsibility (NYLCPR)

The NYLCPR was composed of general standards, aspirational goals, and mandatory rules called Canons, Ethical Considerations (EC), and Disciplinary Rules (DR).

Canons were standards of professional conduct that were never formally adopted by the Appellate Division. In practice, Canons served as outline headings for the DRs. Violation of a Canon did not subject a lawyer to discipline.

EXAMPLE: Canon 2: *A lawyer should assist the legal profession in fulfilling its duty to make legal counsel available.*

Ethical Considerations (EC) were nonbinding, aspirational goals that evolved into best practices guidelines. In practice, ECs were sometimes used as guidance when interpreting DRs. Standing alone, however, a violation of an EC did not subject a lawyer to discipline.

EXAMPLE: EC 2-12: *In order to avoid the possibility of misleading persons with whom a lawyer deals, a lawyer should be scrupulous in the representation of professional status. A lawyer should not hold himself or herself out as being a partner or associate of a law firm if not one in fact, and thus should not hold himself or herself out as being a partner or associate if the lawyer only shares offices with another lawyer.*

Disciplinary Rules (DR) were minimum, mandatory standards of professional conduct that lawyers were to follow. Violation of a DR subjected a lawyer to discipline. The example below is a DR that is a subheading under Canon 2.

EXAMPLE: DR 2-102(C): *A lawyer shall not hold himself or herself out as having a partnership with one or more other lawyers unless they are in fact partners.*

B. New York Rules of Professional Conduct

When drafting the *Proposed New York Rules of Professional Conduct*, COSAC aimed to borrow the best of the Model Rules and the NYLCPR. For example, COSAC adopted the numbering scheme of the Model Rules so that New York's rules could be easily compared to the rules of other states. The adoption of a new numbering scheme eliminated the former distinctions between Canons, Ethical Considerations, and Disciplinary Rules. Further, the text of some Model Rules was also integrated into the proposed code[4] and subsequent adoption. For example, the text of DR 2-102(C) shown above was integrated, almost verbatim, into the *New York Rules of Professional Conduct* as Rule 7.5(C).

EXAMPLE: Rule 7.5(C): *Lawyers shall not hold themselves out as having a partnership with one or more other lawyers unless they are in fact partners.*

For a handy rules conversion chart and extensive commentary, see Roy Simon's comparisons, which often characterize the text of the new rules as "identical," "almost identical," and "similar in substance."[5]

---

4. "An effort was made to adopt the ABA Model Rule language for purposes of national uniformity absent some compelling reason to do otherwise." New York State Bar Association, Committee on Standards of Attorney Conduct, *Proposed New York Rules of Professional Conduct*, at ix, www.nysba.org (click on "Sections," click on "View Committees," click on "Committee on Standards of Attorney Conduct," and click on "Proposed New York Rules of Professional Conduct"). "COSAC endeavored to avoid following the Model Rules slavishly, while also not departing from them lightly." *Id.* at x (footnote omitted).

5. *See generally* Simon, *supra* note 2.

Table 10-2. Legal Ethics Research Steps

1. List the parties involved.
2. List the issues in keyword or short phrase form.
3. List all jurisdictions that could apply to your research problem.
4. Search the New York Rules of Professional Conduct and New York statutes.
5. Search New York ethics opinions and New York case law.
6. Assess whether your research is complete. If not, proceed to Step 7.
7. Seek resources from the ABA; if none exist, seek resources from other states as last resort precedent.
8. Consult relevant secondary sources.

IV. The Process of Legal Ethics Research

Legal ethics research involves pulling together many different primary and secondary resources, beginning at the state level. Table 10-2 is a basic checklist for organizing the research steps.

A. Preparation for Research

Steps 1 through 3 are preparation for your research. First, list the parties involved. Examples may include client, former client, prospective client, and paralegal.

Next, list all of the legal issues in your research problem in keyword or short phrase form. These keywords become your initial search terms in a print index or online database throughout the research process.

Then, consider the jurisdiction. Typically, legal ethics research takes place at the state level, but an ethics issue may involve more than one state. List all of the jurisdictions that could apply.

B. New York's Model Rules, New York Statutes, and Other Laws

Begin Step 4 by seeking relevant rules from the *New York Rules of Professional Conduct*. Selected print resources containing the text of the *New York Rules of Professional Conduct* include the following: Title 22 of the *Official Compilation of Codes, Rules and Regulations of the State of New York* (NYCRR); *ABA/BNA Lawyers' Manual on Professional Conduct*; *McKinney's New York Rules of Court*; *Simon's New York Rules of Professional Conduct Annotated*; book 29 (Judiciary Law) of *McKinney's Consolidated Laws of New York Annotated*;[6] and volume 19B (Judiciary Law) of *New York Consolidated Laws Service Annotated* (CLS). Online sources of the NYLCPR are listed in Table 10-3.

The research process for locating relevant sections of the *New York Rules of Professional Conduct* requires using the keywords created in Steps 1 through 3 of the research process outlined in Table 10-2. Using these keywords and the information you learned about statutory sources in Chapter 5 of this book, consult the print index or search online for relevant provisions. Refer to Chapter 2 for online search techniques. Remember that annotated sources like McKinney's and CLS provide summaries of cases and references to secondary sources below each rule. Other annotated sources, such as *Simon's New York Rules of Professional Conduct Annotated* is an invaluable source of commentary.

Continue Step 4 by researching New York statutes. Four areas of the New York code are likely to be relevant to an ethics issue. In addition to the N.Y. Judiciary Law,[7] thorough statutory research includes relevant portions of N.Y. Civil Practice Law and Rules,[8] N.Y. Penal Law,[9] and N.Y. General Business Law.[10]

---

6. The volume of book 29 that includes the text of the *New York Lawyer's Code of Professional Responsibility* was printed in 2003. Although the code of ethics was overhauled in 2009, the 2011 pocket part was not updated to include the text of the *New York Rules of Professional Conduct*.

7. N.Y. Judiciary Law, arts. 4, 15 (McKinney).

8. N.Y. C.P.L.R., arts. 2, 3, 20, 31, 45 (McKinney).

9. N.Y. Penal Law, arts. 210, 215, 250 (McKinney).

10. N.Y. Gen. Bus. Law, art. 22A (McKinney).

Table 10-3. Selected Online Sources for the *New York Rules of Professional Conduct*

Current Rules	Web Address	Free or Commercial
Bureau of National Affairs	www.bna.com	Commercial source that links to free resource
Department of State (N.Y.)	www.dos.ny.gov/info/nycrr.html	Free
Legislative Retrieval System	http://nyslrs.state.ny.us	Commercial
Lexis	www.lexis.com	Commercial
New York State Bar Association	www.nysba.org (click on "For Attorneys" and click on "Professional Standards for Attorneys")	Free
New York State Legislature	http://public.leginfo.state.ny.us (click on "Laws of New York")	Free
New York State Unified Court System	www.nycourts.gov/rules/joint appellate/index.shtml	Free
Westlaw	www.westlaw.com	Commercial

Federal and state court rules, discussed in Chapter 5, also play a role in regulating lawyer conduct. A research problem may also involve federal laws and regulations. For example, the federal Securities and Exchange Commission (SEC), in 17 CFR part 205, outlines rules regulating the conduct of attorneys appearing or practicing before the SEC. New York attorneys appearing before the SEC are, therefore, subject to these federal regulations. Another useful example is the First Amendment to the United States Constitution because the right to free speech is relevant to issues surrounding lawyer advertising.

Although researching judicial ethics is not covered in this book, it is important to know that professional standards for judges are distinct from the professional standards for practitioners in New York. Judicial ethics are governed by the *New York Code of Judicial Conduct* adopted by the New York State Bar Association, the *Code of Judicial Conduct* adopted by the Chief Administrative Judge of the Courts, and the rules of the Appellate Division.

C. New York Opinions

In Step 5, seek ethics opinions and documents from disciplinary proceedings. Relevant New York case law may also be a useful resource. To locate cases, use a print or online digest or a case law database. Refer back to Chapter 4 for the process of doing a print or online digest search.

1. Ethics Opinions

Ethics opinions, issued by the NYSBA Committee on Professional Ethics, are advisory statements addressing an attorney's anticipated future conduct. They are not binding on New York courts but may be persuasive in disciplinary proceedings. Simple issues are addressed by the committee briefly by phone or in writing to the individual attorney. Complex issues are addressed as formal ethics opinions available in full text on the NYSBA website.[11] There are more than eight hundred ethics opinions dating back to 1964. Browse by ethics opinion number if known. Consult the online index for access to ethics opinions by topic.

NYSBA ethics opinions are available in many print and electronic sources, including Lexis and Westlaw with coverage back to 1988 and 1977, respectively. The *ABA/BNA Lawyers' Manual on Professional Conduct* (Lawyers' Manual) is available as a print or online source. It includes ethics opinions back to 1980. The *National Reporter on Legal Ethics & Professional Responsibility*, published by Lexis, makes available in print and online ethics opinions for every state.

Ethics opinions are also issued by local bar associations. Typically, they are available on bar association websites. For example, the New

11. The formal ethics opinions are available at www.nysba.org (click on "For Attorneys" and select "Ethics Opinions").

York County Lawyers' Association provides the full text of ethics opinions issued since 1912.[12] Advisory opinions for selected local bar associations can also be retrieved online through Lexis and Westlaw. To locate relevant ethics opinions in online resources, run searches using the keywords created in the legal ethics checklist.

2. *Disciplinary Proceedings*

Attorney discipline is overseen by the Appellate Division. Attorneys practicing within a department are subject to the department's rules. There are eight committees of the Appellate Division: the first and third departments each have one committee, and the second and fourth departments each have three committees, divided by county. The eight committees are listed on the Unified Court System website[13] with links to each department's website. Table 10-4 provides the name of each department's committee(s), the applicable rules, and the relevant websites.

Under N.Y. Judiciary Law § 90, disciplinary proceedings are private and confidential, and all documents are sealed. If the formal disciplinary proceedings result in charges or public discipline, the documents relating to the disciplinary proceedings become public record. Grievance committees are established according to the geography of judicial departments. Some judicial department websites provide the text of disciplinary decisions.[14]

D. Precedent from Other Jurisdictions and Secondary Sources

Steps 7 and 8 are optional and should be explored if your research is not complete after the first six steps. Your research is complete if

---

12. These ethics opinions are available at www.nycla.org (click on "News & Publications" and then "Ethics Opinions").

13. The address is www.nycourts.gov/ip/attorneygrievance/complaints_attorney.shtml.

14. For example, the Third Judicial Department makes its decisions available at www.nycourts.gov/ad3 (click on "Search Decisions").

Table 10-4. Disciplinary Committees of the Appellate Division

Appellate Division	Committee(s)	Appellate Division Rules	Committee Website
First Department	Disciplinary Committee	22 NYCRR Part 603	www.courts.state.ny.us/courts/ad1/Committees& Programs/DDC/index.shtml
Second Department	Grievance Committees	22 NYCRR Part 691	www.courts.state.ny.us/courts/ad2/attorneymatters _ComplaintAboutaLawyer.shtml (click on "The Grievance Committees")
Third Department	Committee on Professional Standards	22 NYCRR § 806	www.courts.state.ny.us/ad3/cops/index.html
Fourth Department	Grievance Committees	22 NYCRR Part 1022	www.nycourts.gov/ad4 (click on "Attorney Grievance Committees")

you have enough New York sources to address your legal issue. If your research does not seem complete, try the following sources.

Precedent from other jurisdictions may hold weight in New York courts when New York precedent is lacking. Using your keywords, consult professional codes and ethics opinions from the ABA. Relevant precedent from other jurisdictions may be pursued for guidance but is merely persuasive authority.

Secondary sources are another excellent resource. Consult resources such as the *Restatement of the Law: The Law Governing Lawyers, 3d*; law review articles; and other sources of commentary. The *Restatement of the Law: The Law Governing Lawyers, 3d*, available in print and on Lexis and Westlaw, contains black letter law (i.e., fundamental statements of legal principles) and commentary about ethical issues pertaining to attorney conduct. Use your keywords to search the print index or online in Lexis or Westlaw.

Law review articles and treatises are additional secondary sources for legal ethics research. Locate law review articles by using your keywords in the *Index to Legal Periodicals and Books* or *Current Law Index* in print or online. In addition, Lexis's and Westlaw's law review databases or HeinOnline's Law Journal Library contain the full text of law review articles. Refer to Chapter 3 of this book for the availability of additional online secondary sources.

Chapter 11

Research Strategies and Organization

The purpose of legal research is to solve a client's problem. Doing so is easier if you begin with a clear research strategy and stay organized as you conduct research.

I. Planning a Research Strategy

The research process presented in Chapter 1 contains six steps: (1) generate a list of *research terms*; (2) consult *secondary sources* and practice aids; (3) find controlling *constitutional provisions*, *statutes*, or *administrative rules*; (4) research *judicial opinions*; (5) *update* your legal authorities with a citator; and (6) *end* your research when you have no holes in your analysis and when you begin seeing the same authorities repeatedly. Table 11-1 outlines how you should use these six steps to plan a research strategy.

A. Which Process?

In the initial phases, planning a research strategy means considering these six steps and then deciding where to begin and how to proceed. These decisions will vary for each project. When researching an unfamiliar area of law, you will probably be more successful beginning with secondary sources. If you are familiar with an area of statutory law from previous work, your research may be more effective if you go directly to an annotated code. As a third example, if you are work-

Table 11-1. Planning a Research Strategy

A. Consider the six fundamental research steps, and decide where to begin based on the particular project. Make initial determinations of whether each step is needed and in which order to proceed.

B. Decide which resources to use for each step of your research plan.

C. Determine whether to research in print or online at each step.

ing for another attorney who gives you a citation to a case she knows is relevant, you may want to begin by Shepardizing or KeyCiting the case, or by using the case's topics and key numbers in a West digest. Both steps may quickly provide more cases on point. Finally, if you know that the issue is controlled by common law, you may feel comfortable not researching statutory or constitutional provisions, or spending very little time in those areas. As you consider this phase of research, write a quick strategy for this particular project, listing the research steps you will take in the order you have chosen.

Although your research strategy will be written in a series of discrete steps, the research process is not necessarily linear. Efficient research sometimes requires jumping back and forth between steps. Research terms are useful in searching secondary sources and statutes as well as digests, so circling back to the first step is common. A secondary source may cite a relevant case that you decide to read immediately, not two steps later. Updating may reveal more cases that you need to read, or it may uncover a new law review article that is on point. As you learn more about a project, you may want to review whether your earlier research was effective. Even as you begin writing, you may need to do more research if new issues arise or if you need more support for an argument. Circling back and skipping forward are normal aspects of legal research. Reviewing your research strategy frequently will ensure that you do not inadvertently forget a fundamental research step.

B. Which Resources?

The first question about which resources to use is answered by the jurisdiction whose law controls. Do not search New York statutes if an issue is controlled by Delaware law. After determining the jurisdiction, though, you still have multiple decisions about resources.

Most steps in the research process can be conducted in a variety of resources. In secondary sources, for example, you could begin with a treatise, a practice guide, an article, an encyclopedia, an ALR annotation, or many other sources. In researching New York statutes in print, you could use *McKinney's Consolidated Law of New York Annotated* (published by West) or *New York Consolidated Laws Service* (published by LexisNexis). The relevant chapters of this book suggest which resources are more likely to be helpful for particular projects. In particular, Chapter 3 ends with suggestions for choosing among secondary sources.

C. Which Media?

Many of the resources available for legal research exist both in print and online. Consider which media you have available and their relative costs, as explored in Chapter 2. Then consider your own research experiences and strengths. Some researchers instinctively prefer print or online research media. Many researchers quickly develop a personal preference for either Lexis or Westlaw for online research, even though their search capacities are almost identical. When learning about a new online resource, you may benefit from reviewing the print version first. A few minutes spent flipping through a book can save you time in understanding the online options.

The choice between print and online media should be made at each step. Some attorneys prefer using secondary sources in print, while almost all attorneys use online citators.

II. Taking Notes

A. Research Notes

As you conduct research, take careful notes. Taking notes on your research strategy (the process you wrote out at the beginning of the project) can help you avoid duplicating steps, especially if you have to interrupt your research for a notable length of time.

For each new resource, make notes that summarize your work in that resource. For print research, include the volumes you used, the indexes or tables you reviewed, the terms you searched for, and the search results. For online research, include the vendor or the site, the specific database or link, and the searches that you entered. Note the date that you performed each search. When working with Lexis and Westlaw, use their "History" and "Research Trail" functions to keep track of online searches. Keep track of both successful and unsuccessful index terms and searches so that you do not inadvertently repeat these same steps later, or so you can revisit a "dead end" that later becomes relevant.

B. Analytical Notes

In addition to taking notes on the research process, take notes on your developing analysis. These notes provide a basis for organizing your thoughts and preparing your arguments. Analytical notes do not have to be formal or typed; in fact, you might waste valuable time by following too much structure or stopping to type notes. You should not, however, underestimate the learning process that occurs while taking analytical notes. Deciding what is important enough to include in notes and expressing those ideas in your own words will increase your understanding of the legal issues involved. Simply printing and highlighting do not provide this same analytical advantage. At the least, you should take analytical notes on all relevant secondary sources, enacted law, cases, and updating.

1. *Secondary Sources*

Write a one-page summary for each secondary source you consult. Begin the summary with the title, author, and other citation information for the source. In your own words, summarize the relevant analysis in the source, including references to specific pages. Try to include a few sentences—written in your own words—explaining how this source relates to your research. Does it give the background of a statute? Does it trace the development of a line of cases? Does it criticize the law in your jurisdiction? Does it suggest a novel approach to your problem? Additionally, note any references to primary authorities that may be on point, and include these in a list of primary authorities (explained below).

2. *Enacted Law*

Notes on enacted laws—constitutional provisions, statutes, and administrative rules—should include both the actual language that was enacted and your outline of it. Because the exact words of enacted law are so important, you should print or photocopy the text of these provisions. Be sure to refer to the definition sections of statutes; when important terms are not defined, make a note to look for judicial definitions. Also be sure to read statutes or regulations that are cross-referenced. As noted in Chapter 5 on statutes and in Chapter 7 on administrative law, to fully understand a complex statute or rule, you should outline it. Highlighting is sufficient only if the statute or rule is very short and clear.

3. *Case Briefs and Updating*

If a case is relevant, brief it. The brief does not have to follow any formal style. Instead, the brief for each case should be a set of notes that highlight the key aspects of the case that are relevant for your research problem. You may choose to write this brief on your computer, creating a document or a page of a document for each case. You might prefer to write your brief on your legal pad or create an index card. Each case brief should include the case's citation, the relevant facts, the holding and the court's reasoning, pinpoint pages on which critical information appears, and your thoughts on the case.

Be sure to note on each brief the date that you updated each case with either KeyCite or Shepard's. Printing lists of citing references is an easy and efficient way to compare new citations with other lists of relevant authorities to avoid duplication.

III. Organizing Research

Legal research often produces many documents that must be organized along with your notes. Even in online research, key documents must be printed and properly formatted to ensure careful reading and comprehension. Thus, you need to develop methods of keeping documents organized and sorting out your analysis.

If you decide to print your materials, for a large project you will likely need a three-ring binder or a set of files in which you keep hard copies of the most important authorities. Using tabs can keep you from flipping endlessly through documents.

If you decide that an electronic file system for your documents is more suitable, develop a virtual filing system that is easy for you to remember and to add to as your research grows. You can do this either through the use of files and subfiles, or through extensive "tagging"[1] of your files. Try to label individual documents and files with meaningful titles and the date you added each one to your collection. When using a solely electronic filing system for your research, be sure to back up your research files by using an in-house server, using any of the free web-based cloud services that allow for file upload and encryption, or using a detachable storage device.[2]

---

1. Tagging is a simple method of assigning meaning to a document through self-generated descriptions of its contents. Much of the functionality of tagging is superseded by well-constructed file names, but may be a useful addition for PDFs, images, or audiovisual material.

2. The authors suggest backing up in at least two different ways.

Whether you are working off a printed or electronic filing system, create a list of primary sources that contains the name and citation for all the primary authorities that you need to read. Throughout your research, as you come across a potentially relevant authority, include it on the list. This method will allow you to maintain your train of thought with one resource while ensuring that you keep track of important cites to check later. After creating a list that includes a number of sources, check for duplicates before reading the authorities.

Once you have selected a number of relevant authorities, choose an organizational scheme for reading them carefully in groups. If there is a constitutional provision, statute, or rule on point, begin by reading it carefully and then move to reading cases that interpret the provision. One approach is to read cases in chronological order so that you see the development of the law over time. This may be time consuming for causes of action that have existed for many years. Except for historical research, impose an artificial cut-off of twenty or thirty years in the past, so that you put your effort into recent law. The opposite approach works in many situations: by beginning with the recent cases, you avoid spending time learning old law that has been revised or superseded.

As you read the relevant authorities, look for common themes and group cases accordingly. Pay attention to parts that you may have skipped earlier while skimming. Read carefully the definitions in statutes. Consider organizing cases by which portion of a statute they interpret or apply. As you read through each case, cross out portions dealing with legal issues that are not confronting your client. If you decide that the case is actually not important, mark that on the first page so that you will not waste time reading it again.

When researching several issues or related claims, consider them one at a time. In this instance, you may have several lists of primary authorities, one for each claim you are researching. You may want to create a different section in your binder or a different folder on your computer for each claim.

IV. Outlining the Analysis

Because the most effective research often occurs in conjunction with the analysis of your particular project, try to develop an outline that addresses your client's problem as soon as you can. If outlining feels too restrictive, you may benefit from a chart that organizes all the primary authority by issue or element, such as in Table 11-2. This chart can be easily adapted into an outline of your legal argument following the typical legal analysis format of Issue-Rule-Application-Conclusion (IRAC). In the first column, the chart summarizes the legal rule, the relevant facts, and the court's reasoning. In the right-hand column, the chart applies the cases to the client's problem and reaches a conclusion.

Your first analytical outline or chart may be based on information in a secondary source, the requirements of a statute, or the elements of a common law claim. It will become more sophisticated and detailed as you conduct your research. Recognize that you cannot reread every case or statute in its entirety each time you need to include it in your outline; instead, refer to your notes and briefs to find the key ideas supporting each step in your analysis.

V. Ending Research

One of the most difficult problems researchers face is deciding when to stop researching and begin writing. Only rarely will you find a legal authority that answers the client's question clearly and definitively. Even without finding a clear answer, when your research in various sources leads back to the same authorities, you can be confident that you have been thorough. As a final checklist, go through your research strategy to ensure you considered each step of the basic research process.

If you have worked through the research process and found nothing, it may be that nothing exists. Before reaching that conclusion, expand your research terms and look in a few more secondary sources. Consider whether other jurisdictions may have helpful persuasive authority.

Table 11-2. Sample Analysis Chart

Client's Facts: A synagogue is a client of your firm. Today, the rabbi called to ask about a subpoena requiring her to testify at the upcoming trial of a member of the congregation. The rabbi remembers having conversations with the man about theft, deception, and forgiveness. The conversations took place after religious events when the two were alone as the man was helping the rabbi clean up the meeting room.

Statutory Requirement: Spiritual advisor cannot disclose "a confession or confidence" made to the advisor acting in his/her "professional character." CPLR § 4505.

Issues:
1. Were the conversations "confessions or confidences"?
2. Was the rabbi acting in a "professional character" when talking to the man?

<table>
<tr><th></th><th>Rule and Facts from Cases</th><th>Application to Client and Conclusion</th></tr>
<tr><td colspan="3">1. Confidence</td></tr>
<tr><td>Carmona
627 N.E.2d 959</td><td>Conversation is confidential if defendant intended it to be so; one that took place in the advisor's garden was likely intended to be confidential.</td><td rowspan="2">Conversations between rabbi and defendant in synagogue meeting rooms were likely confidential both because the defendant likely intended them to be confidential and because the defendant had a reasonable expectation of confidentiality. No one was with them to hear the conversation.</td></tr>
<tr><td>Reyes
545 N.Y.S.2d 653</td><td>Conversation is confidential if defendant had a reasonable expectation that it would be kept secret; conversation in church rectory can show expectation of confidentiality.</td></tr>
<tr><td colspan="3">2. Professional character</td></tr>
<tr><td>Carmona
627 N.E.2d 959</td><td>Spiritual advisor acts in professional character when defendant is seeking spiritual advice; praying, crying, and discussing faith after a religious meeting showed defendant sought advice.</td><td rowspan="2">Rabbi was probably acting in a spiritual capacity because the defendant asked about deception, theft, and forgiveness after a religious event in the synagogue.</td></tr>
<tr><td>Cox
296 F.3d 89</td><td>Emotional discussion between members of Alcoholics Anonymous did not show defendant sought spiritual advice.</td></tr>
</table>

Beyond these analytical considerations, often deadlines imposed by the court or a supervisor will limit the amount of time spent on a research project. The expense to the client will also be a consideration.

In conducting research, remember that the goal is to solve a client's problem. Sometimes the law will not seem to support the solution that your client had in mind. Think creatively to address the client's problem in a different way. While you must tell your supervisor or your client when a desired approach is not feasible, you will want to have prepared an alternate solution if possible.

Appendix A

Legal Citation

Lawyers use legal citations to prove that the arguments in their legal documents are well researched and that their analysis is well supported. Legal citations tell the reader where to find the authorities relied on and indicate the level of analytical support those authorities provide.[1] Because citation information is given in abbreviated form, using a uniform and widely recognized format ensures that the reader will understand the information being conveyed.

This appendix addresses the format used to convey citation information. First the appendix addresses the two national citation manuals, the *ALWD Citation Manual: A Professional System of Citation* (the "ALWD Manual")[2] and *The Bluebook: A Uniform System of Citation* (the "Bluebook").[3] Then the appendix turns to the *New York*

---

1. In practice documents like office memoranda and court briefs, legal citations are typically included in the text of legal documents rather than being placed in footnotes or listed in a bibliography.

2. Ass'n of Legal Writing Dirs. & Darby Dickerson, *ALWD Citation Manual* (4th ed. 2010) ("ALWD Manual"). In this appendix, footnote references to the ALWD Manual will include first the rule number and then the page number (e.g., ALWD Rule 12.12(a), pages 94–95). Rule numbers are likely to remain the same in subsequent editions, though the page numbers may change.

3. *The Bluebook: A Uniform System of Citation* (Columbia Law Review Ass'n et al. eds., 19th ed. 2010) ("Bluebook"). In this appendix, footnote references to the Bluebook will include first the rule number and then the page number (e.g., Bluebook Rule 18.1.1, pages 151–52). Rule numbers are likely to remain the same in subsequent editions, though the page numbers may change.

Law Reports Style Manual (the "Tan Book" or "NYSM").[4] This citation manual is used "as a guide for New York judges and their staffs in the preparation of opinions for publication in the Official Reports."[5] It is not binding on lawyers, but "many lawyers find the Manual useful in preparing papers for submission to New York courts."[6] The ALWD Manual, the Bluebook, and the NYSM are reference manuals, like dictionaries and thesauri. The key to good citation format is to learn the general structure of the manual preferred by your office and to know how to use it, not to read all three manuals cover-to-cover.

I. National Citation Manuals

The two most widely used national citation manuals are the ALWD Manual and the Bluebook. Both are large booklets that contain hundreds of pages of citation rules, examples, and explanations.

The ALWD Manual is considered by many the best citation manual for novices and for practitioners because it uses a single system of citation for legal memoranda, court documents, law review articles, and all other legal documents. The explanations are clear, and the examples are given in the format required in the memoranda and briefs attorneys write.

The Bluebook is the oldest, most widely known citation manual. The difficulty with this manual is that it contains two different citation formats: one for law review footnotes and another for practice documents. Most of the Bluebook's explanations and examples are relevant to law review footnotes, which use different fonts (e.g., italics, large and small capitals) than citations in practice documents.

4. *New York Law Reports Style Manual* (Katherine D. LaBoda et al. eds., 2007) ("NYSM"). This manual is prepared by the Law Reporting Bureau of the State of New York and approved by the New York Court of Appeals. In this appendix, footnote references to the NYSM will give just the rule number (e.g., NYSM Rule 2.1).

5. NYSM, Preface to the 2007 edition.

6. *Id.*

Even so, the Bluebook is so well known that most attorneys use the term "Bluebooking" to mean checking citations for consistent format.

A. Navigating the ALWD Manual and the Bluebook

1. Index

The index at the back of each manual is quite extensive, and in most instances it is more helpful than the table of contents. Most often, you should begin working with a citation manual by referring to the index. In the Bluebook, page numbers given in black type refer to citation instructions, while page numbers in blue refer to examples.

2. "Fast Formats" and "Quick Reference"

Many chapters of the ALWD Manual begin with citation examples, in tables called "Fast Formats." A list of these "Fast Formats" is provided on the inside front cover of the ALWD Manual.

The Bluebook contains two "Quick Reference" guides. The one on the inside front cover provides sample citations for law review footnotes. The guide on the inside back cover gives example citations for court documents and legal memoranda.

3. Bluebook "Bluepages"

The Bluebook opens with a section devoted to citations for practitioners; these "Bluepages" appear on pages 3 through 51. The Bluepages provide information for and additional examples of citations used in documents other than law review articles.[7] When using

---

7. The Bluepages are helpful in knowing which font to use in practice document citations. The Bluepages list the following items that should be italicized or underlined in citations in legal memoranda and court documents: case names, titles of books and articles, and introductory signals. Items not included in the list should appear in regular type. Remember to follow the instructions in the Bluepages even when other Bluebook examples include large and small capital letters.

the Bluebook, remember that only the Bluepages and the reference guide at the back of the manual provide examples for practice documents. Thus, a student or lawyer using the Bluebook must use the Bluepages to translate other examples from law review format into the format used in practice documents.

4. ALWD Appendices and Bluebook Tables

The back of each citation manual contains lists of abbreviations and other helpful information. In the ALWD Manual, these are called "appendices."[8] Blue-edged pages at the back of the Bluebook contain "tables" with similar information.[9]

B. Citing New York Material

Because these manuals are designed for national use, their citations for New York material vary from the formats used in the NYSM. A summary of abbreviations for New York material appears in Appendix 1 (on pages 433–434) of the ALWD Manual and in Table T.1 (on pages 253–57) of the Bluebook. Examples are included in Table A-1 in this section. Compare these examples to the New York citations shown in Table A-5 later in this appendix.

C. Case Citations

1. Full Citations to Cases

In both ALWD and Bluebook format, a full citation to a case includes (1) the name of the case, (2) the volume and reporter in which the case is published, (3) the first page of the case, (4) the exact page in the case that contains the idea you are citing (i.e., the *pinpoint* or *jump* cite), (5) the court that decided the case, and (6) the date the

8. ALWD pages 405–625.
9. Bluebook pages 215–473.

Table A-1. Example New York Citations in ALWD and Bluebook Format

Type of Document	ALWD Format	Bluebook Format
State Constitution	N.Y. Const. art. VI, § 35.	N.Y. Const. art. VI, § 35.
State Statute	N.Y. Penal Law § 80.05 (McKinney 2004).	N.Y. Penal Law § 80.05 (McKinney 2004).
State Regulation*	12 N.Y. Comp. Codes, R. & Regs. 23-1.7(b)(1) (2008).	12 N.Y. Comp. Codes, R. & Regs. tit. 23, § 1.7(b)(1) (2008).
State Case	*People v. Moran*, 2 A.D.3d 216 (App. Div. 1st Dept. 2003).	*People v. Moran*, 768 N.Y.S.2d 313 (App. Div. 2003).

* The most common citation format for New York regulations comes from explanatory material appearing at the front of every volume of the *Official Compilation of Codes, Rules and Regulations of the State of New York*: 1 NYCRR 38.9. This format differs from the requirements of the ALWD Manual, the Bluebook, and the NYSM.

case was decided.[10] The key points for citation to cases are given below, along with examples.

Include the name of just the first party on each side, even if several are listed in the case caption. If the party is an individual, include only the party's last name. If the party is a business or organization, shorten the party's name by using abbreviations provided in the citation manual you are using.[11] The Bluebook's list of abbreviations is much shorter than the list in the ALWD Manual, and some of the abbreviations are slightly different. See Table A-2 in this section for a comparison of abbreviations from the three manuals. Note that in the Bluebook "United States" is never abbreviated when it is a party's name.[12] Between the parties' names, place a lower case "v" followed by a period. Place a comma after the second party's name, but do not italicize or underline this comma.

10. ALWD Rule 12, pages 71–118; Bluebook Rule 5.1, pages 15–18.
11. ALWD Appendix 3, pages 527–37; Bluebook Table T.6, pages 430–31.
12. Bluebook Rule 10.2.2, page 94.

Table A-2. Comparison of Selected Abbreviations in ALWD, Bluebook, and NYSM Formats

Word	ALWD (Appendix 3)	Bluebook (Table T.6)	NYSM (Appendix 1)
Associate	Assoc.	Assoc.	Assoc.
Association	Assn. or Ass'n	Ass'n	Assn.
Center	Ctr.	Ctr.	Ctr.
Department	Dept. or Dep't	Dep't	Dept.
Executive	Exec.	*	Exec.
Lawyer	Law.	*	*
National	Natl. or Nat'l	Nat'l	Natl.
Shipping	Ship.	*	*
University	U.	Univ.	Univ.

* The three manuals abbreviate different words, and words don't necessarily appear in all three manuals.

The parties' names may be italicized or underlined. Use the style preferred by your office consistently throughout each document.[13] Do not combine italics and underlining in one cite or within a single document.

EXAMPLE: *Bartlett v. N.Y. State Bd. of Law Exam'rs*, 226 F.3d 69, 80 (2d Cir. 2000).

Next, give the volume and the reporter in which the case is found.[14] Always note carefully whether the reporter is in its first, second, third, or fourth series.[15] In the *Bartlett* example above, 226 is the

13. ALWD Rule 12.2(a) (case names), page 71, and Rule 1 (typeface choice), page 3; Bluebook Rule B1, page 4.

14. For cases available only on Lexis or Westlaw, follow ALWD Rule 12.12(a), pages 94–95, and Bluebook Rule B4.1.4, page 11, and Rule 18.3.1, pages 171–72.

15. Abbreviations for common reporters are found on page 87 of the ALWD Manual; abbreviations for reporters for New York cases are included on pages 433–34. The Bluebook does not have a comprehensive list of common reporters; check Table T.1 on pages 193–242 for reporters in a partic-

volume number and F.3d is the reporter abbreviation for *Federal Reporter, Third Series.*

After the reporter name, include both the first page of the case and the pinpoint page containing the idea that you are referencing, separated by a comma and a space.[16] The first page of the *Bartlett* case above is 69, and the page containing the specific idea being cited is 80. To cite a span of pages, use an en dash or hyphen (e.g., 80–81).[17] If the pinpoint page you are citing is also the first page of the case, then the same page number will appear twice.[18]

In a parenthetical following this information, indicate the court that decided the case.[19] In Appendix 1 of the ALWD Manual and in Table T.1 of the Bluebook, the notations for the courts of each jurisdiction are included in parentheses just after the name of the court. In the *Bartlett* example, the Second Circuit Court of Appeals, a federal court, decided the case.

If the reporter abbreviation clearly indicates which court decided a case, do not repeat this information in the parenthetical. To give an example, only cases of the United States Supreme Court are reported in *United States Reports*, abbreviated U.S. Repeating court notation (U.S.) in citations to that reporter would be duplicative. By contrast, *North Eastern Reporter, Second Series*, abbreviated N.E.2d, publishes

---

ular jurisdiction. Abbreviations for reporters for New York cases are given in the Bluebook on pages 253–54.

16. ALWD Rule 5, pages 36–38, and Rule 12.5, pages 92–93; Bluebook Rule B4.1.2, page 9.

17. ALWD Rule 5.2, page 39; Bluebook Rule 3.2, page 67. For page numbers containing more than two digits, the ALWD Rule allows either the form 113–115 or the form 113–15. The Bluebook allows only the latter. Neither permits the form 113–5.

18. When using an online version of a case, remember that a reference to a specific reporter page may change in the middle of a computer screen or a printed page. Thus, the page number indicated at the top of the screen or printed page may not be the page where the relevant information is located. For example, if the notation *821 appeared in the text before the relevant information, the pinpoint cite would be to page 821, not page 820.

19. ALWD Rule 12.6(a), page 93; Bluebook Rule B4.1.3, page 10.

decisions from different courts within several states, so the court that decided a particular case needs to be indicated parenthetically. Thus, in the second example below, "N.Y." indicates that the decision came from the New York Court of Appeals rather than from another court whose decisions are also published in this reporter.

EXAMPLES: *Brown v. Bd. of Educ.*, 349 U.S. 294, 300 (1955).
People v. Carmona, 627 N.E.2d 959, 963 (N.Y. 1993).

The final piece of required information in most cites is the date the case was decided. For cases published in reporters, give only the year of decision,[20] not the month or date.[21]

Prior and subsequent history can be added to the end of a citation, as shown in the example below.[22]

EXAMPLE: The only time that the Supreme Court addressed the requirement of motive for an EMTALA claim, the court rejected that requirement. *Roberts v. Galen of Va.*, 525 U.S. 249, 253 (1999), *rev'g* 111 F.3d 405 (6th Cir. 1997).

2. *Short Citations to Cases*

After a full citation has been used once to introduce an authority, short citations are subsequently used to cite the same authority.[23] When the immediately preceding cite is to the same source and the same page, use *id.* as the short cite. When the second cite is to a different page within the same source, follow the *id.* with "at" and the new pinpoint page number. Capitalize *id.* when it begins a citation sentence, just as the beginning of any sentence is capitalized.[24]

---

20. ALWD Rule 12.7, pages 97–98; Bluebook Rule B4.1.3, page 10, and Rule 10.5, page 99.

21. For cases available only online, give the month abbreviation, date, and year. ALWD Rule 12.12(a), pages 105–106; Bluebook Rule B4.1.4, page 11, and Rule 18.3.1, page 171.

22. ALWD Rules 12.8–12.10, pages 98–103; Bluebook Rule B4.1.6, pages 12–13.

23. ALWD Rule 12.20, pages 114–118; Bluebook Rule B4.2, pages 13–15.

24. ALWD Rule 11.3(d), page 60; Bluebook Rule B4.2, page 14.

If the cite is from a previously cited case that is not the immediately preceding cite, give the name of one of the parties (generally the first party named in the full cite), the volume, the reporter, and the pinpoint page following "at."[25] The format "*Brown* at 300," consisting of just a case name and page number, is incorrect under both of the national citation manuals. The volume and reporter abbreviation are also needed.

EXAMPLE: The majority of New York courts determine whether a conversation with a spiritual advisor is confidential by asking whether the defendant intended it to be confidential. *People v. Carmona*, 627 N.E.2d 959, 963 (N.Y. 1993). At least one court, however, looked instead to whether the defendant had a reasonable expectation of confidentiality. *People v. Reyes*, 545 N.Y.S.2d 653, 654 (Sup. Ct. 1989). Under either approach, a critical question is whether the spiritual advisor and the defendant were alone during the conversation. *Carmona*, 627 N.E.2d at 963. The Court of Appeals in *Carmona* said the lower court was allowed to consider that the spiritual advisor and the defendant were alone in the garden of the advisor. *Id.*

D. Federal Statutory Citations

The general rule for citing federal laws is to cite the *United States Code* (abbreviated U.S.C. in citations), the official code for federal statutes.[26] Because that publication is published so slowly, the current language will most likely be found in a commercial code, either *United States Code Annotated* (abbreviated U.S.C.A., published by West) or *United States Code Service* (abbreviated U.S.C.S., published by LexisNexis).

A cite to a federal statute includes the title number, code abbreviation, section number, publisher (except for U.S.C.), and date. The date given in statutory cites is the date of the volume in which the statute is published, not the date the statute was enacted. If the language appears only in the pocket part, include only the date of the pocket part.[27] If

25. ALWD Rule 12.20, pages 115–18; Bluebook Rule B4.2, page 13.

26. ALWD Rule 14.1(b), page 126; Bluebook Rule B5.1.1, pages 15–16.

27. ALWD Rule 8.3, pages 50–51, and Rule 14.2(f)(2), page 129; Bluebook Rule 3.1(c), page 66, and Rule 12(e), page 115.

the language of a portion of the statute is reprinted in the pocket part, include the dates of both the bound volume and the pocket part.[28]

E. Signals

Introductory signals placed before citations show the type of support each authority provides. The more common signals are explained below.[29]

No signal	• The source cited provides direct support for the idea in the sentence. • The citation identifies the source of a quotation.
See	• The source cited offers implicit support for the idea in the sentence. • The source cited offers support in dicta.
See also	• The source cited provides additional support for the idea in the sentence. • The support offered by *see also* is not as strong or direct as authorities preceded by no signal or by the signal *see*.
E.g.	• Many authorities state the idea in the sentence, and you are citing only one as an example; this signal allows you to cite just one source while letting the reader know that many other sources say the same thing.

F. Explanatory Parentheticals

Both the ALWD Manual and the Bluebook provide for explanatory parentheticals following citations.[30] Sometimes this parenthet-

28. ALWD Rule 8, page 50; Bluebook Rule 12.3.2, page 116.

29. ALWD Rule 44, pages 370–74; Bluebook Rule B3, pages 5–7.

30. ALWD Rule 46, pages 382–84; Bluebook Rule B4.1.5, page 12, and Rule B11, page 6. The rules for explanatory parentheticals are similar in the

ical information conveys to the reader the weight of the authority (e.g., a case may have been decided *en banc* or *per curiam*). Or the case may have been decided by a narrow split among the judges who heard the case.[31] Parenthetical information also allows you to name the judges who joined in a dissenting, concurring, or plurality opinion.[32] Longer parentheticals can provide short summaries of relevant ideas in the cases, for example, to explain an inference indicated by the signal *see*. When using this type of parenthetical, be sure that you do not inadvertently hide a critical part of the court's analysis at the end of a long citation, where a reader is likely to skip over it.

EXAMPLE: Excluding relevant evidence during a sentencing hearing may deny the criminal defendant due process. *Green v. Georgia*, 442 U.S. 95, 97 (1979) (per curiam) (regarding testimony of co-defendant's confession in rape and murder case).

G. Quotations

In every citation system, the words, punctuation, and capitalization of a quote must appear exactly as they are in the original.[33] Any alterations or omissions must be indicated. Include commas and pe-

---

two citation manuals. However, the Bluebook rule states that parenthetical information generally should not be given in a complete sentence but should begin with a present participle (i.e., a verb ending in "-ing") that is not capitalized. Bluebook Rule B11, page 26. The ALWD Manual is more flexible about the format of parentheticals. *See* ALWD Rule 46.3, page 384.

31. ALWD Rule 12.11(b), page 105; Bluebook Rule B4.1.5, page 12.

32. ALWD Rule 12.11(a), page 104; Bluebook Rule B4.1.5, page 12.

33. ALWD Rules 47.2, page 387; Bluebook, Rule 5, pages 76–79. There is one slight difference in the quotation rules: for the Bluebook, quotations that have fifty or more words must be set off in indented blocks. Bluebook Rule 5.1, page 76. That means the writer must count words to know how many words the quotation contains. In contrast, the ALWD Manual requires indented blocks for quotes that are fifty or more words *or* quotes that span four or more lines of typed text. ALWD Rule 47.5(a), page 390.

riods inside quotation marks; place other punctuation outside the quotation marks unless it is included in the original text. Also, try to provide smooth transitions between your text and the quoted text.

H. Numbers and Spacing

It is most common in legal documents to spell out numbers zero through ninety-nine and to use numerals for larger numbers. However, always spell out a number that is the first word of a sentence.[34]

Ordinal abbreviations are used frequently in citations, especially for showing the series of a reporter. While most ordinal abbreviations in legal citations mirror their non-legal counterparts, two do not. Both the ALWD Manual and the Bluebook use 2d for "Second" (not 2nd) and 3d for "Third" (not 3rd).[35] The letter components of ordinal abbreviations are not superscripted (e.g., 4th not 4th).

Do not insert a space between abbreviations of single capital letters. For example, there is no space in U.S. ordinal numbers like 1st, 2d, and 3d are considered single capital letters for purposes of this rule. Thus, there is no space in N.E.2d or F.3d because 2d and 3d are considered single capital letters. Leave one space between elements of an abbreviation that are not single capital letters. For example, F. Supp. 2d has a space on each side of "Supp."[36]

II. Bluebook Citations for Law Review Articles[37]

While the rules discussed above also apply to citations in footnotes of law review articles that follow the Bluebook, that manual uses dif-

---

34. ALWD Rule 4.2, pages 32–35; Bluebook Rule 6.2(a), page 73.

35. ALWD Rule 4.3, page 32; Bluebook Rule 6.2, pages 81–82.

36. ALWD Rule 2.2, pages 19–20; Bluebook Rule 6.1, pages 80–81.

37. An invaluable source for students working on law review articles in New York is St. John's Law Review Ass'n, *New York Rules of Citation* (William H. Manz ed., 4th ed. 2001).

Table A-3. Comparison of ALWD and Bluebook Formats

ALWD Manual	Bluebook	
All Documents	Legal Memoranda	Law Review Articles
N.Y. Penal Law § 80.05 (McKinney 2004).	N.Y. Penal Law § 80.05 (McKinney 2004).	N.Y. PENAL LAW § 80.05 (McKinney 2004).

ferent fonts—including large and small capital letters—for law review footnote citations. As the example in Table A-3 shows, while there is often little or no variation between the final appearance of citations in legal memoranda and court documents using the Bluebook and the ALWD Manual, law review footnotes under the Bluebook look different. The primary difference is the use of large and small capital letters.

Using the Bluebook to write citations for law review articles is considerably easier than using it for practice documents because almost all of the examples given in the Bluebook are in law review format. Table A-4 summarizes the typeface used for several common sources and gives examples.

Law review articles place citations in footnotes or endnotes, instead of placing citations in the main text of the document.[38] Most law review footnotes include text in ordinary type, in italics, and in large and small capital letters.[39] This convention is not universal, and each law review selects the typefaces it will use. Some law reviews may use only ordinary type and italics. Others may use just ordinary type.[40] Assuming you are submitting an article to a law review that uses all three typefaces, Bluebook Rule 2 dictates which typeface to use for each type of authority.

The typeface used for a case name depends on (1) whether the case appears in the main text of the article or in a footnote and (2) how the case is used. When a case name appears in the main text of the article or in a textual sentence of a footnote, it is italicized. By contrast, if a footnote contains an embedded citation, the case name is

38. Bluebook Rule 1.1, pages 53–54.
39. Bluebook Rule 2.2(a), page 64.
40. Bluebook Rule 2, pages 62–65.

Table A-4. Bluebook Typeface for Law Review Footnotes

Item	Type used	Example
Cases	Use ordinary type for case names in full citations. (See text for further explanation.)	Legal Servs. Corp. v. Velazquez, 531 U.S. 533 (2001).
Books	Use large and small capital letters for the author and the title.	DAVID S. ROMANTZ & KATHLEEN ELLIOTT VINSON, LEGAL ANALYSIS: THE FUNDAMENTAL SKILL (2d ed. 2009).
Periodical articles	Use ordinary type for the author's name, italics for the title, and large and small capitals for the periodical.	Patricia E. Salkin, *Teaching Government Law and Policy in Law School: Reflections on Twenty-Five Years of Experience*, 66 ALB. L. REV. 993 (2003).
Explanatory phrases	Use italics for all explanatory phrases, such as *aff'g*, *cert. denied*, *rev'd*, and *overruled by*.	Legal Servs. Corp. v. Velazquez, 531 U.S. 533 (2001), *aff'g* 164 F.3d 757 (2d Cir. 1999).
Introductory signals	Use italics for all introductory signals, such as *see* and *e.g.* when they appear in citations, as opposed to text.	*See id.*

written in ordinary text. Similarly, when a full cite is given in a footnote, the case name is written in ordinary type. But when a short cite is used in footnotes, the case name is italicized.

III. New York Citation

New York courts follow the *New York Law Reports Style Manual* ("NYSM"). Citations in conformance with that manual look quite a bit different from citations written with the national manuals. Most obviously, citations are enclosed in parentheticals, different abbreviations are used, periods are used less frequently, and brackets sometimes replace parentheses. Table A-5 shows samples of citation to commonly used authorities according to the NYSM. The following introduction highlights key aspects of the NYSM.[41]

A. Citation Placement and Appearance

As shown in Table A-5, the appearance of citations under the NYSM depends on whether the citation appears in parentheses or is part of the text. The difference is most apparent in case citations. Citations that support the text, but are not read as part of the text, appear in parentheses. In contrast, citations that are read as part of the textual sentence are not placed in parentheses. If the citation supports only one sentence of text, the parenthetical containing the citation is placed within that sentence. If the citation supports several sentences, it goes outside the sentence. Compare the examples below.

EXAMPLES:

The appointed attorney in *People v Moran* (2 AD3d 216, 217 [2003]) was allowed to withdraw because the court found no nonfrivolous points to be raised on appeal.

Counsel may withdraw when there are no nonfrivolous issues to be raised on appeal (*People v Moran*, 2 AD3d 216, 217 [2003]).

Appointed counsel are not required to pursue frivolous appeals. The court will review the record to see whether there are nonfrivolous points that counsel could raise. (*People v Moran*, 2 AD3d 216, 217 [2003]).

The appearance of constitutional and statutory provisions may also vary based on placement, but the writer can choose to use abbreviations in both parentheticals and text. The only placement dif-

41. The NYSM references other authoritative books on citation and style, including both the Bluebook and the ALWD Manual, and suggests consulting those authorities for points not covered by the NYSM.

Table A-5. Citation with the *New York Law Reports Style Manual**

Source	Citation in Parentheses	Citation in Text
New York Constitution	(NY Const, art VI, § 35)	NY Constitution, article VI, § 35 *Either abbreviations or full names may be used in text.*
New York Statute**	(Penal Law, art 80, § 80.05)	Penal Law, article 80, § 80.05 *Either abbreviations or full names may be used in text.*
New York Regulations	(12 NYCRR 23-1.7 [b] [1])	12 NYCRR 23-1.7 (b) (1)
New York Case	(*People v Moran*, 2 AD3d 216 [2003])	*People v Moran* (2 AD3d 216 [2003])

* The examples in this table are drawn from the 2007 version of the NYSM.
** As pointed out in the footnote of Table A-1, the most common citation format for New York regulations is "1 NYCRR 38.9."

ference for regulatory citations is that parentheticals use brackets for subdivisions and paragraphs, while text references use parentheses.

A recent change in the NYSM allows writers to place citations in footnotes. When the writer chooses this approach, all citations must appear in footnotes. The NYSM does not allow a combination of styles within one document.[42]

B. Case Citation

Case citations include the same basic information as do citations written to comply with the national manuals: the title of the case (e.g., the names of the parties); the reference to the volume, reporter, and first page of the case in print; the pinpoint page (also called the jump page); and the court that decided the case and the year of the deci-

42. NYSM Rule 1.2.

sion (enclosed in brackets). A citation giving the history of the case can be added to the end of this information.[43]

The titles of reported New York cases are available online in the Official Case Name and Citation Locator at http://iapps.courts.state.ny.us/lawReporting/SearchCitation. The titles of United States Supreme Court cases are provided on that court's website at www.supremecourtus.gov/opinions/casefinder.html. For cases not listed on those cites, and for unreported cases, the writer has some leeway in formulating a title consistent with other citation manuals.[44]

Appendix 1 of the NYSM provides common case name abbreviations. Table A-2, earlier in this chapter, lists selected abbreviations to compare with their counterparts in the national citation manuals. Note that the lower case "*v*" between the parties' names is not followed by a period.

Under the NYSM, citations are given to the official reporters or, in some instances, to West's regional reporters. Table A-6 lists the preferred reporters. Print reporters are preferred over electronic sources.[45]

In addition to providing the first page of the case, the writer should provide the specific page that supports the text. If the cited material covers more than one page in the reporter, the writer must give the page span, separated by a hyphen.

EXAMPLE: (*Scalp & Blade v Advest, Inc.*, 309 AD2d 219, 226–227 [2003])

After a case is cited in full once, subsequent references may be provided in one of three ways: (1) a short-form citation; (2) a repeated full citation, followed by *supra*; or (3) the reference *id.* As for the first alternative, short-form citations include a shortened case title. Typically, this will be the first party named in the case title. If that party is

43. NYSM Rule 1.1.
44. NYSM Rule 2.1.
45. NYSM Rules 2.2, 2.3, and 2.4.

Table A-6. Preferred Reporters under the *New York Style Manual*

Court	Reporter	Abbreviation	Official or Commercial
New York Court of Appeals	*New York Reports*	NY NY2d NY3d	Official
New York Supreme Court Appellate Division	*Appellate Division Reports*	AD AD2d AD3d	Official
New York Supreme Court	*New York Miscellaneous Reports*	Misc Misc 2d	Official
United States Supreme Court	*United States Reports* (if available) *Supreme Court Reporter*	US S Ct	Official Commercial
United States Courts of Appeals	*Federal Reporter*	F F2d F3d	Commercial
United States District Courts	*Federal Supplement*	F Supp F Supp 2d	Commercial

a governmental entity, however, the other party listed is used in the short citation. Any of the following short-form citations is acceptable.[46]

EXAMPLES: (*Scalp & Blade*, 309 AD2d at 225)
(*Scalp & Blade* at 225)
(309 AD2d at 225)

For the second alternative, the writer simply repeats the full citation and adds *supra* if desired.[47] The third alternative can be used only to refer to the immediately preceding citation. To refer to the same page of that citation, the writer simply uses *id.* To refer to a different page, the writer adds "at" followed by the new page number.[48]

46. NYSM Rule 1.3.
47. NYSM Rule 1.3(c).
48. NYSM Rule 1.3(d).

C. Statutory Citation

New York statutory citations begin with a statutory name (e.g., Banking Law, Domestic Relations Law, Penal Law). That name is followed by an article or section number. A more specific citation may include subdivisions, as shown in the examples below.[49]

EXAMPLES: (Penal Law, art 80, § 80.05)
(Domestic Relations Law § 236 [B] [6] [a] [3])
(Town Law § 199 [1] [a])

IV. Citations Not Covered by a Manual

As comprehensive as the ALWD Manual, the Bluebook, and the NYSM are, they do not definitively answer every citation question. When you cannot find a specific rule to cover a source you need to cite, look for rules regarding analogous sources. In creating a citation, always be guided by the purpose of citation: to allow a reader to find a source and to understand the type and weight of support it provides.

49. NYSM Rule 3.1.

Appendix B

Selected Bibliography

New York Research

Robert Allan Carter, *Legislative Intent in New York State: Materials, Cases, and Annotated Bibliography* (1981).

Robert Allan Carter, *Sources of Legislative Intent* (2001).

Joseph L. Gerken, Center for Computer-Assisted Legal Instruction, *New York Primary Legal Research* (2008), www2.cali.org/index.php?fuseaction=lessons.lessondetail&lid=1220.

Kevin P. Gray, *New York Legislative History Sourcebook* (2004).

William H. Manz, *Gibson's New York Legal Research Guide* (3d ed. 2004).

General Research

[Tending to focus on federal material.]

Steven M. Barkan, Roy M. Mersky & Donald J. Dunn, *Fundamentals of Legal Research* (9th ed. 2009).

Robert C. Berring & Elizabeth A. Edinger, *Finding the Law* (12th ed. 2005).

Deborah E. Bouchoux, *Legal Research Explained* (2d ed. 2010).

Morris L. Cohen & Kent C. Olson, *Legal Research in a Nutshell* (10th ed. 2010).

Christina L. Kunz et al., *The Process of Legal Research* (7th ed. 2008).

Amy E. Sloan, *Basic Legal Research: Tools and Strategies* (4th ed. 2009).

Legal Analysis

Charles R. Calleros, *Legal Method and Writing* (6th ed. 2011).

Linda H. Edwards, *Legal Writing: Process, Analysis, and Organization* (5th ed. 2010).

Linda H. Edwards, *Legal Writing and Analysis* (3d ed. 2011).

Richard K. Neumann, Jr., *Legal Reasoning and Legal Writing: Structure, Strategy, and Style* (6th ed. 2009).

Laurel Currie Oates & Anne Enquist, *The Legal Writing Handbook: Analysis, Research, and Writing* (5th ed. 2010).

Helene S. Shapo, Marilyn R. Walter & Elizabeth Fajans, *Writing and Analysis in the Law* (5th ed. 2008).

About the Authors

Elizabeth G. Adelman is a graduate of Albany Law School and the University at Buffalo School of Information and Library Studies. She is currently Director of the Law Library and Vice Dean for Legal Information Services at the University of Buffalo.

Theodora Belniak is a graduate of the National University of Ireland, Galway, State University of New York at Buffalo Law School, and the University at Buffalo School of Information and Library Sciences. She is currently the Head of Collection Management at the University at Buffalo.

Suzanne E. Rowe is a graduate of Columbia University School of Law. After clerking for a federal trial court judge, she was an associate in the tax department of a Wall Street law firm. She is currently the James L. and Ilene R. Hershner Professor at the University of Oregon School of Law, where she directs the Legal Research and Writing Program.

Index